EX : LIBRIS

AROUND INDIA

John Seymour

AROUND

INDIA

ILLUSTRATED

THE JOHN DAY COMPANY
NEW YORK

CONTENTS

Sixteen pages of illustrations will be found following page 152.

AROUND INDIA

1

FAIR WIND TO INDIA

WELL, THERE *was* Hastings," I said. "And who was that chap who stood amazed at his own moderation—Clive, wasn't it? And I believe quite a few others. . . ."

I was talking to the customs officer at Pamban, a small port in South India where I had recently landed. He had just made the surprising statement that no Englishman had ever come to India in a sailing ship before.

"But why didn't you come in the steam ferry like everybody else?" he demanded.

"I can't think of any reason why I shouldn't have come in the steamer," I said. "But it just happens that I came in a sailing ship."

"Yes, but *why* did you come in a sailing ship?"

"Because I wanted to get to India."

"Yes, but then why didn't you come in the steam ferry?"

"Well, I've already answered that question," I murmured deferentially.

But here the port officer, who was also present and if possible more concerned about the whole matter than his customs brother, thought of something. "Ah!" he said. "Ah! You had no right to come in a sailing ship. Such ships are not allowed to carry passengers."

"I was not a passenger," I said.

"How?"

"I was a member, albeit a humble one, of the crew."

"How?"

My fellow members of the crew were standing as we were talking in a group, outside the door, with our captain, Mahomed Aliad. Their own business was finished, but they were plainly not going to leave their shipmate to the mercy of officials before they were certain that all was well. It was clear that there was no love lost between the sailors and the harbor officers. The sailors had a tough and difficult job to do to earn a living from the sea in the face of competition from steamers, and up to that time no customs or harbor official had ever gone very far out of his way to help them. Furthermore, they were Moslems, and the officials were not. And Pamban is predominantly a Moslem place.

I called Mahomed Aliad and asked him to show us the crew list. He pulled this out of the beautifully engraved copper casket in which he carried his ship's papers and, behold, my name was at the bottom of it. The port officer was confounded.

"We must wire to Dhanushkodi," said the customs officer. "We must report this matter. Such a thing has never happened before."

They wired to Dhanushkodi, the port from which the steamer operates to Ceylon, and the reply came that I was to be kept "under escort" until the next day and brought to Dhanushkodi on the train. So the port officer took his leave and so did my shipmates, and the party broke up. Before they left, though, the sailors insisted that I take a loan from them of ten rupees. They knew I was, as ever, short of cash.

The customs office at Pamban is in an old Dutch building, for Pamban was once an important Dutch trading post. The walls of the building are enormously thick, the central part is surrounded completely by a wide *stoep* and is therefore very dark, and the ceiling is extremely high, which was supposed by the Dutch to make for coolness. You need something to make for coolness in Pamban.

The customs officer, his duty now clear before him, became human and introduced me to his children and let me have a fleeting glimpse of his wife. He was a Brahman and very orthodox. He gave me a meal, sat and watched me while I ate it, but of course was far too orthodox to join me.

"You eat with your fingers," he said with surprise.

"Only in countries where people do eat with their fingers," I replied. "If you come to my country you'll probably eat with a knife and fork."

"Your customs and our customs are *quite* different," he said. "*Quite* different. There is nothing the same about them. We are completely different from each other."

"Only superficially, I think," I replied. "After all, what does it matter whether you eat with a fork or your fingers or chopsticks? Or sit on the floor or on a chair? I thought at first I was very different from the crew of the sailing ship, but I found after a day or two in their company that the difference wasn't very fundamental."

"You say, if I go to your country," went on the customs officer. "I will never go to your country. I cannot go away from Pamban. For years I must stay at this hideous place. But I must live. What to do?"

Pamban is indeed unprepossessing. Built on the sandy point of what is practically a desert island, about half its buildings are empty and deserted and falling into decay. The remainder are occupied by poverty-stricken people, hanging on in sheer inertia to a dying town. For Pamban's day is done.

We had crept into Pamban Bay that morning, feeling our way with the lead along the narrow and winding channel through the shoals, until we had let go our anchor and handed our fore-topsail about a mile from the shore, the nearest we could get. Taking to the boat, we rowed for half a mile, grounded, and then got out and waded the rest, splashing with our bare feet through the warm, shallow, greenish water, watching the crabs and small fish spurting away for the shelter of the soft weed forests (which I personally avoided walking through, for fear of prickly things).

On the shore were some small naked boys to greet us, and to follow us as we crossed the dirty sand of the beach and entered a land of scattered palmyra palms that alternated with patches of dried-up, goat-nibbled scrub. The coconut will not grow in that arid country.

After perhaps a mile we came to Pamban.

A jumble of mud-brick huts and houses, narrow, dirty streets, everything decaying and falling to bits beneath the glare of the relentless sun. We met and greeted several men in the streets—sailors some of them, or merchants—and Moslem women pulled their shawls over their faces and stood aside to let us pass. We went by an ancient Dravidian Hindu temple, which had small trees bursting their way out from between its stones, we passed the place where craftsmen were building a boat—the kind of open sailing craft used almost exclusively for smuggling between Ceylon and India—and finally we arrived at the shop of the local agent of our owner.

The agent, a Moslem gentleman dressed like my shipmates in a sarong and cotton jacket and with a fez on his head, asked us in, and we squatted on low stools and were given glasses of tea.

It was shortly after this that two peons came from the port officer and I was carried away to be questioned by the officials.

After my meal as the guest of the customs officer, however, I was allowed to wander out, and I walked along the waterfront of the old town.

Besides Dutch buildings there was a big and crumbling warehouse with the sign of a British trading company over the door. I wondered when the last Englishman had lived in Pamban, and what his name was. I doubt whether an Englishman will ever live there again.

The island of Rameswaram, on which Pamban stands, is part of that string of low sand islands and sandy shoals called Adam's Bridge, which stretches like an umbilical cord between Mother India and Ceylon. The only channel through which small ships can pass between the two countries runs between Pamban and the mainland of India, and a swing bridge in the railway causeway that now connects Rameswaram with India allows vessels to get through.

It is the railway, partly, that has killed Pamban. In the old days Pamban was a steppingstone on the journey from Ceylon to India. Now the trains just rush straight through without stopping, on their way to Dhanushkodi at the other end of the island from which the steamers complete the journey. And then, of course, Pamban, being on an island, was a safe place for the Dutch—and later the English—to build a "factory" for carrying on trade with the mainland. In how many forgotten nooks and crannies of the Indian coastline, I wonder, would you find the crumbling but solid remains of Dutch forts and factories, and their gabled churches?

From the south side of the island I could see the *Deyvada-highi,* our noble ship. With her squared yards and enormous bowsprit she looked very like a pirate vessel as she lay there out on the bay, and I wondered how many real pirate vessels had lain there before her, and how many Dutch East India-men and British men-o'-war. She is a brigantine: she has two masts, the mainmast fore and aft rigged, and the foremast square-rigged. Not far from her lay a much larger ship: a three-master, square-rigged on all masts, and some distance farther lay a fleet of much smaller lateen-rigged vessels, tile carriers from the coast of Coromandel. They were waiting for the swing bridge to be opened in the railway causeway, so that they could make their way north along the coast.

Ships like *Deyvadahighi* are to be found all round the coasts of Ceylon, up the Indian west coast as far north as Karachi, and—when there is a trade—they will go as far east as Burma to fetch rice. They are among the few remaining square-rigged sailing vessels in the world.

We had sailed from Colombo four days before landing at Pamban. At six in the morning, on the day of our departure, I had been put aboard the brigantine, and the captain, who had been waiting for my arrival to cast off, gave the order to make sail. The square foresail and fore-topsails were broken out, our four small headsails set, the mooring lines, which had held us to some other vessels, cast off and, with a freshening early morning breeze on our port beam, we started slowly to thread our way between the hundred or so vessels, large and small, which lay at moorings in Colombo harbor. We must have looked rather fine in the early light, and as we passed a large tramp steamer registered in the Port of Lon-don, some members of her crew gave us a cheer.

As we passed out of the harbor mouth, our bows began to lift to the monsoon swell and the breeze freshened, coming from about seven points off our port bow. As the sun came up behind us, the breeze got stronger and soon, with all sail set, we were ramping through the waves at a great pace, the deck below us at a steep angle, and the great system of spars, sails, and cordage over our heads, swaying over and staying over.

The *Deyvadahighi* was maybe a hundred feet long. She was flush-decked, but forward there was a low fo'c'stle head, under which there was just room to creep and lie down, and aft there was a poop deck, which formed a small cabin. You could not stand up in this cabin but you you could sit down. I tried sleeping in it one night but was bitten by bugs.

In the waist of the ship lay a large and heavy boat. Forward of the foremast was the galley, a dog-kennel-like arrangement fastened down with ropes to eyebolts on the deck. Inside the galley was the stove, a simple platform of brick with three indentations in it to take small wood fires. There was a large steel water tank on deck, and abaft the mainmast was an old-fashioned capstan. Right aft, on the raised poop deck, was the crudest steering wheel I have ever seen. But I saw that it had the virtue that, if it broke, as it must obviously have done quite often, it could easily be repaired with more string.

The mainsail was a big fore-and-after, set loose-footed on a boom, with a heavy gaff, which took the combined efforts of the crew to raise. We always half lowered it to jibe it. Between the masts there were five small staysails, and on the foremast were the two squaresails—the foresail and the foretopsail. I was surprised to find that they would set closer than the mainsail when we were close-hauled. Then out on the very large bowsprit were four jibs, or headsails. So that we could set twelve sails in all.

I had always heard that to put a square-rigged ship about takes half an hour from the time when the captain shouts for the cook (whose job it is to tend the jib sheets) to the time when the braces are coiled down and the men can go below again. But we could come about on *Deyvadahighi* in two minutes. First the main sheet was hauled in close and several men would shove against the boom to push it back. Meanwhile the helm was put down and the ship's head would rapidly come up into the wind. As soon as the squaresails were taken aback, her head would fall quickly away on the other tack, the mainsail would come over, and we would quickly tend the braces to bring the squaresails over and haul them close. Then, at our leisure, we could tend the staysails.

But for the first day and night we did not have to go about. We held on, full and by, on the port tack, heading for the port of Tuticorin, over on the Indian side of the Gulf of Mannar.

As night came on, the wind increased and we handed most of our staysails. The captain insisted that I sleep in the only bed on board, a rickety camp cot, and so I wedged this between the boat and the main hatch and turned in. I would far rather have slept on the deck, for it was extremely difficult to hold my berth on the camp cot, at such an angle were we and so violent our motion. There was a really big sea running from the southwest. But our ship, being light, lifted beautifully to the waves and never shipped a drop. As the wind increased, she went like a train—we *flew* along.

At midnight the mate called us up to hand the mainsail. It was too much for her. We got the big sail down and she went along beautifully under squaresails only. I spent a couple of hours standing on deck, entranced by the eager squaresails that bellied out above our heads, swaying against the stars, lifting us along across the waves. Did man ever build a finer thing than a sailing ship? All the works of art in all the galleries and museums of the five continents are dross compared to it. All the fast airplanes, with flames shooting out of their backsides, are silly toys. And the record-breaking steamers—built of tin, tearing backward and forward across the Atlantic, driven by streetcar motormen—they should not be allowed to float on the same ocean!

As the sun rose the next day, we could just see a low, hazy coastline, and two old steamers lying at anchor about five miles from the shore. They were being loaded from small sailing vessels from Tuticorin. We made for a gap in the coral reef that runs parallel to the coast there, and sounded our way in carefully with the lead; then, after standing in close to the shore, we brought up in three and a half fathoms of water. We had sailed a hundred and seventy miles in twenty-four hours.

Our crew were probably not as piratical as they looked. The captain, Mahomed Aliad, was a dignified figure, especially when he went below and got his smart red fez. He could spit farther than any man I have ever seen, although sometimes he failed to make due allowance for the wind. The mate, Moidin Chini Assana, was the driving force of the ship. He had held a command himself once, and I hope he soon gets one again. Whatever work there was to be done, the mate was sure to be there doing it first, and he instilled energy and enthusiasm into all of us. He was also our chaplain. At five o'clock every morning he woke us up with the Call to Prayer, and at different intervals during the day he was to be seen performing his devotions up on the poop; but he was not, I noticed, above interrupting his communion with the Almighty to shout an order if he saw that a sail wanted trimming.

The bosun was a fine old man with large, drooping white mustaches. He reminded me very much of an old Essex fisherman I knew at Tollesbury. He was entirely reliable, a sound seaman, but not, perhaps, one born to command. He had that straight and steadfast look in his eye that can only be achieved by a lifetime at sea, or deep in the country, away from money-grubbing.

There were ten of us altogether, most of the men I have not mentioned being fairly young. The captain's son was aboard, a likely lad, and our cook was a small, dwarfish man, rather the laughing-stock of the younger and more thoughtless of us. He spent most of his day squatting on deck beside the galley rolling out curry stuffs (chillies, dried fish, peppercorns and other spices) with a stone rolling pin on a concave stone slab. For meals we always had a plate each of rice and curried dried fish and vegetables, and very good it was. The tea was pernicious, but we drank it nevertheless.

Oh, and the ship's cat! She was not fed, to encourage her to catch mice. This was obviously effective because there were no mice. And by now I fear there is probably no cat.

The rest of the crew like having me on board. I break the monotony. I pull my camera out at times and take their photos. As soon as they see the camera, they all dive below and put on their shirts—normally they wear only sarongs or shorts. With their shirts on they stand and pose for me, beaming from ear to ear. They are delighted to find that not only will I heave in a rope, but furthermore I know which rope to heave on. They point out to each other than I can even tie a bowline.

But my bath is the highlight of the day.

As soon as I produce my razor, the captain bellows for the crew; it's a case of "all hands on deck!" The better to supervise the operation himself, the captain, who is often at the wheel, hands over to the mate and comes forward. Hot water is rushed up from the galley for me to shave with, and the captain's very own piece of mirror is held before my eyes

by the captain's son. I shave. Then comes the dramatic part
of the business. I squat down in the scuppers and have bucket
after bucket of cold water poured over me. Members of the
crew dash backward and forward between me and the water
tank as if they were putting out a fire. No one else is allowed
this lavish use of fresh water and I feel guilty, protest, but
the process goes on. And when I am all but washed out of a
scupper the captain gives the order to cease and I am allowed
to dry myself.

When I sit on the hatch and write in a large book I have,
the captain and various members of the crew leave whatever
they are doing and come to watch me. They watch every
single word I write down. When the page flaps about in the
breeze, the captain holds it down for me. He is fascinated.
Every now and then he makes some conjecture in Tamil as
to what I am writing. And I make mental conjectures as to
what *his* conjectures are. I know not one word of Tamil.
And he knows not one word of English.

And yet, somehow, we converse. There is nothing that any
of us want to say to each other that we do not eventually suc-
ceed in saying. We make each other laugh at each other's
jokes, we tell each other tall stories, we compare the size of
our families or our lack of families, we compare the relative
advantage of various sailing rigs, and we express what we
think about customs officials and their kind. I do not know
how we do this, but we do.

Well, after we have let go our anchor in three and a half
fathoms of water, we have our breakfast, launch the boat,
and, leaving two shipkeepers aboard, row ashore. We run
through small breakers onto a steep sandy beach, and I jump
out onto India.

We are on arid shore indeed, where even palmyra palms
find it hard to exist. But in places there are patches of plan-

tains, or banana trees, irrigated from wells. Small fishing canoes are drawn up on the beach, and some big, graceful surf boats—fast sailing craft used for fishing or smuggling. Smuggling between India and Ceylon is the main industry of that coast. The smuggling is largely in human beings—illegal immigrants. Wages are slightly higher in Ceylon than they are in India, and for this reason there is a constant stream of human traffic going from India to Ceylon.

We walk along the dry, dirty sand and eventually reach a group of fishermen's huts. They are not ostentatious buildings. Each one consists of a tiny oval shelter of *cadjan,* or woven coconut fronds, into which a man and a woman and a few kids can just crawl.

There are no men about, only some women and small children bathing at a well. Two of the women are very pretty: I regret the fact that we are not pirates. They bathe by pouring water from a bucket over themselves, but alas, their charms are covered by thin, cotton, sarilike garments, which they wear while bathing and pull up over their breasts when they see sailors coming. Their black hair hangs down, wet and glistening, and they giggle and flash smiles at us. They hand us the bucket, which is made of woven banana leaves, and we strip to our loincloths and bathe in our turn.

After the bath we go and squat near a hut, and a woman brings us palmyra nuts. These are disappointing things really, especially unripe ones like those they bring us. You cut off one end of the large, green nut about the size of a coconut and you find three objects about the size of hen's eggs made of clear jelly embedded in the inedible white interior. If you are a sissy, you laboriously cut these out and eat them. If you are a sailor off a brigantine, you have a different approach. Holding the nut up to your mouth, you force your thumb into one of the jelly cavities and then, working your thumb vigorously back and forth, you suck violently and noisily, and most of the refreshing but rather tasteless jelly goes into your mouth. Some of it, though, runs down your chin.

After this refreshment, and after casting a last look at the fairer of our hostesses, we decide to walk inland to a village where there is a famous Moslem shrine. The sun is now high up and hot, and we walk slowly along the sandy track through the flat, arid countryside. The country is verging on being a desert. Large flocks of goats ravage what little bit of scrub or bush there is, and sand dunes are beginning to form and encroach on the countryside.

We arrive at a big and dirty village and are welcomed by the village headman. He speaks a little English and is delighted to find an Englishman to talk to. A large crowd collects; we sit on the porch of a shop and drink glasses of tea. The headman pours out his troubles to me. He wishes the English were back, ruling India. He is a Moslem and he fears that the Hindus will victimize him.

I point out to him that if he had been a Hindu living in Pakistan he would not exist. The fact that large villages populated entirely by Moslems still exist in India surely disproves his allegations of ill treatment. He admits that so far there has not, really, been ill treatment, but taxes are high and living hard.

Of course the abolition of toddy tapping has hit this part of the world. Madras State has prohibition, and this has killed, or forced underground, the most flourishing cottage industry of large parts of the country. In the place where we are, the palmyra, or toddy, palm is about the only plant that will grow satisfactorily. And about the only thing you can do with a toddy palm (besides squish the jelly out of its nuts with your thumb!) is to tap it for toddy. You can ferment this toddy and make delicious and nourishing beer out of it or you can boil it down and make *jaggery*, a coarse but very nourishing kind of sugar. But now the government has set its face against tapping the palms at all. How do they know, if a man taps a palm ostensibly for sugar, that he does not make toddy out of it? A few licenses are given, it is true, for jaggery making, but only rarely. The fact is that you see miles and miles of palms that used to be tapped, which are now no longer tapped. They just stand there, taking up space, doing no good to man at all.

And the people who used to draw a living from them—the vast army of toddy tappers—are unemployed. Nor is there work for them to do, in spite of government efforts to supply it.

And furthermore, the inhabitants of the country have lost a valuable source of food. Good toddy, sweet or fermented, hath no fellow. It has practically everything in it that the body requires, including all the vitamins in the alphabet. In the Jaffna district of Ceylon, where for part of the year toddy is king and where there are no sniveling prohibition laws, men, women and small children drink toddy early every morning, and they are the healthiest and most vigorous and enterprising people you will find. There are Jaffna Tamils in half the countries of the globe; they are often called the Scotsmen of Ceylon.

But there. There are many arguments both for and against prohibition in India and we will deal with them in their place.

Meanwhile we drink our tea and then go and look at the mosque, which is unimpressive, but no doubt holy.

We return to the beach and admire the sight of our vessel lying out at anchor, in the company now of some small dhows which are running back from Jaffna empty, to fetch more tiles from Tuticorin. Our boat is still there, and we launch her and pull out to the ship. We up-anchor and away. But the wind has now turned dead against us—the last puff of the northeast monsoon perhaps—and we have to tack to windward. I am amazed at how easy this unwieldy vessel can be handled, and how close she will point.

The getting up of the anchor, by the way, is a picturesque business. A heavy coir line, called a "messenger," is fastened to the anchor cable up in the eyes of the ship and led aft to the capstan, which is set between the mainmast and the break of the poop. We then seize hand spikes, insert them in the sockets of the capstan, and, led and urged on by the mate, who works harder than anyone, we do a devil's dance around the windlass, pushing against our spikes and singing for all we are worth.

The singing is led by the little cook, who squats on deck a short distance away and coils down the messenger as it comes in. When we have pulled in a length of the heavy chain cable we unfasten the line, take it forward again, and take another bite. The process was exactly the same in Nelson's day, and little boys were employed to "nip" the capstan line onto the cable with spun yarn as it came in—hence the word "nippers"!

Every night, in the narrow channel between the land and the coral reef, we have to anchor, and during the day we must turn against the head wind. So it takes us three days to do the hundred miles to Pamban. But we get there, and that is the important thing.

Well, there we were in Pamban, with myself, if not under arrest, at least under a cloud.

I slept that night on a camp cot on the *stoep* of that old Dutch building, with the customs department peons sleeping on mats not far away. And next morning the customs officer and I caught the train for Dhanushkodi.

There I was exhibited to various officials and they all asked me the same questions. *Why* had I come in a sailing ship? *Why* had I not come in the ferry? And I gave them the same answers. And then of course, again and again, the old question: "What was I?" A man, of course, John Seymour. *Homo sum*. Yes, but what did I *do*? Well—anything that I thought worth doing. Yes, but what was my *work*? Anything that presents itself when I have to work, but work is a means, not an end. When I want something that requires work for its attainment, I do the necessary work—unless of course I can contrive to get somebody else to do it for me. The *Bhagavad Gita* says that work can be good, if it is done in a spirit of sacrifice: "Save work done as and for a sacrifice this world is in bondage to work" is part of the advice given by Krishna to Arjuna. (Radhakrishnan's translation.) Work should be done if there is work to do, for: "Not by abstention from work does a man attain freedom from action; nor by mere renunciation does he attain perfection." And again: "The renunciation of works and their unselfish performance both lead to the soul's salvation. But of the two, the unselfish performance of works is better than their renunciation."

This I explained to the officials, but it was not enough. What was my profession? They had to write it down on a piece of paper.

The steamer came in from Ceylon, and we went on board to search for the head immigration officer. I ran into a huge man, a Bengali, the second engineer. We had a beer together.

He told me of the time he was on a pilgrim ship taking hadjis to Mecca. They had struck a storm in the Red Sea, the ship had been overloaded, the fine-weather ports down near the water line were unprotected because the steel doors that had been supplied for them had been dismantled in Bombay, and the ship took great quantities of ocean through these apertures and developed a dangerous list.

The women and children were hustled out of the way into various saloons, which were then kept locked, and the men were exhorted by the captain to carry water up from below in any vessels they could find and put it over the side to help the pumps.

Panic, if there would have been panic, was averted by this order, for the men felt that they were doing something at least to help themselves, and eventually the ship made the lee of one of those little rock islands that you find in the Red Sea with lighthouses on them. There they were able to find holding ground and lie for a day or two to sort themselves out.

Just as they were sorting themselves out, though, my customs officer came along with the immigration officer. The latter looked at my passport. Nothing wrong. What was all the trouble about? I'd come in a sailing ship? Why shouldn't I come in a sailing ship? I could swim if I liked! Or come in a balloon. What was all the trouble about?

So shortly afterwards I caught the train for Madura.

As we drew slowly out of the station, we passed a small group of officials standing on the platform. One of them was waving his arms about.

"Yes, but *whyee?*" I heard him say, in very South Indian English. "Whyee? Whyee? Whyee he did not come in the ferree?"

For all I know, they may be still standing there on the platform at Dhanushkodi, arguing about it now.

2

THE HOLY CITY

As the train approaches the ancient city of Madura, you look out the window and see, standing up above the scruff of light-brown brick buildings in the distance, four towers with inward-leaning walls, reminding you perhaps of the cooling towers of a great power station. From a distance of several miles they look enormous: they soar over everything else.

They are the four *gopurams,* or gate towers, of the Temple of Minakshi.

I spent four days wandering about at Madura, and during that time I spoke to very few people. The people were willing to be friendly enough—it was just that I did not want to. I wanted to stroll slowly about the streets, wander through the gloomy galleries of the enormous temple, sit in little cafés and watch the world go by. Just generally to recover from the shock of being taken from a manageable little island like Ceylon and dumped down in the middle of the twentieth century, but *not* the twentieth century A.D.—the twentieth century B.C.!

Of course, Madura is quite an up-to-date city in some ways. There is a large post-office building and one or two big office blocks, one or two long, glaring, hot, wide streets. But the large areas of little winding alleyways north of the Temple are residential areas for people who live as their ancestors lived. What of them?

The people of Madura, of course, like most South Indians, are of Dravidian stock; and nowadays it is believed by some people that the Dravidians were the race that lived at Mohenjo-Daro, the people of the Indus Valley civilization who were among the most ancient city dwellers in the world. And I would be willing to place a small bet that if you could bring back to life a Mohenjo-Daran, say, of the fourth millennium B.C., and put him down in modern Madura, he would feel very much more at home there than I did.

Certainly in their dress, their dining habits, their way of sitting and sleeping and talking, the modern Madurans resemble far more closely the Mohenjo-Darans than they do, say, the modern New Yorkers. I mean no disrespect to them. They have found a manner of urban life suitable to the climate and the land. Why should they alter it?

The modern Brahman gentleman of Madura wears a white cotton dhoti about his hips and legs, his chest is bare except for the Thread of Life—a white string passed over his right shoulder and under his left arm—and he generally carries another piece of white cloth, which he may fling over one shoulder or, if he feels the occasion warrants it, use as a shawl. His feet are bare, the front half of his head is shaven, but the hair is left very long at the back, and heavily painted on his forehead is his caste mark, varying in shape according to the sect of the Hindu religion to which he belongs.

If he is a businessman, or a landowner—certainly if he is a priest—he will be on the plump side, even fat. His essentially

urban life does not call for exercise, nor does his way of thinking; and his diet, being deficient in proteins and having a
superabundance of starch, is fattening. In order to eat enough
of it to maintain his energy he must fill his belly very full
indeed. Try to eat rice against a Brahman gentleman of
Madura, and see where you come in!

Now—disregarding the Thread of Life, the caste mark
and the hairdo, which have a mystical significance—it is hard
to see how his clothes could be more suited to his needs.

The dhoti is cheap, clean, cool, comfortable, and graceful.
If you have seen the relief with which a westernized Indian
changes from his hot tight trousers into his dhoti at the end
of his day's work in the office, you will realize what a comfortable garment it is. An old-fashioned Hindu gentleman,
when he takes his early morning bath at the well or at the
tank (a *tank* in India is a pond, or surface reservoir) takes his
dhoti off and washes it, lays it on the grass in the sun to dry
as he washes his body, then puts it on again and goes home
to his breakfast. What can be simpler, cleaner, or more suitable than that?

Why then should our Dravidian gentleman change his
ways? Supposing his Indus Valley ancestors also dressed like
this, why then should not he? If a mode of dress is found
suitable enough to remain at the height of fashion for five
thousand years there can be very little wrong with it.

But to a Westerner these Brahmans, with their shaven
foreheads and their heavy white caste marks, look exotic indeed. They look like people from another world—certainly
from another age. And the uninitiated foreigner is surprised,
when he speaks to one, to find that, in all probability, he is
answered in impeccable English. For English is the second
language of South India in a way that it has never been of
the North.

And the houses. They have narrow, unpretentious frontages for the most part, maybe with a little porch on which
the women of the house can sit and gossip during the day and
watch the passers-by, for there is no purdah among South
Indian Hindus. As far as the frontages of the houses are concerned, there is little to distinguish them from houses anywhere else.

There are two features that are distinctive, though.

One is an elaborate geometrical design drawn in chalk,
fresh every morning, just in front of the front doorstep.
Nearly every house in Madura has this. Formerly it was
drawn in rice flour, or some other foodstuff, but now chalk
is the general rule.

And the other is the vista of doors.

Through the modest front door, which is always kept open,
you find yourself looking through a diminishing vista of
doors, one behind the other, maybe seven or eight of them,
right to the back of the house. All these doors are kept open,
and they are always built in line. You realize then that there
is far more to the house in question than its modest and narrow frontage would lead you to expect. The dwelling house
is almost certainly single-storied, and you will find, if you
are lucky enough to be invited into it, that the rooms are
dark and cool and sparsely furnished, for most of the living is
done on the floor, and that at the back there is an open courtyard with some small bushes growing in it, around which the
kitchen and other offices are ranged. One of the bushes is
called the *tulsi,* and people walk round it when they pray.
There will probably be a well in the courtyard, around which
people bathe and where the women scrub the big copper
cooking pots until they shine. There will be a latrine with
a bucket in it that does not bear contemplating. The almost

fanatical cleanliness of the caste Hindu does not extend to his latrine.

I made one friend in Madura, a young clerk who had recently joined the Communist Party. He lived in a house such as I have described with his father, his newly acquired wife, and one or two brothers and sisters; it was more or less a joint family, as many South Indian families are.

He took me to a Communist meeting, held in another house not far away. I was not well received there. Indian Communists apparently have never heard of *swaraj*, or independence, and they still spend half their time flogging the dead horse of British imperialism. I was a Briton; *ergo,* I was an Imperialist. Probably I ate babies for breakfast.

They more or less made this attitude clear to me, so I said, "We have Communists in England, you know."

"Yes, but you're not one of them," perceptively remarked one young man.

"Furthermore," I went on, "your kind of Communism started in England. Where do you think Marx and Engels lived?"

"Well, anyway, we must free India from foreign domination," they said, doggedly, looking pointedly at *me*. I couldn't dominate a rabbit. I asked them if they were not afraid of foreign domination of another kind—from Russia? And, of course, I got the stock reply.

I asked them how it was that Communism was doing so well in such a holy city as Madura. How did the devout Hindus find it compatible with their religion?

"Communism is nonsectarian," one of them said. "It is not concerned with religion. It encourages religion, in fact, and leaves religions in peace."

I wasn't arguing seriously, of course, only baiting them a bit. Politics is not my cup of tea.

They mostly worked in the big Madura cotton mill, these ardent young men. This is one of the biggest mills in India— British-owned, incidentally—and one of the few big spinning businesses in the country. I had a look at it, and got mixed up with the workers as they were going home, some thousands of them, with cotton fluff on their hair and on their clothes.

This mill owner is a model employer, as employers go, and the workers are paid good wages. And yet, why do they look so small and thin and pinched? I followed them to their homes, which were mostly in some huge slums which have sprung up on the wrong side of the railway line. These South Indian slums are rural slums really, not urban slums. They are just huge congested villages crammed into whatever space people can find in the towns. Most of them are, like the ones in Madura, quite innocent of any form of sanitation. It struck me that working in a cotton mill all day, no matter what an efficient one it was, and going home at night to live in a leaky shack in those slums was not quite the ideal life.

But if the Communists get their way, there will be more of such mills in India, of course, not fewer.

In a café I met a man named Vustad. He was a teacher in a local school. About thirty, wife and two children, very westernized for a Madrasi, for he wore white trousers and shirt and a blue tie.

We talked of the English language.

Vustad deplored what he thought was the decline of English in India, owing to the government's policy in the schools. English was to take third place; the local language, first; and Hindi, second.

Now in South India, Hindi just does not seem to have a hope. It is a North Indian language and bears no resemblance whatever to the Dravidian tongues of the South:

Tamil, Malayalam, Kanada and Telugu, for example. Government servants in the South may be forced to learn Hindi, but they will learn it as English schoolchildren learn Latin, as a task only, something to be used for passing examinations. English is the lingua franca of South India, no other language. Every man with the least education knows some English, and every man has every intention of seeing that his sons will know some too. Even while I was at Madura someone defaced with tar the Hindi place name at the railway station, part of the agitation then going on against the introduction of Hindi into South India. Vustad had a novel solution to the language problem: the revival of Sanskrit and the making of this the official language, while English remained the real lingua franca. Sanskrit is, of course, a dead language, like Latin or Greek, but it is the language at the root of the North Indian languages, and also to a large extent of the Dravidian tongues. It is a rich language, highly adaptable, by all accounts extremely difficult to learn, and I should think that the chances of getting three hundred and sixty million Indians to learn it are slight indeed.

Meanwhile, English is to cease to be an official language within fifteen years, and every government servant is by then supposed to be going to know Hindi. In South India, at least, one can visualize the fifteen years being renewed from time to time and extending away into the future like tomorrow and tomorrow and tomorrow.

But my friend Vustad, as a teacher of English, was very concerned with the falling off of the standard of English speaking that was a result of the government's educational policy.

English was not now taught until the ninth class at school when the child was about thirteen years of age. And so he never really learned it properly.

"If the British had stayed in India another ten years," said Vustad, "we should all have spoken English by now. English would have become the real Indian language, and nothing could ever have stopped it."

I asked him why this was, and he said, "Because for the previous ten years people had been making a tremendous effort to learn English. English was becoming the only path to any sort of success in anything, and therefore parents were making any sacrifice to see that their children learned it. In another ten years the bulk of the population would have known it."

I do not know what the answer to this language problem is. If I were an Indian, I would want to read in English, but talk and write in my vernacular. For not to be able to read English is to be cut off from all but a fraction of the world's thought and feeling; but not to talk and write in one's mother tongue is never to be able to express oneself really fully and deeply, to put into one's own utterance the finer and subtler shades of meaning, or to feel really and finally happy among one's own countrymen.

Vustad told me in shocked admission that his wife did not speak English. Nor did his children, in spite of his own efforts to make them. Tamil was their language.

"My wife is backward," he said, "and this holds me back. A man cannot get far ahead of his wife. In this country we still do not realize this, and we do not spend sufficient on our girls' education. It is this that is holding us back."

I asked him in what way his wife was backward, and he told me that, for one thing, she quarreled with the other women at the well when they were drawing water. She would not, of course, let people of inferior castes draw water from the common well that she used at all, but she would not permit even people of other respectable castes. When she had her bucket down the well, they were not to put theirs in. There might be some sort of cross-pollution between the buckets. She would wait until they had finished and then draw her water, or if she had started first, would rail at them if they attempted to come near. What was this, Vustad asked me, but rank and deplorable superstition?

"Then," said Vustad, "she will give any money to a beggar —if he comes and threatens to put a curse on her if she doesn't give him money. You have seen those so-called *sadhus* and holy men; well, most of them are just rascals, and they go from door to door when they know the husbands are away, and threaten the women. First they call blessings on the house, and then, if the wife doesn't come and give them money, they call curses, and my wife then will always give."

I asked Vustad how he had met his wife, and he said that his had not been a "love marriage." In this he meant that, like ninety-nine point nine or so per cent of his fellow countrymen, his wife had been chosen for him by his parents.

"I was westernized, though, you see," he said "because I went to a mission school at Ootacamund. And so I told my father that I would not marry without seeing my wife first. And my older brother supported me; we made a pact about it. But when the time came, you know, and I tried to hold out, even my brother turned against me. His own marriage is a failure—his wife was chosen by my parents, of course—and they are unhappy. But even so, he helped to force me to do what my parents wanted."

"Why?" I asked.

"Because we must," he answered. "We just can't get away from it. Our family ties are too strong. We *cannot* break away from the family. It is too strong for us."

In the West we do not have any conception of the psychological power that an Indian family has over its members. To break away from it is almost impossible. Very few people achieve it. I have heard Vustad's story over and over again in India. Time and again I have met people who deplored the system of arranged marriages, and yet submitted to it themselves and will always bring their weight to bear on other members of their family to force them to submit to it also.

"You see, I did not wish to choose my own wife," said Vustad. "That would have been impossible. I belong to a very small subcaste of Kshatriyas; in the whole of India there are only a few thousand of us. And we have very strict rules about consanguinity. I couldn't marry anyone even remotely related to me. Then I had to marry someone with about my standard of wealth. So this brought the only possible choice down to one girl. My parents made all the usual inquiries and discovered only this one girl in India that I could marry: the right subcaste, the right age, the right riches, and not too closely related."

"But did you have to marry inside your subcaste?" I asked. "You say you are westernized. Couldn't you have made a break and married outside your caste? What was to stop you from choosing any attractive Hindu girl you met at college, for example?"

"I could *never* have married outside my caste," he said with some vehemence. "That would have been quite impossible."

"But why?"

"Well, in the first place it would have *killed* my parents. Without any doubt the shame would have killed them. Then, how could such a marriage work? All the girl's customs and ways of living would have been different from mine."

"But what terrible differences could there be?" I asked. "She would have been a Hindu, she would have spoken Tamil, she would be used to the same food as you. . . ."

"No, she would have been quite different," he said. "How would she ever have got along with my family and relations? She wouldn't know what to talk to them about, even. No, I was quite willing to let my parents choose my wife, but the thing was I wanted at least to *see* her once before we were married."

"Why didn't you then?" I asked.

"Because, as I say, my whole family were against me. It is against our custom, you see, to see one's wife before marriage. And all our family collected—my uncles from Bombay, even, they made a special journey to talk to me. I held out, though, even when my brother went against me, but then my father got ill with the worry of it and the doctor told me if I went against him any more he would die. So then I said all right, I would accept her without seeing her, but must see her before the wedding. And that they agreed to."

"And *did* you see her before the wedding?"

"Not really," he said. The wedding, apparently, had begun at the railway station, because he had had to go to Mysore to marry his wife, and the wedding party had met him at the train and the ceremonies had started straight away. "What could I do then? I couldn't make a scene there in public, and put everybody to shame. So I just had to go through with it."

"Were you lucky?" I asked.

"Yes, I was lucky. My wife was only fourteen—I was twenty-four—and I find she is a good wife. She is never impertinent." And what more can a man ask?

In theory, I found, he was not only for "love marriages" but for intercaste marriage as well. But when it came to practice, he would always be against these things.

"Do you know," he said, "so backward are we still that I cannot go for walks in the evening with my wife as I would like to? And she could never go to the post office by herself;

people would stare at her. And I have a neighbor whose wife meets him at the gate and takes his bicycle from him when he comes home from work, and even this makes the people talk. They are shocked at this behavior. Of course, Madura is an old-fashioned place. This would not be so in other parts of India."

I do not know whether Vustad is right in his theoretical (even though totally ineffective) opposition to arranged marriages. Our Western love matches do not seem to me to be conspicuously successful. I think I have seen more really happy marriages in India than in the West, although it is true that it is hard to assess the happiness of an Indian marriage, for quite often the couple may suffer in silence. But I am not convinced that a marriage is more likely to be happy because the couple chose each other. In arranged marriages, of course, the people concerned never have the thrills and pangs and heartburns of young love-making, courting, and suffering from an occasional broken heart and the feeling of insane jealousy once in a while; all such things add to the spice of life, if not to its tranquillity.

But I sometimes wish that my parents had foisted a good match on me when I was twenty. I might now be living in a comfortable villa standing in its own grounds, the father of a large family, a prosperous wholesale grocer perhaps, instead of as it is, spending my time sitting about in cafés in places like Madura, asking perfect strangers impertinent questions about their love lives.

3

THE TEMPLE OF THE FISH-EYED GODDESS

THE CENTER AND CORE of Madura is the Great Temple. The Great Temple of Minakshi, the fish-eyed Goddess and the consort of Siva; and also of Siva himself under his name of Sundareswa. In his Sundareswa form the god fell in love with the daughter of a chief of Madura and married her, and once a year now this event is celebrated by a ceremony in the great Marriage Hall after the god and the image of the chief's daughter have been paraded through the streets in a juggernaut.

Going in through the gate under one of the immense *gopurams*—one of the four that you see from the train from far away across the plains—you find yourself between two high stone walls, the outer of which, according to my *Murray's Handbook of India, Pakistan, Burma and Ceylon*, forms a parallelogram about 847 feet by 729 feet. The four great *gopurams*, according to the same source, are about 152 feet high. Their inward-leaning sides are covered with tier upon tier of fantastic statuary, right up to the strange shell-like or hornlike ornaments at the top. In spite of the profusion of rather crude and irrelevant detail I find these structures strangely impressive.

High up on the inner wall, by the way, there is a tiny window, and if you stand in a certain position you can see, through this window, the glint of the largest of the gold-covered domes of the interior of the temple. This is the only place from without the inner wall from which this dome can be seen. I was told that the window was cut so that Moslems, who may not enter the inner wall lest they defile the temple, can catch a glimpse of the glory that is inside. It does not require much deduction to suppose that it was not only Moslems for whom this window was cut. Hindu untouchables also, until recently, certainly would not have been allowed to enter.

You can wander where you like nowadays inside the temple, excepting of course into the two *adyta* where the two principal gods themselves are kept.

And what an edifice it is!

There is the Hall of a Thousand Pillars, and it *has* a thousand pillars (although some quibbling fellow counted them once apparently and found only nine hundred and ninety-seven, but as far as I am concerned there are a thousand pillars. I never believe bookkeepers and mathematicians). And what pillars! Nearly every one of them has some figure or figures carved on it: stately, graceful, horrific, humorous, or plain bawdy. "This hall was built *c.* A.D. 1560," says *Murray*, "by Arianayakan Mudali, Minister of Vishvanath Nayakka, Founder of the dynasty. He is represented on the left of the entrance sitting gracefully on a rearing horse. In the row behind him are some spirited figures of men and women, or male and female deities dancing."

And there they are, and you could wander for a week among those thousand pillars and still see something new.

The pillars represent, of course, a grove of a thousand coconut palms in the middle of which the god Sabhapati was once found seated. And on some of the pillars, if you search diligently enough, you will find some very naughty things indeed. A guide who attached himself to me said, "Only for decoration. Only for decoration, you see. Not religion."

But the Hall of a Thousand Pillars is as nothing compared with the rest of the temple. You could spend weeks wandering about it, seeing new things.

Dravidian architecture did not use the arch or the vaulted roof very much. The roof is of flat stone slabs supported by the walls or pillars. This necessitates either long narrow corridors or forests of pillars, for none of the stone slabs of the roof can be very long. The pillars in their turn lend themselves to sculpture, for what more suitable than that gods or goddesses should adorn them, or figures from mythology, or that heraldic animals should leap out from them into eternity?

And so you can walk, apparently for miles, along the dark, stone corridors, obtaining glimpses into the eerie, lamp-lit recesses, where priests perform strange rites for minor gods, emerging sometimes into great, pillar-supported galleries, rich in fantastic and often very beautiful carving. You come sometimes into the open and see towering above you, against the blinding blue of the sky, the great forms of *gopurams;* for the four hundred-and-fifty-foot *gopurams* are not the only ones in the temple by a long way. I managed to get permission to climb one of the big four, and took some photographs from the top.

What masters of stone these old temple builders were! Apart from the uncounted statues and reliefs—all competently done and some of them exquisite pieces of sculpture—there are the most amazing monoliths, pieces of sheer virtuosity, whole set-pieces, with gods and heroes and subsidiary figures, surrounding pillars, gorgeously ornamented stone canopy overhead, all carved in some miraculous manner out of one enormous rock! How could they have got these enormous masses of stone there in the first place? How could they have hollowed them out so completely, leaving only the slender pillars and other delicate elaboration, without a single disaster in the way of something breaking off which should not have done? For sheer virtuosity in rock carving, these old sculptors will surely never be equaled.

There are bunches of slender pillars carved out of one rock, and when you strike each pillar with a stone, it gives out a clear, musical note. There are the fantastic *yalis,* mythical beasts with bodies like lions but faces rather like elephants, or tapirs perhaps, inside whose open mouths you will find loose round stones. Short of smashing the *yali* you will never get these stones out. For they were never *put* in there: the carver carved them out of the rock from which he excavated the mouth!

Now so many statues are there in Minakshi Temple alone that I believe that if all the sculptors in the world today—the really good ones, that is—were put to work and told to spend the rest of their lives sculpting, they could not produce the sheer volume of carved stone that is to be found there. And none but really first-class artists could produce work of equivalent standard. This makes one wonder what has happened. Why is it that when Minakshi was built there were sufficient anonymous sculptors in South India alone to produce this huge volume of exquisite work, while now it would be impossible to find enough if you searched the entire world?

The golden age of Indian sculpture was the medieval period, a couple of centuries before Minakshi was built. But sculpture in the South of India went on flowering later, and in the sixteenth and seventeenth centuries fine temples were being built in many places there. This period was the South Indian equivalent of the time of the building of the great cathedrals in the West.

What are the conditions required to produce great popular anonymous art like this? Certainly the mass of the people must have been interested in sculpture in those days. One gets the impression that the cathedrals of the West and the sculpture of India arose spontaneously somehow from the people as a whole, and were not just the work of a few architects and artists backed by sufficient money.

The guide I mentioned before, who one day attached himself to me, was an enthusiast. He had been a clerk in the temple employ, but had lost his job, and now he earned a few rupees now and then, fastening himself onto tourists, like me. But he really knew his gods, and his mythology too. And once or twice he came out with some surprising statements.

"This statue," he said, "is half man, half woman. This side god Purusha, that side goddess Prakriti." And indeed, the statue did appear to be lopsided. "This proves," went on my guide, standing as he was among this multitude, this plethora of gods, "this proves there is only one God. All gods really only one God."

We debouched into an open space, which contained a large open-air swimming pool. People were bathing in it and the water was pea green. "Even though it looks dirty," said my guide, "it is good to bathe in it. Very holy. The water is changing once in three months." It looked to me as though the three months were nearly up.

Of course it must not be supposed that the temple was empty of people. The corridors and galleries were thronged with temple servants, uniformed guards, minor priests and major priests, and plenty of worshipers. The latter were

mostly simple village folk, by all appearances, who had probably walked in from the surrounding country to pay homage
to the gods. Some, perhaps, had come from the farthest corners of India, visiting Madura on their tour of the holy places
of the South.

Always there were things going on in the temple. Strange
wind instruments—serpents and trumpets and conches—were
being blown, drums were being beaten, groups of people
were chanting, sacrifices were being made before the gods. It
must not be supposed that Minakshi and Sundareswa are the
only gods who get attention in this particular temple, just
because it is dedicated to them. There are no less than one
hundred and forty idols of Ganesh, the elephant-headed god,
alone. Wherever you go you will find people pouring oil
on lesser gods, or performing *pujas* before them; you will
find, perhaps, a line of toil-worn peasants craning forward
to see into a door that a priest has opened for them, a door
that leads into some deep, lamp-lit recess where sits some
special god which these peasants have paid their hard-earned
annas to see.

You will see very few worshipers of the educated classes
here. If they come at all, it will probably be for political reasons: it is necessary to impress the masses that they are reli-
giously minded. Or they may come, of course, as I came, as
sightseers.

I went late in the evening once, just before the temple
was to be closed for the night. There were few people in it,
and the long corridors and galleries were dimly lit with oil
lamps, or not lit at all. From somewhere far away in the interior I could hear the eerie music of strange instruments, and
I made my way toward the sound. Eventually I came to where
they were engaged in putting Sundareswa to bed. The god
was in a palanquin, hidden from sight; temple servants (you

could tell them because they were thin) were carrying the palanquin, in stages, to the *adyta* where the god would spend the night; musicians blew instruments as weirdly shaped as they sounded; one or two priests (you could tell them because they were fat) chanted *mantrams* and performed rites. Later on I assisted at the putting-to-bed ceremony of the gods in another temple, so I will give a more detailed description of it there. I caught only a glimpse of this one in Madura.

One of the priests caught sight of me and, before I knew what was happening, rushed at me and clapped a garland round my neck. This, I thought, is going to cost me money. It did.

After rattling off some facts about the love lives of some of the gods, the priest asked me point-blank to give him some money. (The priests, by the way, are dressed like the Brahman gentlemen I described earlier on in this chapter, only more so.)

I fished out two rupees.

No head waiter in a famous restaurant could have given such a performance. A look of amazement at the money in my hand, a short laugh: of course! it was a joke! I was toying with him. Ha, ha, well, well—time's getting on—let's be serious now.

Sheepishly I fished out another three chips. I know when I have met my master. Again a virtuoso performance. Ah well, never mind, I see that not only are you a poor man of no account, but you are also completely ignorant of proper behavior, but let it be. I hold you no ill will, and in any case money means nothing to me. Come, let me tell you some more about the gods! Money is no object. Maybe, when you come again, you will have learned better how to behave.

This man was one of the ten high priests who guard this greatest of Indian temples. The image flashed through my mind of the Archbishop of Canterbury haggling with an American tourist as to how much he was going to drop in the offertory box.

Now this book is not going to be another "Verdict on India." I came to India with a completely open mind about it —inclined to be doubtful perhaps—and I left it completely won over, a convert. I am, if nothing else, pro-India. But that is no reason why I should suppress the truth. It would be doing no service either to India or to Hinduism were I to do so.

Educated Indians are quite well aware of what goes on in their temples, and uneducated ones are too, for that matter. The most ardent pilgrims will assure you that all the priests in the temple they are visiting are rogues, and out for money. Laws have been passed recently to try to put temple finances on a dignified footing—but what was ever achieved by passing laws? So in writing like this I am not telling Indians anything they did not know before. Nor am I, in the long run, doing Hinduism a disservice, so far as its reputation among foreigners is concerned.

For centuries foreigners have been judging Hinduism by visits to just such temples as Madura. They see the, to them, meaningless rites, they hear the tales of the often not very orthodox love lives of the gods, and, above all, they see, and suffer from, the rapacity of the priests. From the time that a foreign tourist leaves his shoes in the care of the grasping old woman as he goes in to the time that he finally gets them away from her on his way out, he is beset from all sides by touts, hagglers, beggars, and priests who insist on showing him things he has already seen and telling him things he already knows, and charging him heavily for the service.

And when he talks to these priests, he finds that they are

not learned men. They are not well read in Sanskrit literature. They are certainly not ascetic.

And so he condemns Hinduism in his mind as a sink of
superstition, cupidity, and idolatry. And he cannot understand how some of the most intelligent, broad-minded, and
scholarly men in the world can profess themselves to be
Hindus. And he learns nothing of the subtlety and beauty
of this oldest of all religions, and the profundity of its philosophy.

What, of course, a Christian or a Moslem or a Jew finds
so hard to understand, is the limitless *tolerance* of Hinduism.
It will embrace anything. If some tribe of jungle people have
some weird forest god of their own, right! says the Hindu, to
them he *is* God! Let them set up his idol in our temple if
they like, let them perform whatever rites or sacrifices to
him they please. God appears to them in that aspect; to us
perhaps He appears in another. Some of us can see Him in
idols, some in nature, some imagine Him in the sky, some
have highly abstract and intellectualized conceptions of Him.
Some of us just think He is Truth, or the Life Force. Some of
us seek Him in temples, others in works, others within ourselves. But whatever happens we must not deride or decry
another man's conception of God, just because that man is
unlettered and has a simple mind that cannot move on an
abstract plane. If such a man thinks God is a stone idol with
arms emerging from where its ears ought to be, well then,
that idol is indeed God.

This idea of tolerance has always been at the basis of Hinduism. It is laid down in the *Gita,* as well as in other works,
that it is *wrong* to weaken a more ignorant man's faith in
whatever may be his religion. The great temples, like the one
at Madura, are primarily for simple people, and they find
satisfaction there. There, they get their glimpse perhaps of

the One True Light. More educated Hindus seldom go to such temples, but they also are none the less Hindus. In fact, when you get to know them, you often find them extremely devout. They need not, to be Hindus, worship specifically any god of the Hindu pantheon. They need not even *believe* in it, in the sense of believing that it is anything more than an intellectual conception. Many of the greatest Hindu thinkers and writers have been agnostics and some, to all intents and purposes, atheists. The Buddha, born a Hindu, became an atheist, and his religion has been reabsorbed into Hinduism.

So we should not judge Hinduism by what goes on in the Madura temple any more than we should judge Christianity by the antics of its more extravagant sects in the mountains of Kentucky or the cities of California. And meanwhile we should not allow such things to divert our attention from the glorious art and sculpture that make the great shrines of Hinduism the equal, in their different way, of the finest creations of the medieval cathedral builders of Europe.

4

THE FOOD OF THE GODS

O N THE WAY NORTH to Madras city I might have made a diversion to Pondicherry, but I did not. But this is no reason why I should not say something about Pondicherry in this book, for I did go there during the war.

We used to get leave from where we were, and we could go to any part of India that we wanted provided that it was a "hill station." Now one visit to a hill station was enough for me, as I should think it would be for anyone, and so after my month in Naini Tal (or "Naughti Naini") with a visit to Ranikhet (or "Randi Rani") I used to cheat. I used to obtain a pass to a hill station but not go there. As we were given an allowance of traveling time I would pick a hill station as far away from where I was serving as I could, so as to have longer away from soldiering, for my love for the army was not so overpowering as to make it distasteful to me to be away from it for a while.

So one day, when my leave became due, I asked the adjutant for a pass to Ootacamund (or "Snooty-Ooty"). But I did not go to Snooty-Ooty. I got off the train at Madras.

From Madras it is a short journey to the French enclave of Pondicherry, and thither my curiosity led me. I only stayed there a day and a night. The hotels were full and I had to spend the night in a very peculiar sort of a flophouse, and I saw that to get more value from Pondicherry than a two-day visit could give I would have to stay there several weeks. And so I moved on.

But in two days I savored something of the flavor of the place, the quietness, the grave dignity. Large, rather somber and boxlike houses stand in shady, high-walled gardens; one imagines a leisurely nineteenth-century type of existence in them. Strolling in the streets in the evening, relaxed by the warm and balmy night air, I came upon some young people singing. There must have been twenty boys and girls, and about half were French and half Indian. They stood together under a street lamp, in a close bunch, singing with tremendous gusto, "When the Lights of London Shine Again"! This was a song which before that time had always failed to impress me very favorably, but which now affected me considerably. Not only was it a dozen years since I had seen the lights of London, or even London in the dark, but it seemed to me at that time that I was very unlikely ever to see London again. Not only this though, but never before had I seen such a sight as I now witnessed. Young people, pinkish-white and brown, Indian and European, singing together in perfect amity if not perfect harmony, standing in a group with their arms round each other's shoulders.

Another thing delighted me at Pondicherry, and this was a conversation that I had, in my peculiar French, with a harbor official.

Pondicherry is, of course, a port. I asked the official how many Frenchmen there were working in the customs and port offices, and he said two hundred. I asked him if there was much work to do and he told me that there was quite a lot—when a ship came in. I asked him how often a ship came in and he said that the last one had come in in 1939. It was then 1944.

Well, having seen these wonders in Pondicherry I decided to go a little farther, so I took my pack on my shoulder and shambled out of the town. And before I had gone far I beheld a strange sight: an omnibus was being pushed along the road by a crowd of people, with dense clouds of black smoke coming from the back of it. It was a bus driven by a charcoal burner, or producer-gas plant. Finding a gap among the pushers, I applied my weight also, and after we shoved the vehicle for a hundred yards or so, it started and we all jumped aboard.

This bus was very crowded; in fact, it was with difficulty that we all got in. Fortunately my companions were mostly thin men, and I found that the reason for this was that they were schoolteachers. I sat between two of them: a Vaishnavite gentleman in a dhoti and with the caste mark of the largest sect of the Vaishnavites on his forehead (a white **V** divided by a red vertical line), and a Christian gentleman in a white European-style suit. They could both speak English fluently, but with the quaint South Indian accent, and it did not take them five minutes to find out my name, what I was doing, where I came from, whether I was married, and a dozen or so other facts and figures concerning my existence.

Normally Indians, though strangers to each other, will start talking quite freely without hesitation when they come together; but when there is an Englishman in the party there is generally some reserve. They do not quite know what line he is going to take. However, when they see that he is human like themselves, they lose their reserve and start asking him questions forthwith.

I am not talking about very westernized Indians now, but the ordinary minor official or small businessman, or school-master, with a good secondary or college education, who speaks English out of doors but his own language in the home.

Now this asking of questions annoys some Englishmen, because we are reticent in this respect, and the questioning is looked upon as impertinent. But of course there is nothing impertinent about it, and it is simply the Asian equivalent (you get it right through the Middle East as well as in India) of our fatuous opening remarks about the weather. Two Englishmen will be closeted together in a railway carriage from London to Aberdeen, and when they get to Macclesfield one of them will open the conversation by saying, "Wet again, eh?" But two Indians in the same circumstances, by the time the train has drawn fairly out of Euston Station, will have asked—and received replies—about each other's jobs, states of matrimony or otherwise, numbers, sexes, and ages of any legitimate issue, monthly salary, and whether or not they are receiving traveling allowances.

Now personally I find this very sensible. Conversation is one of the better things of life, and if one is going to engage in it satisfactorily with a stranger, surely it is as well to begin by knowing some of the essential data about his life. These are all the superficial things about a man, which are not worth keeping secret. Why not get them sorted out straight away before engaging in the serious conversation? It is an effective way of breaking the ice, of satisfying one's immediate curiosity, and of displaying a friendly interest in a fellow mortal.

Well, these people gave me betel nuts to chew, asked me personal questions, and told me all about themselves. They were schoolteachers, the advance guard of a teachers' conference that was to be held at a place called Mahabalipuram. They introduced me to several other teachers in the bus, and all of them could hardly have been more friendly.

Well, when my schoolmasters had found out that I had not the faintest idea where I was going, they said I must go with them to Mahabalipuram, and, of course, I agreed. They argued and talked the whole time, mostly in Tamil but sometimes in English (for my benefit or to show the other people in the bus they knew English) and I was very surprised to find out what a well-informed lot of people they were. You see, up to that time I had never really come in contact with Indians and might well have made the same sort of mistake about them as the man who said to a Chinese at a dinner party, "Likee soupee?"

The teachers were determined, of course, to drag me into an argument about British Rule, and a very hot and lively argument it proved to be. It was a pleasure to argue with them. They so obviously *enjoyed* arguing; their wits were sharp, and they never lost their tempers or their sense of proportion.

They were very keen on pointing out places of interest to me—mostly places where one or other of the gods had had some strange adventure in days of old. I remember one hill with a temple at the foot of it called The Place of the Beautiful Vultures. I was assured that every day at noon a priest climbs the hill with food, and the vultures, beautiful or not, according to one's aesthetic values, come and take it from his hands.

We stopped to eat at wayside villages, and our bus broke down at intervals—we would all have to get out and push— and once the driver had to tie up some part of the inside mechanism with a piece of bark that he pulled off a tree. But late that evening we got to Mahabalipuram, and we all went to the schoolhouse where we were to spend the night.

Various dignitaries were there to meet us, and they had a meal ready. We sat on the ground outside the school—that is the Christians and I did, and such of the Hindus as were sufficiently Low Church to eat with us, the more orthodox ones, of course, having to go off and eat elsewhere. The meal consisted of a huge bowl of rather sloppy boiled rice, placed on the ground between us, and several smaller dishes of curried vegetables of different sorts and curried dried fish, all as hot as fire. For plates we used banana fronds, and we ate with our fingers, carefully washing our hands first, of course. My own performance was perhaps not pretty to watch, for this was the first time that I had eaten sloppy boiled rice with my fingers. However, my hosts got some amusement trying to teach me, and I love curry, the hotter the better, so I got it into me somehow and thoroughly enjoyed it.

People, of course, get as much fun from being traveled *at* as they do from traveling. In most countries I find that the inhabitants will go to endless trouble to show you the ways of the land, and they obviously enjoy doing so.

And what a lot of fun people miss by refusing to try the customs of strange countries. People will insist on eating, for example, watery boiled cabbage and stringy overcooked meat on the coast of Coromandel, where all the spices of the Indies are theirs if they want 'em. That is one of the reasons why I do not like hill stations. They are an attempt to create the atmosphere of a London suburb in the heart of India.

Well, after his meal we went into the school building—a very remarkable wattle-and-mud hut it was—and there we bedded down for the night.

I discovered that these people do not really go to bed in the same way that we do. They do not make, well, such a *business* of it, with sayings of good night and going into special rooms and complicated undressing and all the rest of it. We just went into the school and sat about on the benches and went on arguing. After a time one man pulled his feet up and wrapped his dhoti about him and laid his head on his arm. Someone else took his shirt off and rolled it up for a pillow and stretched himself out on top of a table, and like this, one by one, we all got down to some sort of a night's rest.

But even then my companions did not *really* get down to it. At frequent intervals during the night I awoke to hear two or more of them arguing. One of them had suddenly awakened and thought of a telling point. Three of them leaped up (it must have been about two in the morning) to have a look at some part of the proposed camping ground; they had got to decide where they were going to put the kitchen of the members of one of the Sudra castes. Then back they came, woke the others to argue with them a little, then all lay down on the tables and benches for some more sleep. In that very hot climate perhaps people get used to sleeping more lightly than we do.

Early in the morning they all went off to start laying out the camp, but they still found plenty of time to show me the sights.

Mahabalipuram is an amazing place. It was once the capital of a Hindu kingdom, and it is strewn with old temples and rock carvings. There is only a small village there today, inhabited by peasants and fishermen; but in the granite hills round about are the most amazing remains. When I say remains, I do not mean *ruins*. These temples are carved out of the solid rock and they are in as good repair today as they were a thousand years ago. There are five big pagodas, each carved out of a separate hill of granite, each of an entirely different shape and yet all seeming somehow to keep each other company. They are simply beautifully done; their surfaces are covered over with an intricate pattern in bas-relief illustrating incidents from Hindu mythology. There are several places on the hillsides, too, where lofty vertical faces of rock have been carved all over with gigantic pictures—gods and men and elephants and horses—all perfectly hewn out of the living rock, full of life and movement. They seem to be alive. I am not an art critic, and I cannot say what an art critic would think of it; I only know that personally I think these carvings are so good, so lively and well done, that Mahabalipuram alone is worth going round the world to see.

That men can give such life and significance to lumps of dead and senseless rock that a thousand years later people from another race can come and marvel at them and feel that they know just what these old fellows were getting at, this is a thing to wonder at. It makes one realize that we are all one sort of animal really, whatever age we happen to be born into.

And, of course, while we gazed at all this, my schoolmaster friends told me all the stories that the carvings told. Since then I have read the sacred books; but at that time it all seemed something very rich and strange to me.

After a few days the schoolteachers left with heartfelt good-byes and exchanges of addresses, and I felt that I was losing some really good friends. I had got to know and like some of them so well that I was entirely at ease in their company; we might have known each other for years.

After their departure I moved from the school to the rest house, where there was a bed. I had come to know one of the local priests who spoke some English, and also the village squire. This squire, or landlord, was a charming old gentleman. He spoke good English, although he dressed in Indian fashion and was an orthodox Brahman. He used to come and visit me every afternoon at the rest house and we would sit out on the veranda and have long discussions. About four-ish we used to retire into my room to do a little secret drinking, but it was only tea drinking. For, of course, it'd never have done for the squire to have been seen by his tenants drinking tea with a non-Brahman. When the priest was with us, of course, I had to drink my tea alone.

I do not think that I ever enjoyed conversation more than I did those talks with the squire and the parson of Mahabalipuram. The squire particularly. One felt in him a deep and ancient culture, and he had a very keen and urbane wit. The parson was a bit, well, inhuman. He was always faultlessly turned out with a clean-shaven head—just a tuft of hair near the back, of course—and his caste mark newly painted on his forehead. He wore a snowy-white robe, flung with perfect grace over one shoulder, leaving the other bare. But his face never altered its aloof expression, and he never smiled. I asked him once what his job was in the temple. "I am a cook," he said rather surprisingly. "What do you cook?" I asked. He answered, "The Food of the Gods."

The Food of the Gods! No wonder he stalked about as though he did not really belong to our old planet at all!

In the evenings I used to stroll round near the modern temple (the locals did not seem to look upon the ancient temples as holy any more) and from inside the high stone wall, which I was never allowed to see behind, came weird, unearthly sounds of conches and drums and strange instruments, and the chantings of age-old ceremonies like voices from the buried past of the earth.

I left Mahabalipuram on a canal barge when the time came. It was drawn by coolies, who took it in turn to walk along the bank, for the wind was against us and we could not set sail. We kept going night and day until we reached Madras and I had to get back again to the world of smelly railway compartments and the war and the various other manifestations of our western civilization.

This little interlude was my first glimpse of the Indian India. It was enough to make me wish to see more.

5

MADRAS: THE WORLD OF KUTTI

We must now move forward in time, but not in space. From Madras to Madras, but from 1944 to 1952.

In the latter year I arrived in Madras by train, and not by canal boat, and having by this time no visible means of support, was without very much money. Now during my infrequent and transitory periods of solvency, I sometimes spend a little money on a camera, and maybe on one or two subsidiary lenses. At other times these cameras have to go. They leave me. When I reached Madras this second time I realized that the moment had come for parting with a lens or two.

A good friend of mine in Ceylon had lived for many years in Madras, and he had given me the name of a friend of his there, one G. K. Vale, a professional photographer. So I decided to go to see this man and find out if I could not sell him a couple of lenses.

There are said to be three climates in Madras city: hot, hotter, and hottest. When I arrived there it was hottest. I had to walk a long way from where I was staying to the establishment of G. K. Vale, and the streets were hot and dusty, beggars were frequent, traffic was noisy and troublesome, and, after a mile or two, life began to pall. I arrived at Mount Road, the main shopping street, and after inquiry discovered the shop of G. K. Vale. It was obviously the premier photographic business in the city.

Inside I inquired for the proprietor. I was introduced to a thick-set, apparently rather phlegmatic, middle-aged man, who looked at me through thickish spectacles in a hard sort of way, as though he were trying to see right inside me. He wanted to discover how things were with me, what I thought about it all, and what life added up to for me. Later I found that he looks at everybody like this. He is desperately interested in people and how they approach life. I little realized, when I was haggling with him over the price of a Summar f/2 and an Elmar Wide Angle, that in meeting G. K. Vale I was being handed the keys of the city of Madras.

After I had driven a surprisingly satisfactory bargain with him over the lenses, he asked me where I was staying. I told him that, although I could hardly describe myself as young, and am not altogether a Christian, I was staying at the hostel run by the Young Men's Christian Association. My intention was to remain there until I could find something very much cheaper. He said, "If you are a friend of Cooray's, you are a friend of mine, and if you do not mind Indian food, you had better come and stay in my house." I said that I thought that I might manage to stomach some Indian food and told him that I would be delighted to stay in his house. We collected my kit from the Y.M.C.A., drove south along Mount Road into an area of large houses, and turned into a palatial driveway. In front of us was an ostentatiously large house. On the lawn in front of it a concrete water nymph stood in the middle of a small pond.

Inside the house was first a large living room with easy

chairs and sofas, fans overhead, framed photographs, and landscape paintings done by Mr. Vale's retouching artists on the
walls, and one or two small statues on pedestals. The room
looked as though it had never been lived in. There were no
newspapers lying about, no books, no odds and ends, no un-
tidiness. It had nothing of India in it, this room, and yet it
was not specifically western. We were met by one of my host's
daughters.

Mr. Vale has three daughters, all, alas, married; and two of
them live in their father's house, together with their husbands and children. Where will you get women like South
Indian women? They compare in beauty with any women in
the world, and withal they have a kind gentleness: a submis-
siveness that is yet firm and possessed; a poise and, yes, *self-
assurance,* which you will find nowhere else in the world.
They know exactly where they are, and have no wish to be
anywhere else. Whether this is because they are the products
of the longest unbroken run of civilization man has had, or
whether it is because of the peculiar manner in which they
are brought up, I do not know. Later, when I got to know
Kutti better (Kutti was Vale's nickname), he said to me, after
we had both drunk a fairish amount of whisky I must admit,
"If I had another daughter, I would marry her to you, John!"
Well, Kutti, if you had, I would take her, mark my words!
But the secret of being a bachelor is always to fall in love
with women who do not exist, or else with ones whom you
cannot marry.

We sat down to our meal together and I was delighted to
find that my host was not a vegetarian. I like vegetarian food
well enough, but I like it best when I have a half pound or
so of good meat to eat with it. Kutti told me that he personally always ate meat with his meals. There was one day a week
on which his wife would not cook meat, even if he ordered

her to do so, because that day was particularly holy among Hindus. So on that day he went and ate at the Jimkana Club.

At Kutti's we always had rice, good fluffy dry rice, large heaps of it; meat, curried mutton perhaps, never beef, of course; fish, either fresh or else dried and salted, but in all cases curried, and maybe half a dozen different kinds of vegetables. Tropical vegetables, like the hideously named "lady's fingers," the eggplant, or many other kinds of gourd-like vegetables. The disadvantage of this sort of food is that it is so good that you tend to eat far too much of it.

After this first course we had the second: more rice. But this time eaten with pepper water. We ate from plates, sitting at a table, not from plantain fronds on the floor. The pepper water was delicious. We poured it over the rice and scooped the wet rice up with our fingers, or we took a mouthful of rice and then a sip of pepper water. Then came the third course. Rice. But this time with curd. We dumped the curds on top of the rice and ate this again with our fingers. I was expected at first to eat with a spoon, but never did so. The fact is that to eat good rice with a spoon is a sacrilege. This sounds like nonsense, but it is not. Eat rice for a month or two as it should be eaten: with your fingers, and then try to use a spoon. You will see what I mean. It tastes entirely different. For one thing you can taste the spoon. For another, it—well—it's different. I can't say why, but ask anybody who is used to eating rice with his fingers.

After the third course came mangoes. Large, juicy, completely delicious mangoes. Wherever you eat mangoes in India you will be told, "These are nothing! You should have been here a month ago, at the height of the season. Or you should eat mangoes in North India. Or in South India. Or in East India. Or anywhere in fact but here." I was given this sort of talk at Kutti's, but this did not stop me from eating a great many mangoes.

The meal I have described we had twice a day, every day without exception. South Indian food varies a lot as to individual dishes, but not as to the general layout of the meal. Always rice. Always three servings of it, the second eaten with pepper water and the third with curd. But the side dishes with the first helping occur in great variety.

Breakfast, now that we are on the subject of food, consisted generally of rice cakes of one sort or another—*appemrs, pitu,* cakes made from rice flour or else from whole rice steamed inside hollow bamboos. This is eaten with *sambar,* hot curry of one sort or another, grated coconut perhaps with plenty of chillies in it, sometimes delicious dried fish. At first there were always two fried eggs for me, for the belief is widely held in India that an Englishman *must* have two eggs for breakfast: his survival depends upon it.

After a midday meal such as I have described above there was but one thing to do, and I did it. I went upstairs, turned on the fan in my room gently, and fell fast asleep until some tea was brought to me at the civilized hour of four o'clock.

Kutti's household was not a typical joint family system, because his daughters had remained with him after marriage, with their husbands. Kutti had no sons. If he had had, no doubt the sons would have stayed on in their father's house and the daughters gone to live with their in-laws, which is the usual arrangement.

One might feel appalled at the prospect of spending one's life with one's in-laws, if one did not know the conditions which prevail inside the average Hindu joint family home. You see, the various subunits of the family do not impinge very much upon each other. They live in different parts of the house, probably get up and go to bed at different times of the day, meet only at certain times, and, in fact, remain a certain distance from each other.

The joint family system of the Hindus not only involves living in the same house. Often, in fact, the various branches of the family do not live in the same house. The brothers split up and go to various places to earn their living. But the family does not split up. It remains an indivisible economic unit. All the sons of the family, when they begin to earn money, send some of it back to the head of the family. This head is, of course, the father, until he dies, and then it is the eldest brother. But whoever it is keeps and spends this money as a trust for the rest of the family. As long as Hindus retain the joint family system the average man will never need social insurance, or indeed any other kind of insurance. The family is its own insurance. If a boy needs educating, and his father cannot do it, then the family will do it. If he leaves school and cannot find a job, then the family will support him. Or find him a job. Lands and houses belong to the family, not to any individual. Wives are found for the young men of the family by the family, and husbands are found for daughters. The individual's very identity is merged with his family.

Whether this system is good or bad I have no way of knowing. I do not belong to a joint family myself, and find it hard to imagine doing so; in fact, I think that I would be unsuited for it. But one must appreciate the security and stability conferred by such families. There may also be, of course, a certain stifling of personal initiative.

Probably the joint family system in India is breaking up. There was a system very like it in England, a hundred years ago, and that has certainly broken up. The big difference about the English system was primogeniture, the passing on of the bulk of the estate to the first-born. The Hindus have never had this; the property either has been retained by the

unbroken family, or else has been divided equally between
the sons, the daughters first having been fitted out with
dowries. This difference in law and custom has certainly had
a profound effect on the whole of the life and society of the
two cultures.

I am not holding Kutti's family up as an example of a
typical joint family, for it was not, but merely making a di-
gression about this important Eastern phenomenon at this
point.

The evening meal is usually taken very late in South
India, but in Kutti's household it was preceded by a pleasant
and civilized ceremony. We sat about on the lawn, near the
water nymph, and drank whisky and iced soda water.

Now Madras, as I have said before, is a prohibition area,
but this did not prevent us from drinking whisky and soda
near the water nymph. For Kutti and most of his friends had
permits, which they had obtained by saying that they needed
whisky on medical grounds.

Kutti moves in a very civilized, pleasant, urbane society.
I think of his circle of friends as "Kutti's Club." There were
some dozen people, perhaps, all mature men, middle-aged,
and representing the higher civil servants and the more solid
businessmen of the city. There was no one in Madras to
whom I could not have had access through Kutti or his
friends, if I had been interested in having access to the sort
of people one has to have access to. But as it was, every evening during the two weeks that I stayed there we had a pleasant party at one house or another, during which we drank
whisky and soda, engaged in sound, sensible, civilized conversation, generally got as far as a little song, and broke up
at one or two o'clock in the morning.

The first evening we sat by the water nymph and discussed
the sexes. There were some half-dozen of us—a grand little

man I will call Number One, who is a very senior civil servant; the Major, a retired official of the Prisons Department;
a Brahman businessman named Narayana; an Indian Christian civil servant, Bob; Kutti, and myself. These are neither
their real names nor nicknames, but near enough.

Kutti started on a subject dear to his heart, the incompara-
ble perfection of South Indian women. He always stressed
South Indian. I do not think Kutti would have admitted
much good of anything far north of the Godavari River. Bob
said women should be emancipated. A girl should be brought
up exactly as a boy is, have the same rights and the same
duties, find her own husband if she wished to get married,
and then have equal status with her husband. Men and
women were equal. They asked me what I thought about it.

I thought that it was impossible to compare two different
things. You cannot say for example, "This apple is equal to
that orange." You might say, "I like apples better than
oranges," or you might say, "An orange has more nourish-
ment, is sweeter, is brighter, than an apple," but you cannot
possibly say that these two things are *equal.* They are different, and different things can never be equal.

Kutti asked me whether I thought that girls should receive
the same education as boys. I asked him whether he thought
that apples should receive the same cultivation as oranges. I
said that I thought that girls should receive *as much* education as boys, but not *the same* education. Kutti said that he
was seeing that his granddaughters grew up to be good wives
and mothers; he was not giving them as much education as he
was his grandsons. They had a different role to fulfill; why
give them the same preparation for it?

Bob, the Christian, indignantly championed what he
thought were Women's Rights, and reiterated his belief that

men and women were equal. He asked me why I thought
they were different.

I said that I could demonstrate to him very easily that
women were different from men, if he would just bring me
one along. I further said that there were many things which
a woman could do, but which neither he nor I could do. Was
it not reasonable to suppose, I added, that there were certain
things that he and I could do which a woman could not do?

The Major then said that he knew of an emancipated girl
who had ruined her youth by addressing herself to the study
of the higher mathematics. She had managed to remain in her
class only by excessive effort, and had thus missed all the fun
of being young, and then—she was an attractive girl—she had
got married. Where were the higher mathematics now? Gone
and forgotten, the best thing that could have happened to
them.

Number One asked me why I thought that women should
have as much education as men if it were not to be the same
education. Did I mean that they should be taught domestic
science and how to look after babies for fourteen years?

I said that of course they should be taught how to look
after homes and babies—how could anyone think that they
should not?—but they should also be given a very full liberal
education. They should concentrate on literature, the arts,
languages. If they were musical, they should be able to play
some instruments; they should know a great deal of poetry
and perhaps be able to compose it; they should be, even more
than men, cultured people. For the culture of society depends more than anything else upon the culture of its women.

Kutti said that no women in the world could be more truly
cultured, more entirely satisfactory, than the South Indian
women. Some of them, perhaps, did not know how to read,

but reading was not everything. One could still have culture and not be well read.

How truly Kutti spoke! He himself never read anything, so far as I could find, but American comics, which are not comic but tragic. And yet one could not have found a more really cultured person. He had the culture of five thousand years of civilization behind him, and it was discernible in every gesture he made, in every word he spoke.

The next evening our meeting was on the Major's roof garden, and there we drank more whisky and soda, and this time talked about God. You cannot go very far in India without talking about God.

But first we set about poor Narayana and pulled his leg.

Bob did not like Brahmans. He attacked them (present company excluded; of course, nobody could fail to like Narayana) but Bob blamed them for all of India's alleged backwardness. It was the Brahmans who kept the Harijans down; it was the Brahmans who perpetuated the stupidity of caste; it was the Brahmans who kept women in subjection and men in ignorance. The best thing that had happened in the new India was the discomfiture of the Brahmans.

For to a certain extent they have been discomfited.

Brahmans originally were priests, of course. Any adult male Brahman is automatically a priest, and qualified to perform any of the rites of Hinduism. This is true to this day. But, as the Brahmans increased in numbers and the amount of money that could be extracted from the laity by priestcraft diminished, more and more members of the caste took to other jobs, and these were mostly jobs of an intellectual nature. The Brahmans are a clever people, used to working with their brains, not with their hands. As time went by, most of the better jobs in the country fell into the hands of Brahmans.

But now, with New India, they were being placed at a disadvantage. Firstly, Harijans (the people who used to be called "Untouchables") were being given preference in admission to colleges, universities, or to posts. An all-out effort is being made in India, and very rightly too, to raise up the depressed classes. Secondly, now that India is a democracy, the Brahmans, being a minority, are losing their important position. The first minister of Madras is a Brahman, C. R. Rajagopalachari, but he is there for other qualities than that of being a Brahman. ("That old fox!" people say when they hear talk of Mr. Rajagopalachari. But they say this with a strain of affection in their voices, unless they happen to belong to the Communist Party.)

Now Kutti, who is not a Brahman at all but a Mudaliar, or member of a trading caste, stood up stoutly for the Brahmans. The Brahmans had *earned* their favored position before Independence, he said, and it was unfair to discriminate against them now. Just because they were cleverer than other people, was this a reason why they should be victimized?

Narayana sat in his chair, sipping his whisky and soda, with a smile on his fat, good-natured face. I must say he did not look very victimized.

Bob disagreed with Kutti. He said that Brahmans were not really clever, but fools. They were terribly superstitious, for example. Look at old Narayana there. He wouldn't do a deal in business without going first to his astrologer.

Narayana, who enjoys being a butt, was persuaded to tell the tale of the time he died.

His astrologer had told him that he must set his affairs in order, for on a certain day he would die. "He has a weak heart, you see," said Kutti in an aside. "The doctors keep telling him that he will die within six months if he doesn't stop drinking whisky, and they told him that ten years ago and have been telling it to him ever since."

"Yes, Kutti, but I really *did* die," said Narayana, in his rather fruity voice. "You see, our teaching tells us that we each die twice. The first is our real death, and after that we're just ghosts, although our bodies keep on going. Since that day I've just been a ghost."

"A pretty substantial ghost!" said Bob. "I never thought a ghost could turn the scale at a hundred and eighty pounds and put down a bottle of Scotch whisky every evening!"

"Ah, you laugh," said Narayana.

"But, John, the astrologer really did tell him that he would die on a certain day," said Kutti. "And as the day got near he wouldn't eat, wouldn't drink, wouldn't have a whisky. He spent all his time doing *puja* in the temple, didn't you, Narayana?"

"Yes," said Narayana happily. He loved having this story told.

"He even began to get thinner," said Kutti. "And he's got a lady friend in a certain part of the town, you see, John," he went on. "So we told him to go to see this lady. Now the lady told him, 'Look here, Narayana, you come and spend that day with me. Come and spend the day here. I will look after you, I'll feed you and make you happy, and you'll be all right. And if you *do* die, then you'll at least die happy.' Isn't this true, Narayana?"

"It's quite true," said Narayana, smiling and wriggling a bit in his chair and taking a sip of whisky.

"And did he go to the lady?" I asked.

"No, at the last minute his courage failed," said Kutti. "He didn't go to the woman. He stayed at home and did *puja* all day. We all took turns at going to see him to cheer him up, but he wouldn't talk to us. He spent the whole day in front of his shrine doing *puja* to the Gods. Didn't you, Narayana?"

"Of course, that's what I did," said Narayana.

"And did you die?" I asked Narayana.

"Well, you see, John, I didn't die really, I suppose. But afterward the astrologer explained it to me. He said that some people *do* die twice. I am one of them. We Brahmans say we are born twice, so this was my first death. The next time will be the real one."

"He's dead scared of dying," said Bob. "Aren't you, Narayana?"

"Well, Bob, I must admit I do enjoy this life, you know."

"That's because you think you'll be a snake or a cow in the next one, isn't it? Look at the sins you've committed in this one! Look at the whisky you've drunk! Look at the meat you've eaten! Look at the women you've been after! Look at the lies you've told!" I must say that Narayana did not look like an ascetic by any means. He was a sort of Eastern Falstaff.

Then the conversation turned to God. "We Hindus," said Number One, "are the only really free people. Provided you believe that God exists—that is all—then you can be a Hindu. Narayan believes his astrologers and all that stuff about dying twice, but he's no more a Hindu than I am, and I have never been in a temple, except to look at the sculpture. I never pray, I have no household Gods, I never do *puja!*"

"Do you believe in God?" I asked.

"As Voltaire said, 'If God didn't exist, it would be necessary to invent Him!' The word *God* is simply a convenient way of expressing a conception that one cannot think very far without. If you think far enough, you eventually have to invent something, which is best called God."

"But in what way are you a Hindu?" I asked. "You never take part in any Hindu worship."

"The Hindus have no corporate worship," said Number

One. "The only thing they do in their temples is to pay the priests to perform *pujas,* or sacrifices, to the Gods. This is an entirely individual matter, not a corporate one." (I believed this then, but later on I took part in what seemed very like corporate worship to me.) "But I am a Hindu because I was brought up in the Hindu philosophy and way of thinking," he went on. "Hinduism is a way of life, and an attitude to life. I have that attitude. It is an acceptance. I have that acceptance. Narayana has it too, although he believes many things that I do not believe. Or, at least, I believe them insofar as I think that they're true for Narayana. I support temple worship too, because I know that less educated people than myself must have a simpler, more direct religion. So must women. My wife performs daily *puja.* She can conceive of God better if she can see Him sitting on a shelf. I can conceive Him only by intense and prolonged meditation, which alas, I don't get time for. But her God is just as true and as real as mine is."

"Idolators!" said Bob, who was a Roman Catholic. "What about cow worship and monkey worship and *lingam* worship and caste and not being able to eat with this one or that one and untouchability? What about all those things? Aren't they the things that are holding this country back? You talk about tolerance. What is tolerant about a religion that won't let a man sit down and have a meal with another man because they're not of the same caste?"

"These things are not the real things of Hinduism," said Kutti, mildly. "These all started later. You will not find about them if you read the Vedas."

"The Vedas, the Vedas! Always the damn Vedas! If you believe the Vedas, why don't you act on them? The Vedas continually talk of killing cows and eating beef—yet why all this nonsense about cows being our mothers and we can't kill

them? It's mainly due to this: we're the poorest country in
the world. The Vedas talk on nearly every page of drinking
soma ras. That was an intoxicant. Yet what about all this
nonsense of prohibition, because drink is against Hinduism?
What about child marriage and sutteeism and temple prosti-
tution?" demanded Bob.

"He's been reading *Mother India,*" said Number One with
a smile.

Number One was Bob's boss, among other people's.

There seemed to me to be nothing very intolerant about a
country that five years after it had achieved independence
would keep a man like Bob on in a high position and allow
him to say the things he does say about the religion of ninety
per cent of the population. I can think of other countries not
a million miles away where this would not be the policy.

But Narayana began to sing. He always does sing sooner or
later. Bob and I sometimes sang English songs, for Bob had
been educated in England and was as English as I was, and
yet I believe he liked the Indian songs best. Kutti and his
other friends sang only classical Indian songs, Karnatak or
South Indian songs. These are very strange to a Westerner's
ears until he gets used to them. They always seem off the
note somehow, and there is a lot of trilling and warbling in
them. But by that time I had heard enough Indian music to
have got to like it, and there is no missing the intense sincerity with which these songs are sung.

Our friends would take turns singing songs, sometimes ex-
temporizing about some particular occasion perhaps. The
people not singing would sit about with wrapt expressions,
at times wagging their heads in their inability, real or as-
sumed, to control their emotions, breaking sometimes into
vocal exclamations: "Ah! ah! ah!" or "Woh! woh! woh! woh!
woh! woh! woh!"

But the song that Narayana sang was not extemporary; it was an old song, no one knows how old. It was supposed to be the song of an untouchable, one who is not allowed within a hundred yards or so of the temple lest he defile it with his presence.

Kutti translated it for me. The words meant: "O God, even though you will not allow me to come near you, even so I want to worship you. Let me worship you from afar!"

One song followed another, argument was interspersed with song, and it was well into the morning before we left the Major's roof garden.

6

THE SEAMY SIDE AND THE DANCE

As in all big cities of the world there are slums in Madras, and people who are never quite sure whether or not they are going to get anything to eat. Give a man his fair share of the earth's surface, and, if he survive one good harvest and is not a fool, he never need fear being hungry again. But take him and dump him down in a huge city like Madras and he immediately becomes dependent on factors outside his control—the prosperity or otherwise of trade, the demand for labor, the price of rice.

In Madras there are many rickshaw pullers, and also hand-cart pullers—human beasts of burden. Human beings are much cheaper than horses or oxen in Madras, and one does not have to buy them. There is no initial cost, but only a trifle for maintenance. One has no capital locked up in them, and when they founder, it is no loss. There are plenty of others.

A great part of the cargoes of this thriving port are taken to the dockside or away to the city on handcarts. Two or three men in loincloths pull and push these loaded carts, with the

sweat running down them and actually dripping onto the
street, for it is hot in Madras, and sticky. They get quite good
money when they can get work, three or four rupees a day
even. But they do not last long. The work puts an unbearable
strain on the heart. As for the rickshaw pullers, surely they
must have sinned terribly in a former existence? We should
hate them, for their sufferings in this life show that they must
have been wicked in the last. Free enterprise works perfectly
among the rickshaw pullers. Competition keeps prices down
beautifully.

There is always some wretch willing to pull you five miles
for an anna less. The more enterprising ones take to pimping,
of course; in all walks of life it is the enterprising who come
to the top.

In all South Indian cities there are beggars. Many of these
are highly paid professionals, reared to the trade. Some take
the religious or mystical line; they play on the fears of the
ignorant by threatening to curse them. Others, also professionals, are maimed by their parents while young; there are
very many such. Their legs are withered or deformed, their
arms are still those of babies. Then there are the shammers,
about whom one cannot be too severe. They are not properly
maimed at all; they only pretend to be maimed, binding back
one leg so as to hide it, for example, and painting a suppurat-
ing stump-end on the knee. In North India there are the
pinheads, but they are the result of a vow. There was a
Moslem saint who was afflicted with this condition of pin-
headedness, and nowadays a man sometimes will make a vow
that if such and such a thing is vouchsafed him he will dedi-
cate his next child to be a pinhead. Then the baby's head is
encased in an iron helmet as soon as he is born and he is
allowed to grow up like that. His body grows big—larger often
than the average adult's—but his head and his mind stay the

same. The creature dribbles and whines as he walks about, led generally by some woman or child who asks alms for it.

But most numerous of all are the real beggars: people normal but for the fact that they have no way of eating unless someone gives them an anna or two. They beg at first because they must, but afterward get used to it and would never wish to do any other work. As they become more proficient, they employ more art. Most of them hire the small children, who are always available for a few annas a day. A thin baby, kept howling by an occasional shrewd prod, preferably with a few sores and certainly with his eyes completely obscured by flies, is worth his weight in gold.

What is the reason for this phenomenon of begging? Partly poverty, of course, but also partly religion. For it is meritorious to give alms. And to simple people it is most meritorious to give alms directly—to the final recipient—not to give money to a charitable institute and do good at three or four removes. As long as the demand exists, to acquire merit by giving alms, so long will there be people willing to satisfy this demand by begging.

As for the slums, the Madras slums are rural slums, like those of Madura. They are not the big dilapidated tenement buildings of the big cities of industrial countries, but slummy villages of shacks or hovels, which have been dumped down in vacant lots in the city. They are preferable to the tenements, I think. Your roof may leak (in fact, it almost certainly *does* leak), the road outside your front door may be a latrine, your hovel may be full of flies, but at least your slum is not so all-pervading. You can always get out of it quite quickly. And, of course, in Madras one is never far from the sea, and where the sea is, no man need give up hope. For the sea can never be bought by some rich man and built upon. You can always bathe in it and sniff the fresh breezes from it and, if you have the skill and the courage, go out on its waters and catch some fish to give to your children.

I saw something of these slums, and the people who live in them, because I met a man named Dr. Sambandam, who was director of an institution called Ashok Vihar. This was started in Madras after the war on the style of a health center. I went to Ashok Vihar in the evening the first time, and there I found Dr. Sambandam playing volleyball, a game that has become very popular in India. He left the game to come and talk to me, and I fancied that he felt just a touch of elation when he saw, as we stood and watched the game, that the side on which he had been playing, and which had been winning, now began to lose.

There was a lot of activity going on besides volleyball. Maybe fifty or sixty children of all ages were playing other games or engaging in physical training, and I could not help noticing that their standard of fitness was well above that of others whom I had seen in the streets of Madras. The children were clean also, and each one wore a clean uniform, which I was told he put on, after a shower, when he came to the center, and took off and left behind when he went away.

Later on we saw a cinema show, saw women being taught handicrafts, watched boys studying in light and spacious rooms (because there was no place in their slum homes to study), watched others playing ping-pong and other indoor games.

The next morning I went there again and saw a procession of poor parents bringing their children along to the day nursery that is run there. These were little children up to four or five years old. They also were washed and dressed in clean overalls; their rags were put away in a cupboard. They were cared for by some very efficient ladies dressed in nurses' uniforms.

During the day I saw these little children being fed good food, being allowed to play with lots of fascinating toys, having their minds stimulated and awakened by simple teaching and by play. Supposing every poor child in India could be brought up like this for the first four or five years of his life? In one generation India would lead the world in everything worth leading it in.

But, of course, Ashok Vihar can cope with only a negligible fraction of the children of Madras.

Dr. Sambandam with his assistant, Dr. Chitra Bai, spends his morning going round the slums on foot, visiting the homes of those families which are members of his health center. Ashok Vihar admits only families to membership; individuals are not accepted.

For several days I went round with these two doctors and saw parts of Madras that I would not have seen otherwise.

It must not be thought that Madras is doing nothing to improve the lot of its slum dwellers. In the first place, it has started Ashok Vihar. Then we saw many "improved slums," some improved to the point where they have ceased to be slums at all.

The unimproved slum is just a piece of wasteland, the owner of which charges from four to ten rupees a month for the privilege of erecting a hovel on an area of ground about the size of a small living room. The lucky tenant scavenges around for some mud bricks, some old bits of rusty corrugated iron, some flattened gasoline cans, some pieces of woven coconut fronds, and erects himself a shack. The doctors and I worked out what the owner of one slum was making per annum from about half an acre of such land, and I must say I rather envied the man. How does one set about becoming a slum landlord?

But slums on city land have been, and are being, greatly

improved by the city. The roads have been paved in most cases, sometimes there are electric street lights, water mains have been opened in every street, and when I was there a big drive was on to install waterborne sanitation in every house —surely the first essential and *sine qua non* of decent urban living.

In some cases the city itself had built *pukha* houses: genuine houses of burnt brick. In other cases they had marked out plots and allowed the people to build their own houses, but to a proper design and with some financial help from the government. In one case, alas, zeal for sanitation had outrun aesthetics to such an extent that enormous concrete latrines had been built in a row down the street in front of the houses, which seemed to cower behind them. It was like a city of public lavatories.

The pleasantest so-called "improved slum," to my mind, was one in which masonry plinths had been built by the city and the people had been allowed to build their own houses on them to their own designs, provided only that they fitted the plinths. Sufficient room had been left for small gardens, trees had been planted, the little houses, although uniform in size and ground plan and standing perforce in line, were sufficiently varied not to be monotonous, and altogether I would not have minded living in one myself.

In the afternoon the two doctors returned to the center, and there they were busy until evening doing medical examinations; for each member of every member family is subjected to a periodical medical checkup. If there is anything seriously wrong with him, arrangements are made for him to go to a hospital.

Ashok Vihar costs a lot of money, and affects only a small part of the slum population of Madras. Some people would

like to multiply it, start such centers in others parts of the
city until the whole city is covered.

But others would not. Of course, institutions like Ashok
Vihar start with a big disadvantage in that they have no
figures to offer. And where can you get, in the world today,
with no figures? For you can prove *anything* with figures.
And, of course, you can prove nothing. But if you have no
figures, where are you? Whom can you impress?

And Ashok Vihar depends on preventive medicine. And
preventive medicine can have only negative results. How can
you prove that a boy who grows up into a healthy man might,
under other conditions, have grown up to be a consumptive?
The people who attend regularly at Ashok Vihar just do not
get ill, that is all. They have nothing to show for it. No
figures.

When you scrutinize the annual budget of Madras, you
realize that it would be difficult for the city to spend more
money on such ventures as Ashok Vihar. But when you walk
or drive around the streets of Madras, you realize that there
is wealth enough in the city to establish and support a hundred Ashok Vihars. The difficulty is to extract and apply this
wealth. I hope that this difficulty is soon overcome, for if
Democrats cannot overcome it, there are others who are willing to try.

Another place I used to visit in Madras was Adiyur. This is
a place on the coast some miles south of the city where the
Theosophical Society have their headquarters. I did not go
to see the Theosophical Society, but to visit Kalakshetra, a
school for teaching dancing and art to children whose parents can afford to send them there.

I used to watch dancing in the company of Shankar Menon,
the brother of the more politically minded Krishna Menon
who generally tries to live in London. Shankar Menon helps

to manage Kalakshetra, which was founded by Rukmini Devi, one of the greatest of Indian dancers.

The place delighted me. There was a children's school in the same compound, and there seemed to be a lot of coming and going between the school and Kalakshetra. The school was run on what is known as "modern" lines. The teachers do not control the children by punishing them. The atmosphere of the place is delightful.

But the dancing!

Of the two schools of dance of South India, Kathakali is the best known. To my taste it is too formalized, too artificial. The other school, Bharatya Natya, had almost died out when it was revived by Rukmini Devi, and it can be seen today at its best only at Kalakshetra.

Most of the Bharatya Natya dances are based on incidents from the life of Lord Krishna.

The Krishna cult is the expression of personal love in Hinduism. Many of the god's followers feel the intense, almost passionate, love for him that some Catholics feel for the Virgin. Young girls worship him particularly, for they look upon him as the ideal man and lover. A great deal of Indian art—painting, song and dancing, particularly—is inspired by Krishna, and among the Hindu pantheon he is by far the most human and understandable of the gods. He seems friendly and approachable.

Originally, it is probable that his legend was based upon a historical figure, a king who took part, passively, in the great battle described in the *Mahabharata*.

When he was a small child, Krishna's life was threatened by the king of his land. This king had been warned by an astrologer that this particular baby would grow up to kill him and assume his throne. The baby Krishna was therefore smuggled out of his father's house and hidden in the house of a cowherd, by whom he was brought up, and later did in fact return to kill the wicked king and mount his throne.

The most delightful of the Krishna stories are about his doings as a boy among the cowherds. They are tales of mischief —of how he used to steal the milk and the butter, of how he played the flute, and of how he used to tease the *gopis,* or milkmaids, and incidentally make love to them!

One of the Bharatya Natya dances that we watched was based on this teasing of the *gopis.* This dance is the enactment of a *sloka,* or stanza, of the *Karnaamrita,* or book of Krishna. It describes how Krishna came one day to where the *gopis* were bathing in a pond, having taken off their saris and laid them down on the bank. Creeping up unobserved, Krishna stole the saris and climbed a tree with them. He then began to play his flute and laugh at the *gopis.* The *gopis* became embarrassed and begged Krishna to give them their clothes back, but he would not do so. When the *gopis* chased him, Krishna took refuge by hiding in the middle of the herd of cows.

The dance was performed by one girl, a consummate dancer named Sarada Devi, who was twenty-one but had spent most of her time dancing since she was a little girl. The music was provided by two men and two young women, who sat on mats playing drums and a flute and singing.

If one had any idea of the story, it was not necessary to understand the words of the song, the actions of the dancer were so expressive.

One saw the *gopis* coming to the water and laying off their saris. This taking off of the saris was indicated with an inexpressibly graceful gesture. One saw them place their saris on the ground. One saw them enter the water, pushing the water away from them with their hands as they entered it. One saw them hold their noses and duck their heads! One saw the naughty Krishna leaning on his stick, one leg up, in a position very characteristic of Indian herdboys.

In some cunning way the dancer made you see all this, and she conveyed the impression that Krishna was watching the *gopis* all the time that they were bathing. And meanwhile the intensely graceful movements of the dancer and the insistent rhythm and sweet line of the song combined to make you oblivious of the rest of the universe.

The milkmaids bathe their cows: Left hand held out represents a cow; forefinger and little finger held up are her horns; right hand cups the water and pours it over the cow. You did not have to be told what they were doing; anyone who has seen Indians bathing their cattle (which they do every day) would know immediately what the gestures meant. The Lord Krishna creeps up unseen, carefully watching the *gopis* as he does so. He stretches out his hand and pinches their clothes!

The *gopis* come out of the water and look for their *saris*. They are amazed to find that they have gone. Suddenly they see Sri Krishna sitting in a tree, playing his flute and laughing at them! Gracefully, appealingly, they beg him to give them back their clothes. If a *gopi* appealed to me like that, I would give her the moon! The hardhearted Krishna, though, leaves the clothes in the branches of the tree and runs into the midst of the cattle, where he is shown standing, one hand held up on each side of the face in the cow position to indicate that he is surrounded by cattle.

I have given the impression perhaps that this dance is just a series of miming positions. Nothing can be less true. It is a dance full of life and movement. The positions I have described occur only momentarily; the dance would stand up as something perfect if the miming meant nothing. Such joy was in this dance, such lyrical movement, such consummate art, that I wanted to cry.

As Krishna worship developed, Krishna became less of a man and a hero and more of a god. The *Bhagavad Gita* was interpolated into the *Mahabharata,* in which Krishna not only exhorts the hero Arjuna to fight against evil (in spite of Arjuna's protestations that he does not believe in action) but also reveals himself to Arjuna as God, and warns Arjuna to surrender himself to Him. Later still in time Krishna was made one of the nine avatars or reincarnations of Vishnu.

But to the Hindu laity, and particularly to the young, he is still the herdboy. Another dance performed by Sarada Devi described how a young girl tells her girl friend how she saw Krishna, and what he is like—how she was amazed by him, how he paid no attention to her, how he played on his flute, how he flirted with other girls but not with her. The dance culminates in a spirit of ecstasy, for the teller of the story is completely overwhelmed by the beauty of Krishna. This dance, too, any reasonably sensitive person would understand without the aid of a running commentary, such is the extreme expressiveness of the action.

Puritanism has a lot to answer for. Bharatya Natya dancing was suppressed because normally it was performed by temple dancers, and these dancers were sometimes also temple prostitutes. Because some of the dancers were considered bad, therefore dancing must have been bad.

Hinduism gives rise, from time to time, to waves of Puritanism that make the Plymouth Brethren look like playboys of the Western world.

7

GOOD-BY TO MADRAS

Kutti's wife sacrificed her son-in-law's hair.

"He had typhoid," Kutti told me, "and so my wife vowed that if he recovered she would sacrifice his hair."

"But who was supposed to be making the sacrifice?" I asked. "Your wife or your son-in-law?"

"Well, she took him to the temple when he got better," said Kutti, "and sacrificed his hair. But one day it will grow again, and he will look better."

I never saw Kutti's wife, because all the time I was in Madras she was in Bangalore, where Kutti had another house.

"My wife is very religious," said Kutti. "She does *puja* in the house every morning. She often goes to temple. She will not cook meat on Thursdays and I have to go to the club to get my meals. Women are always superstitious."

That evening, at the session by the water nymph, we discussed Indian women.

"I do not know how it is," said Kutti, "Indian men are supposed to be the lords of their women. But the men are *crippled* before them!"

I asked him what he meant.

"Well, look at my sons-in-law," he said. "They come back from work; their wives take off their shoes for them and clean the shoes themselves. Even though we have plenty of servants, they clean the shoes themselves because they think it is their duty. They never question anything their husbands tell them. And yet—I tell you this is true with all South Indian married people—the women always have their own way. We men are crippled before them. They never set up against us and yet they get every time their own way. I don't know how it is. Because they are submissive, they seem to have a power over us. We are crippled."

"Well, our Western women seem to get their own way fairly often," I said.

"Yes, but they are not like our Indian women. Here in Madras we see the troubles you Englishmen have with your women. We see the divorces and quarrels and separations. We see the people who take to drinking too much, owing to the troubles with their women. And yet in spite of this freedom I don't think your women have as much real power as our women have. We South Indian men are *crippled* before our women."

"How does one know," I asked, "how happy Indian married couples are? If our Western marriages are unhappy, we see it. If the partners are unfaithful, we see it. But your marriages don't show. How does one know that a lot of your married couples don't just suffer in silence?"

"Very few of our marriages are unhappy," said Kutti. "You have not as much freedom as we have in marriage. It is hard for you to get a divorce. In Travancore, if a wife wants to divorce her husband, she just gives him back the two garments that he gave her on marriage and says, 'Here is your *mundu* and *kundu!*' And she is automatically divorced. And if he wishes to divorce his wife, he just has to say, 'Give me back my *mundu* and *kundu!*' And he is divorced. And yet, hardly ever do they do it. So often are our marriages happy. In Hindu law we can have polygamy. A man can have more than one wife. And yet I do not know of one man who does. Not one! Excepting some coolies and maharajahs. Sometimes a coolie will have two wives and make them work. Sometimes a maharajah will have more wives because it is expected of him. But ordinary men—never! Although it is allowed to them."

I had to admit that by all appearances Indian marriages seem to be very happy. There is a naturalness, a lack of strain and neurosis, about them. The two partners know exactly where they are. There is no constant mental struggle for supremacy. The woman never thinks that she has made a bad choice in marriage, because she is brought up from childhood to know that her parents will choose her husband for her, and then it will be her life's task to accept what she has been given and make a happy marriage of it. And, as there is no question of extramarital love affairs (for wives, at least) or, in spite of what Kutti said about the *mundu* and *kundu,* of divorce, the wife's mind is at rest. She is not all the time half wondering if she could not do something better for herself, and then suffering remorse, perhaps, for having such wonderings. One cannot imagine an Indian wife with a complex.

"Ah, there comes Number One," said Kutti, and Number One's car drove up before the house and he got out of it and very soon had a glass in his hand. He was shortly followed by the Major.

We talked of prohibition.

"For us," said the Major, pouring himself another whisky, "prohibition is absurd. But not for the working class. A friend of mine who has a textile mill told me that now there is prohibition his workers do twice as much work. Or they would, at least, if only prohibition were properly enforced."

Number One reached for the bottle. He was not the one to nurse a drink. "For simple villagers, maybe, prohibition is good," he said. "You see, John, we Indians, when we drink we do not know where to stop. *We* do, of course. We are educated men. But the villager does not. You will see in a village the wealthier *ryots* will take to drink. A respected man will put a towel over his face so that he cannot be recognized, and make his way to the tavern. There he will find a group of hangers-on. They will drink half the night, and soon he will not bother about the towel. All the world can see him there. And they will talk loud and sing—and sometimes fight—and he will spend all his money, and soon his children will have to go without food."

"Yes, so many of our families are ruined like that," said Kutti.

"And here in the city," said the Major, "even the rickshaw coolies spend all their earnings on drink. As soon as they've earned a rupee, they go and drink it. And also the mill workers. Prohibition is to see that their children get enough food. And also to see that they are fit to work."

"Does it do what it's supposed to?" I asked.

"Of course not," said Number One. "Nobody takes any notice of it. It just gives employment to a huge army of prohibition guards, who are without exception the biggest rascals in the state. How can you have prohibition when there's a toddy palm every few yards of the landscape? The only difference now is that the government loses the revenue. What used to be our biggest source of revenue is now gone. That's why we are heading for bankruptcy. And nobody drinks any less."

"In Bombay there are special people for going to jail," said

Kutti. "The bootleggers carry on their business; every now and then the police have to make an arrest, so one of these men comes forward and gets himself arrested. He goes to jail for six months, and the bootleggers keep his wife and children and pay him a lump sum when he comes out."

They argued the matter back and forth, and all agreed that it would be better if the poorer classes of India drank less, or were prohibited from drinking at all, but that in fact prohibition failed to achieve either of these objects. Prohibition just did not work, and that was that. And furthermore it was encouraging a contempt for the law that would prove dangerous.

How was it that those present could sit out on the lawn in full view of a main road, drinking whisky? Because we all had permits. For me it was easy. A humane government had ruled that drink-addicted foreigners can, without much difficulty, obtain permits; the inhabitants of Mother India are to be kept pure even against their wills, but the foreigner can be allowed to go to hell in his own fashion. And then also it has decreed that even the Indian addict can, on presentation of a doctor's certificate to say that he requires alcohol for his health, also obtain a permit. And so every Indian who can afford to pay a doctor has a drink permit. And most of them drink far more than they would do if there were no prohibition; because, having a permit for so many units, it is human nature that they should wish to consume the permitted number of units.

The arguments of the antiprohibitionists are founded, in my opinion, on false premises. Their chief contention is that it is ruining the state financially. Which, of course, it is.

But the prohibitionists very rightly reply to this by saying, "Let it ruin the state! If our state is to be founded on vice, then it deserves to founder! If drink is wrong, then we must stop it. There can be no question of finances."

The antis' answer to this is, "Yes, but you can't stop it! You've tried and, like every other country that's ever tried prohibition, you've failed."

But the prohibitionists answer to this, again rightly, "Even though we may fail, we must try. And we must go on trying as long as we are in office."

But the *real* case against prohibition is seldom stated. It is that there are two points of view about whether drinking is an evil. Some people think that it is not an evil. And as long as this is so, then (provided that in doing so they are not harming other people) the drinkers must be allowed to drink. As long as there are two points of view about it, then men must be free to follow their own consciences. The holders of either point of view do not have the moral right to impose their morality on the holders of the other by force.

We went to the house of the father of one of our party whose birthday it was. He was an old man, over eighty, and very much loved and respected in the city.

We had a meal, the usual buffet supper served to guests in better-class Indian houses (rice and various curries, of course), and then we settled down to the business of the evening, saying things that we thought would please the old gentleman whose birthday it was. Prose gave way to poetry. One of the party recited a long Tamil poem he had written specially in honor of the occasion. There were some pompous speeches, in English, in the English after-dinner manner. Among the blessings we have conferred on India, besides the thunderbox and all the statues of Queen Victoria, is the habit of giving pompous, windy, insincere speeches. Speeches gave way to song. Narayana sang a long song in Tamil extoling the virtues of our host, and the "Oh, oh, ohs!" and "Ah, ah, ahs!" showed the deep effect it had on such of the listeners as could understand it. Then Number One got up and went and prostrated himself before the host and touched his feet. Tears came to the old man's eyes and to several other people's. Several others followed the lead of Number One. "It is our custom," said Kutti to me.

After we had said good-by and were taking our leave, Kutti went back into the house just as we were getting into the car. I happened to stroll back that way myself, and I beheld Kutti on his knees before the old man, touching his feet. When Kutti rejoined us I heard him say to Number One: "I went and touched the old boy's feet, you know. It is right. We should do it. He is a fine old man, you know. It is what we should do."

We stopped for a drink or two at Narayana's house, and Narayana sang a song that meant: "Although I am too poor to have gone to bathe in the actual Ganges and Jumna, I have done so in the spirit, and therefore am purified."

When Kutti and I got back to the house after these evening sessions we had a little custom. We sat on some cushions on the floor of Kutti's veranda, under the electric fan, and each drank a Drambuie. And we talked. Kutti did not sleep much, and he liked to supply himself with company for as much of the night as he could contrive to do, at least when his wife was away.

He never slept on a bed. He slept on the hard tiled floor of his veranda, under a fan, clad in nothing but a thin dhoti around his loins.

"You know, John," he said on that particular evening, "the only luxury I ask from life is that fan up there."

"But, Kutti," I said, "you live in a most luxurious fashion."

"Do I?" he said. "John, if this house and all my money were taken away from me tomorrow, d'you know I would be

quite happy? What do I want with it all? What do I ask from
life that a coolie does not get? The only luxury is that fan.
For food I ask two simple meals; you know I don't take more.
I may have good meals, but the ingredients are cheap. I could
do just as well with less—some rice and some fish. And for
accommodation I want a patch of hard floor two feet by six
feet. This patch of floor here, for example. If I were out in
the street I would sleep just as I am sleeping now."

"Why do you have this big house, then?"

"It is expected of me. I have made money—I enjoy my work
and have made money—and it is expected of me to have a
large house. My daughters and my grandchildren live in it.
But I do not need it. I need two simple meals a day and two
feet by six feet of hard ground, nothing more, nothing less."

"You like your whisky." I said.

"I can do without it. But, unless I have to, why should I?
I like my friends, and we all drink whisky. That's why I drink
it. It keeps us friendly. I don't need it."

Of course, he was right. The Indian is much less *entrenched* than the Westerner. No matter how much luxury
he surrounds himself with, inside it all he lives simply. He
does not become so terribly dependent on his comforts as a
Westerner. He is as much a slave to habit as any Westerner.
He must get up at daybreak, have his bath, have the food he
is used to, go through a fairly elaborate ritual throughout the
day, in fact. But it is the same ritual that is gone through by
the sweeper or the gardener. When a Westerner becomes
rich, he alters his entire habit of living and of thinking. The
Easterner hardly changes. The luxury with which he surrounds himself does not really touch him. It is for effect. It is
because "it is expected" of him. He still sleeps on the floor,
has a cold swill from a bucket, eats much the same food. And

he still talks much the same language, and holds the same type of philosophy, as his servants.

Travel is a perpetual bereavement.

No sooner do you make real friends, and become settled and happy in an environment, than you have to move on.

And one day I had to say good-by to Kutti and to his friends and to Madras, and move on to worse places.

8

THE MALABAR COAST

PERHAPS IT WAS AS WELL that the next place I visited was
Travancore, that green and fertile country of the Malabar coast, because it is there, perhaps, that India's problems
and worries are at their worst; and so, by going there, I was
prevented from getting too optimistic a picture of the country.

It is a mistake to suppose that fertile countries are richer
than infertile ones. The countries themselves are richer, of
course, but the people living in them are often much poorer.

For it is a sad fact that human beings, like lesser animals,
breed up to their level of subsistence. People living in the
most fertile countries in the world do this, and therefore the
inhabitants of such countries as Travancore, Bengal, the Nile
Valley, the rice bowls of China, to mention a few very fertile
areas, are as miserably poor as any people on the globe. By
rendering country more fertile—by irrigation, for example—
you give only momentary relief. After a few generations the
population catches up with the increased food supply and the

people of the country are just as hungry as they were before, only there are more of them. More hungry people.

In Travancore there is poverty as bad as anywhere; amid plenty as lavish as anywhere, there is a caste system as entrenched as anywhere; Communism as rampant as anywhere, and corruption that could hold its head up even in the Middle East. And I was not lucky enough to see there much of that kind of practical idealism that in other parts of India looks as if it will eventually move mountains.

My reason for going to Travancore at all was, that in several trips by B.O.A.C. *Speedbird,* I had looked down out of my comfortable airplane and seen, while flying along that southwest coast of India, a strange mixture of land and water. Not only could I see that the world down there was green and closely planted with coconut palms and dotted with red-roofed cottages, but all along the coast there was a chain of lagoons, broad rivers, canals, and inland waterways such as I had seen nowhere else in the world. I had promised myself that I would have a frog's-eye, as well as a bird's-eye, view of this semi-aquatic never-never-land.

It is the fashion nowadays for people who write travel books to travel third class, sometimes with strange animals like half-wild tiger cats to bear them company. But in India I only travel third class when I cannot find enough money to travel second class, which is often enough as it happens. The reason is that in second class I can always find somebody who speaks English.

So I clambered into a second-class carriage to go to Travancore.

There were three youngish men in the compartment, one of whom had a revolutionary past. He had not taken the path of nonviolence but had joined the Communist Party before the war, and had been jailed by the British for creating a disturbance. But now he had left the Communist Party and was a congressman. Hence he wore *khadi*, or homespun cloth. The other two wore white drill trousers. We had a political argument. The *khadi* man had not forgiven the British.

"Why did you get out in such a hurry?" he asked. "Leaving everything in a mess. Why couldn't you have taken enough time and carried out the transfer decently?"

I explained to him that I had not had the ear of Lord Mountbatten personally, and therefore I refused to accept responsibility. But I pointed out that, in 1946, when I left India myself, all I could hear from the likes of him were cries to "quit India!"

"Yes, but you shouldn't have quitted it so hastily," he said.

I said that the people who were shouting, "Quit India," should have made that clear at the time. They should have shouted, "Quit India—but not just yet!" And in any case, India seemed to be getting along quite nicely as far as I could see.

"The corruption is terrible," said one of the trouser-men.

"The corruption was terrible before Independence," I said.

"But it's worse now," said the trouser-man, who was a Travancori, going to his home in Trivandrum. "Whatever the British were, they were at least—most of them—above corruption. Now *everything* is a matter of bribes or nepotism. It's terrible."

And everyone except the *khadi* man started telling tales of corruption and "plums for pals," which is the Indian equivalent to telling snake stories in South Africa.

The *khadi* man, whose name was Natraj, thereupon expounded a theory that what looked like corruption in India was not really corruption at all. It was merely a simple and effective way of doing business. In the old days, because the various governments did not have such a strong organization as they have now, officials used to be appointed on the understanding that they would not receive salaries but would be paid for their services as and when they rendered them by the members of the public to whom the services were rendered. The doorkeeper of an office, for example, received no pay from his master, but expected a tip from every applicant for an interview. This was not a bribe, but a payment for a service rendered. And even now, if a poor man wanted an interview with an official he knew that he had to tip the peon at the door. Otherwise no interview. And this system held all the way up to the top.

Now I believe that Natraj summed the matter up quite correctly, although I did not agree with him as to what ought to happen now. For he then went on to say that he thought that it was a mistake to judge such things by Western standards and condemn these old Eastern practices as wrong. They were a simple and efficient way of running the country, and India should not try to ape the West, but should develop along her own traditional lines.

The rest of us did not agree to this at all. We unanimously condemned this giving of tips. One of the trouser-men said that, while he agreed that corruption might not have gone right to the top in British days—because British officials drew high enough salaries not to have to worry about asking for bribes—all the same, underneath, corruption had been as bad as it was now. And at least now, with self-government, there was a chance perhaps of eradicating it.

The other trouser-man said that nepotism was the worst thing in the country. It was futile to apply for any job on your own merits. And, he said, this was the fault of the joint family system. A man's first loyalty lay to his family, not his country.

I expounded my theory that this was inevitable in a country where government, for many hundreds of years, had been government by one or another kind of despotism. Under a despotism every man's true duty lies to himself and his family. Why *should* he be local to the despot? His loyalty should lie to his family and his circle of friends. But in a democracy the family should become less important.

And the first trouser-man agreed that this was so, and pointed out that in India today there is at least a great outcry against nepotism. People cannot engage in it without risk of being exposed. The fact that everyone in India will talk to you about corruption and nepotism is a sign that public feeling is beginning to be aroused against them. At one time these things were taken for granted. Now things are becoming harder for the "contractors," and the *bhai-bundi* boys. They have to look out.

And of course he was quite right. Corruption has been like a chronic disease in India, never breaking out to the surface, always working away quietly underneath, weakening the body politic and lowering the country's vitality. And nobody heard much about it. But now, since Independence, it is breaking out to the surface. One hears of nothing else. And because this is so I believe that Indians will take really drastic measures to cure it. They will perform whatever operations and injections of penicillin are necessary to destroy the germs of this filthy disease forever.

After this the conversation fell down the drain of the Cold War, and I turned my attention to the landscape.

The coast of Coromandel, for the most part, is a dry country. The winds of the southwest monsoon have shed their water by the time they reach it, for they have been forced upwards by the Western Ghats. This coast gets some rain in the northeast monsoon, for the northeast winds pick up a lit-

tle moisture in their passage across the Bay of Bengal, but
this is a pittance compared with what the southwest can give.
So in all the places that I had so far passed through—from
Pamban to Madura and Madras—the country was dry and
dusty, and the only crops were those grown under irrigation;
for big rivers flowing eastward from the Western Ghats are
tapped by *anicuts* or weirs; surface catchments, large and
small, speckle the map, and well irrigation is universal. From
very ancient times these South Indians have been masters of
irrigation.

But as we approached the Western Ghats, we began to feel
a difference in the atmosphere. The intense dry heat of the
plain began to be tempered by a cooler, moister breeze, which
was coming at us through a gap in the mountains. Then the
train began to climb into spectacular and jungle-covered hills,
and if I had had a pullover I should have put it on. It began
to rain. We saw elephants hauling big teak logs down to the
railway line, and the forest on either side of us was grand indeed. Then, after crossing a pass, we began to descend into
another world altogether.

When we reached the plain again, I thought I was back
in Ceylon. The country, instead of being dry and open, was
green and lush, and tree-covered. Most of the trees were coconut palms, but there were jack and breadfruit trees, mangoes,
trees that bear a score of different kinds of tropical fruits
(mostly fruits which do not have English names, or if they
do have I don't know them), and interspersed with the higher,
wooded country were level, terraced paddy fields, not relying
on irrigation but depending on rainfall only. The sky was
full of large rain clouds, and every now and then we ran into
a shower. We were in the land of the southwest monsoon.
At the time of it, too.

At Quilon I got off, pushed my way across the crowded

platform, and emerged into the station yard. There I was surrounded by a shouting and struggling mob of rickshaw pullers, *jutka* (small horse carriage) drivers, and the owners of those pleasant little carriages pulled by trotting bulls. If I had thought that there was far to go, I would have taken one of the latter, but as it was I put my luggage in a rickshaw and said, "Dak bungalow!"

Now I do not know any Indian language, certainly not Malayalam, the language of the Malabar coast. But I know my Kipling. So I said "dak bungalow" with complete confidence. The rickshaw puller nodded his head in delighted comprehension and motioned me to get in with my luggage.

The British may have done much that was good in India, and much that was bad; but the one unforgivable thing they did was to condone, and to exploit themselves, the use of rickshaws. It is the ultimate lapse of good taste.

If the rickshaw puller can walk, then why the devil can't *you* walk? Unless, of course, you happen to have a broken leg, in which case there is an excuse for you. I feel like shouting rudely to every able-bodied man I see riding in a rickshaw, "What's the matter with you, can't you walk?"

I believe that every person fresh from Europe who gets into a rickshaw feels a sense of shame as he does so, and feels degraded sitting up there being pulled along by another human being. But because he thinks, "Well, I'm in the East now, and this is the usual thing here," he does it, and after a time perhaps gets used to it. People can get used to any sort of degradation in time.

For it is degrading for one man to be pulled along by another man. If there is anyone who cannot see this, then there is something very lacking about his sensibility.

So I stalked along beside my rickshaw, and a fleet of other rickshaws followed behind, hoping that the mad European

would weaken and summon one of them for a ride. Finally
we reached a large house standing in a spacious garden, and
the puller of my luggage waved his hand at it and said something which might have been "dak bungalow."

He drew up in front of the front door and, unloading my
luggage, carried it in and dumped it in the middle of a very
beautiful carpet. This, I thought, is something like! I was
used to the rest-houses of Ceylon, which are excellent, but
they are nothing up to the standard of luxury of this beautiful "dak bungalow" into which I had entered. I gave a bellow
for the rest-house keeper. "Dak bungalow keeper" sounds
stilted, so I used the Ceylon term.

"Rest-house keeper!" I bellowed. "Rest-house keeper!"

Nobody came, so I made myself comfortable in a very fine
armchair. Every now and then I gave another bellow.

Finally a servant appeared, looking not just frightened but
plain terrified. "You the rest-house keeper?" I asked cheer-
fully.

For answer he pointed overhead.

"He's gone to heaven, has he?" I said. "Oh, he's upstairs?
All right, go and fetch him, my good man!"

He muttered something in Malayalam, and pointed again
towards the ceiling.

"All right, go and get the damn man!" I said, my patience
wearing a bit thin. "I suppose he's asleep, is he? Well, wake
him up! Tell him there's a customer. A man who wishes to
take his ease at his inn." The servant uttered some gibberish.

All right, I thought, I'll go and wake the fellow myself. I
strode to the staircase, surely a magnificent one for a municipal rest-house, and climbed up to the floor above. "Rest-
house keeper!" I bellowed. I had arrived on a porch, and
walked along it looking in doors. "Rest-house keeper!"

I turned a corner to find a man, a white man, a white man

with a sizable mustache, sitting dressed in a dressing gown in an easy chair. He looked as though he had been having an afternoon sleep. He also looked like a man who was wondering just exactly what was happening. . . .

It was at this juncture that my self-possession began to leave me. I began to have doubts as to whether all was as I had thought it.

"Are you—" I began, but then changed this to, "Can you tell me where the rest-house keeper is?"

"The what?" he replied. "What the devil d'ye mean, the *rest-house* keeper? This isn't a damned rest-house! This happens to be my home!"

The ground, as always on such occasions, stubbornly refused to open up and so I just had to take it. This house, it appeared, had thirty years before been occupied for a short time by a doctor. Therefore it was known to all in Quilon as the doctor's bungalow, and would be so known forever more. Now, "dak" is pronounced almost like "doc." And so that was that. In fact, I had arrived at the dwelling place of the chief accountant of a large British firm.

And of course, as one would have expected, he was extremely kind, and directed me to the European Club. I told him that all I wanted was the municipal rest-house, but he said, "Can't have pale-faces staying in a place like that. That wouldn't do. You go to the club. Probably see you there myself tonight—have a drink."

So to the club I went.

There were two fellow pale-faces staying at the club, members of a large British trading firm. They were not impressed with Travancore or its inhabitants. They considered that India was galloping downhill very rapidly and that Travancore was leading by several lengths. I was quite prepared to believe this, but decided that I had better go along on my journey and find it out for myself.

And so accordingly I left Quilon the next morning and—again in procession with a luggage-carrying rickshaw and a fleet of hopefuls—made my way down to the port on the Malabar Backwaters. For Quilon is at the southern end of the great system of inland waterways called the Malabar Backwaters, which I had seen from the B.O.A.C. airplane, and I was determined to go for a voyage along them.

Quilon was an uninteresting place, I thought, but then I was not there long enough to see much of it. It was flat. There were a few tumble-down streets of shops and some large warehouses, because Quilon is in two senses a port. It is a port on the Backwaters, and during the time when the southwest monsoon is not blowing, it is also a seaport.

The houses in all that part of the world have one distinctive feature: they have Chinese roofs. Their roofs sort of sag in the middle of the ridge but come up at the ends, and under the ends the gables are filled in with often beautifully carved woodwork. It is quite distinctive, a style that fits in beautifully with the surrounding country. The roofs, by the way, are of red tile.

The people are chiefly remarkable from a superficial view because there are so many of them. Wherever you go along the level coastal belt of Travancore, you cannot get away from crowds of people. Towns and villages are choked with them, the main roads are never free from processions of pedestrians, the numerous buses are always loaded far beyond capacity, and the very fields are populous.

Most of these people are on the small side, and many of them look underfed. As for clothes, they are all dressed in white cotton dhoties and shirts, and during the monsoon nearly every mother's son carries an umbrella. Very wisely too, for one gets constant heavy showers of rain, coming down without any warning at all.

They say that every Californian you meet tells you that California has the finest climate in the world. Well, every Travancore person tells you that "Travancore has the highest literacy rate of any part of India."

But personally I found them strange people. They are very cut off geographically from the rest of India, for the great barrier of the Western Ghats runs parallel to the sea. Even now, excepting for the one railway that I came along from Madura, there is little communication with the other side of the hills, and there is no coastwise railway. Coastwise communication—to Bombay, for example—has hitherto been chiefly by steamer, and the steamers do not run during the monsoon.

In days gone by, before the railway and the steamers, they must have been even more cut off than they are now. They developed, under their maharajahs, separately from the rest of India. Many of their customs—caste customs, for example —are unique, as I discovered later in my travels.

But meanwhile I followed my baggage-carrying rickshaw down to the Backwaters, and there bought a ticket and boarded my motor launch.

If there is one of these passenger launches, or water buses, on the Malabar Backwaters there must be hundreds. They are very long; they are driven by diesel engines, which often appear to be tied together with string; they are roofed over —decked I should say, but roofed, although landlubberly, describes it better—with corrugated iron. Perched on top of the corrugated iron just forward of amidships is a tiny wheel-house, inside which the helmsman just has room to squat cross-legged. Hanging over the stern is a large structure, also of corrugated iron: the latrine.

But if there are hundreds of these vessels, there must be thousands—if not tens of thousands—of a kind of craft called the *wallam*. These *wallams*, like the roofs of the houses, are Chinese. And not only do they look Chinese, but they really are Chinese, or at least the design of them came from China. Centuries ago Chinese junks used to trade regularly to the Malabar coast, and the present-day design of the houses, the *wallams*, the hats that fishermen wear, and the "fishing machines" with which they fish, all owe their design to this Chinese influence.

These *wallams* are open boats, nearly flat-bottomed, hard-chined, double-ended, made of planks sewn together with twine. They are perhaps forty feet in length, although they vary, and they carry up to twenty tons. Their Chinese design is most manifest in their stems (you cannot talk of their sterns because they can be propelled with equal felicity either way). So the stems at both ends are very raking, and they terminate at the top in beautiful scrolls. An alongships plank rests on thwarts at either end, and backward and forward along these two planks the two operators of the *wallam* walk, punting with long poles. The amidships section—perhaps four-fifths of the boat—is taken up with cargo space and is covered with a roof, sometimes rounded and sometimes triangular, a roof of *cadjan*, or woven coconut fronds. Lying on top of this roof is a short mast, which can be stepped at one end of the vessel to support a ridiculous little sprit-sail, also made of *cadjan* matting, or sometimes of split bamboo.

Wherever you go in the hundreds of miles of Backwaters you will see these *wallams*, with their crews of two, generally a man and a boy, one of them doing the poling and the other squatting in the shelter of one end of the *cadjan* roof preparing the next meal over a fire of coconut shells. Or sometimes, in the middle of the great open stretches of water where you lose sight of the shore, you will see a fleet of them running with their little sprit-sails before the wind, their skippers leaning on large oars, which they are holding over the sterns. *Starboards* like the Vikings used. The *wallams* are generally heavily laden with cargoes of paddy or rice (rice is paddy that has been hulled); copra; coconut husks going to Alleppey to be turned into coir; a kind of gray sand called monazite, which is used for the manufacture of paints and other purposes, to say nothing of its being useful in the production of atomic bombs.

Occasionally you see a string of *wallams* being dragged along by a noisy and stinking motorboat, their crews squatting, wet and shivering and no doubt heading for pneumonia, under what little shelter is left them under the roof by the cargo, instead of standing up keeping themselves fit and warm with their punting poles. Such is progress.

As for the Backwaters themselves, of course it is infuriating only to be able to see them from a water bus driven by somebody else. You want your own craft, to be able to sail around to explore the fascinating channels and creeks and canals and to race across the open waters.

Long canals have been constructed, leading away from the Backwaters proper to various towns and villages, but most of the Backwaters consist of large, very shallow lagoons, separated from the sea only by a narrow but unbroken strip of coconut-planted sand. There are some thousands of islands in them, all just a foot or two above the level of the waters, flooded in fact for part of the year when the monsoon is at its height. People *make* islands. A man will find a place where the lagoon is unusually shallow and build up a little wall, throw in some sand, plant some coconut palms, build a *cadjan* hut, and, lo, he has an island. Of course, it is wonderful country for growing coconuts, probably the best in the world. Coconuts love to have their feet in the water, and the warm, moist climate is perfect for them. There is an English family which owns an eight-hundred-acre island, all planted with coconuts. Eight hundred acres of coconuts make you a very rich family. They have a large house on the island, in which they have lived for several generations, and at one time of each year the entire island is flooded, except for the plinth upon which the house stands. One often finds these strange families in India. Europeans whose ancestors came out generations ago obtained a concession of some sort, perhaps from a rajah, started an estate, and there they still are, still Europeans and yet as much a part of India as any Hindu family. They have merged completely. Probably they do not mix very much with whatever English community there may be in the vicinity. They look upon themselves, and really are, a part of the Indian landed aristocracy, although they have possibly adopted few of the Indian ways of living. That fine novel *Indigo* was about such a family.

Well, our water bus started and stopped and started and stopped, as often as any country bus in England, and each time people jumped on and off. And after about eight hours of it we got to Alleppey, the home of the coir industry.

Alleppey is similar to Venice in that most of its transport goes by water, but it is like Venice in no other way. The whole place is cut up by canals; there is no railway, and it is not particularly easy to get there by road. When the monsoon is not blowing, it is a seaport, for ships lie off at anchor and surfboats put out to them.

In Alleppey are many large factories, mostly European-owned, all producing coir rope, matting, carpets, and other goods made from the husk of the coconut. Most of the factories were working part time when I was there, owing to lack of markets, and the poverty of the place was indescribable. I watched a large procession carrying hammer-and-sickle banners; I endured the scowls of nine-tenths of the population, because in Alleppey Britons are not popular; and the English manager of a factory told me that he could no longer work unless there was a mob shouting Communist slogans outside his window; otherwise it seemed too quiet.

I was told hair-raising stories about how, a couple of years ago, the state forces were obliged to come and mow down a Communist army not far from Alleppey, an army that had announced its intention of marching on Delhi. They would have had a long way to go.

I spent the night in the Majestic Hindu Hotel, where they charged me two rupees (about forty-two cents) for a double room, and left on another water bus the next morning.

Here, again, my pronunciation brought me to grief. Although again the grief was only temporary and soon turned to good.

I said I wanted a water bus to Cochin. Now, at sight, an Englishman would pronounce that word *cochin*. Which I did. It is actually pronounced *ca-cheen*. There is another place spelt Kottayam, which is actually pronounced *cochin*.

Hence, after all day chugging along through the fascinating Backwaters, when we arrived at our destination, I eventually found that instead of Cochin I had arrived at Kottayam. I *thought* we had been heading too far east when we should have been going due north.

Anyway, one place is almost as good as another.

9

THE ANCIENT CHURCH OF INDIA

I N KOTTAYAM I fell among Christians. Not Anglican Christians, but members, possibly, of the oldest Christian church in the world. For their church was founded, they believe (and more and more evidence seems to be coming to light to support their belief), by no less a person than St. Thomas, in the year 52 A.D. Some people even place it as early as 51 A.D.

I had heard, of course, of the Syrian Christians of the Malabar coast—supporters of the Nestorian heresy—who had existed in India from very early times. When I got to Kottayam, I fell into conversation with a man who knew something about them, and he fired my curiosity. He advised me to go and see Father K. Philipos, as one who would give me some information.

Father Philipos's house was in the compound of an ancient church, built in the Portuguese baroque style. The house itself was of wood, and was obviously hundreds of years old. The massive door had hand-wrought hinges and fastenings, the windows were closed by wooden panels, the teak roof

beams were carved and painted, but, alas, beginning to
crumble. Father Philipos was out, so I sat down in a chair
on the upstairs veranda to await his return.

What sort of a figure from the past was I going to see? I
had been told that he knew some English, but I imagined
that it would probably only be a few words. If St. Thomas
himself had walked slowly up the stairs to greet me, I would
not have been very surprised.

Finally, the Father arrived. He bounded quickly up the
stairs, and I saw that he was a very tall man, quite young, and
was wearing a gown and a sun helmet. His brown face was
largely covered by a beard.

I prepared a few words of simple English to introduce myself to this priest from a bygone age. But he cut me short.

"My dear fellow!" he said, in perfect upper-class English,
no exaggerated drawl. "So pleased to see you. They told me
you had come. Come in and make yourself at home!"

Father Philipos, it appeared, had spent many years in England, and had incidentally studied divinity at Canterbury.
He loved my country, and had pleasant memories of two dear
old maiden ladies with whom he used to stay in their large
house overlooking Regent's Park. He showed me some photographs of them, driving out in an open one-horse carriage
along the lanes of Devonshire. "Every year they used to go to
Devonshire and spend their time touring the woods picking
bluebells," he said. "They packed the bluebells in boxes and
sent them to their friends who were not able to leave London.
But last year," he added, "when I went to England again,
one of them had died. And the other, poor old soul, was living all alone in that large house, and perfectly miserable. No
servants of course, and queues, and no holidays in Devonshire. I felt as though part of my world had gone."

But that was several days later. Meanwhile he asked me

where I was going to stay in Kottayam, and I said I did not know, but had only arrived there by a mistake anyway, and so he very kindly asked me to stay with him. He showed me the room that his deacon had occupied, but now the deacon had gone away. It was a little room of beautifully carved teak; the door had huge teak bolts and fastenings, and out of the strange little windows I could watch the slowly moving world.

Kottayam is an attractive town. It was at one time, I imagine, on the Backwaters; but for centuries men have been reclaiming the shallower lagoons to make paddy fields, and now Kottayam is just connected to the Backwaters by a river. The town itself is on some high ground; in fact, it is quite hilly. The whole place is closely overgrown with coconut palms and other tropical trees. One sees far more of the trees than the houses. The houses themselves are attractive. Most of them have the sagging, high-ended ridgepoles I described before, with the lavishly carved teak gable-ends. The warm, red tiles look attractive under the dark green tropical trees.

It is an old town, and has often been the capital city of kingdoms, and princely states. Near the church, Cheria Palli, where we lived, was a large area of ancient masonry—city walls, fortifications, palaces and temples; but all knocked down, overgrown, and built over.

It is a town of churches and schools. The Church Missionary Society (now merged with the Church of South India) built a large college there, and there are churches of a dozen Christian denominations. The college was used in December, 1952, to accommodate a World Conference of Christian Youth. But most of the churches belong to various branches of the Syrian Orthodox Church.

Unfortunately, they are all in the Portuguese baroque style. I have nothing against this style; in fact, I like it. But when one sees some of the ancient Syrian churches in Travancore (there are very few left), churches built before the Portuguese and not altered, one deplores the activities of these zealous colonizers. For, with few exceptions, they knocked the grand old churches down and put up their baroque.

The streets of Kottayam, like those of every other town in Travancore, are packed with people. You would think that every day is a market day there. There are thousands of people, all dressed in white cotton, all carrying umbrellas, and most of the young men in couples, arm in arm or with their arms placed lovingly around each other's necks. And it is obvious that the vast majority of these people never do any manual labor; they are clerks, shopkeepers, students, and lawyers.

I went for a stroll along the river soon after my arrival and passed a group of youths, lounging about like our drugstore cowboys, who giggled as I went by. This staring and giggling is infuriating when you first go to Travancore; but later you learn that it is not unfriendly: it is just the custom. Later, when I returned, the youths were still there, and one of them asked me the time. I got talking to them—they spoke school English—and we went across the river in a small *wallam* to their house to have some tea.

One of them owned the house, and was head of the family. He was a timber merchant. He bought teak and other timber from the hill country, had it brought to Kottayam in lorries, and had it made into rafts and floated them down the Backwaters to the port of Cochin.

The rest of the young men were his brothers, cousins, and hangers-on. And not one of them had a job. They all had left school and were just lounging about, hoping one day to get work as clerks. To be a clerk was the height of their ambition, and they had all struggled at school to obtain the necessary educational qualifications.

The elder brother supported them all, and he, I gathered, made little-enough money. He told me that had it not been for the fact that he owned a few coconut trees they would all have starved.

I believe that there are far more young men who have been to school in that country who do not have jobs than there are those that have them. But it costs little to live there, you see, and the joint family system ensures that the idle are fed. Their fathers or brothers or uncles must keep them. Nearly every jobholder in India has to support not only himself but some unemployed relatives as well.

These young men told me that sometimes they could not even afford to buy fish, the staple food of the country. Their house was actually on the bank of the river; you could fish out of the window. I asked them why they did not catch fish themselves? They replied, aghast, that although members of their caste could *eat* fish, they certainly would not catch them! Besides, fishing was a coolie's job. How could they expect to obtain posts as clerks if it became known that they spent their time fishing? The brother owned two *wallams,* which he used in connection with his timber trade. At the moment they were idle, and he told me he was thinking of selling them. I asked him why his jobless brothers did not take them and go in for carrying freight? He said that the men they would have to employ to navigate the *wallams* would rob them and swallow up all the profit. I explained that I had meant that the boys should navigate the *wallams* themselves. They all laughed, deciding that the stranger had at last made a really good joke! People who had been to school paddle *wallams* indeed!

I wondered if the missionaries, who came in such large numbers to Travancore to teach all the boys how to read and write, were really doing a good thing.

As if there were not already enough churches and religions in Kottayam, there is a big colony of Moslems there, and they have some fine old timber mosques. As far as one could make out, there has never been any persecution of them, or indeed even mild victimization, even during the slaughter and rapine in the Punjab after Partition. They live there perfectly peacefully.

I attended many ceremonies of the Syrian Church.

These ceremonies were long and complicated. The normal service consists of the celebration of the Holy Kurban or Eucharist. It is performed by a priest, assisted by several deacons and servers, with much burning of incense, waving and rattling of silver fans, ringing of bells, a long liturgy in Malayalam with parts of it in Greek, and while the Holy Mysteries are being performed, a curtain is drawn in front of the altar.

The congregation stand, and it is nothing for them to stand like this for four hours! Once or twice during the service they bow down to the ground, but for the rest they just stand. It is not surprising then that they become restless, particularly as small children are taken to church, and often the priest has to compete against howling babies, *shushing* mothers, and murmuring children—also people strolling out occasionally for a breath of fresh air and strolling in again.

The Host is of leavened bread, and Father Philipos showed me a device which he himself had invented for baking it. He also showed me the yeast he used, and said; "We're very conservative people in our church, you know, and we don't like to change things very much. Our liturgy hasn't altered one word, so far as we know, for well over a thousand years. I got this yeast from my predecessor, and he got it from his, and we all guard it extremely carefully. There isn't any reason why it should not be the living descendant of the yeast brought out by St. Thomas himself, and which he may have received from the hands of Christ."

And certainly, what reason is there? But, however old the yeast is, I noticed that Father Philipos cooked it on an electric grill!

I went to one very long service—Pentecost, celebrated in the Old Seminary by no less a person than His Holiness the Catholicos himself. It lasted three and a half hours. Everything had to be gone through three times, to honor each member of the Holy Trinity. Three times His Holiness called down the Holy Spirit from above, and three times he walked around the nave in procession, sprinkling the congregation with holy water, besides doing a lot of other things. I sat part of the time up in a loft, from where I took some pictures, and talked to some small boys who were up there for the purpose of ringing a bell as the Holy Spirit descended. They were naughty and inattentive to the service, and when one of them went out of the room the other hid his shoes. They missed their cue once and the bell did not ring at the proper time.

These services are impressive. The male part of the congregation is all clad in white, and they stand in front; the women are in a group right at the back. The priests for the most part stand with their backs to the people, for they face the altar. I was told that the Easter service goes on from midnight to sunrise, and a silver cross, which has been buried on Good Friday, is resurrected. It is strange to hear such phrases as *Kyrie eleison* and *Barekmore* coming from these people, who have kept their ancient liturgy down the millenniums even when for centuries they were completely cut off from the rest of Christendom.

The history of this church is interesting, whether one is interested in a general way in churches or not.

There was a big Jewish community at the place the Romans called Musiris (the modern Cranganur) for some time before Christ, and recently many Roman remains have been found there. There was close connection between this port and the Roman world. There is an old legend that says that the Lord appeared to St. Thomas and said: "Fear not, Thomas, go to India and proclaim the Word." St. Thomas replied: "Wherever thou wishest to send me, send me elsewhere; to the Indians I am not going." While he was speaking, there came a man named Abbanes sent to the Holy Land by King Gondophorous to fetch a carpenter. Our Lord handed him St. Thomas and sold him for three pieces of silver! And so the Apostle was taken to India.

However this may be, there is such a strong and ancient tradition all over South India that St. Thomas did go there that it seems difficult to believe that he did not. And of course he found the community of Jews waiting for him, part of which he converted (there are plenty of unconverted Jews still left; afterwards I met some of them), and later he converted a number of high-caste Hindus. Many Indian Christians, who were originally converted by European missionaries, were drawn from the untouchables and lower castes. But the "Syrians," as they are called, consider themselves and are considered by Hindus to be of the highest caste.

The first thing that is definitely known about the Indian Christians is that in the year 190 A.D. one Pantaneus was sent to India by Demetrius, Bishop of Alexandria, in answer to a plea from the Indians. He found that they had a copy of the Gospel of St. Matthew in Hebrew. He reported that this gospel had been taken to India by St. Bartholomew, but it is likely that he was confused by the expression "Mar Thoma," which is what the Syrians call St. Thomas. Pantaneus returned to Alexandria, and his disciple, Clement, has left a secondhand description of his master's tales of Yogis, Brahmans, and Buddhists.

Later, at the Synod of Nicaea, in 325 A.D., a bishop named John signed himself, "John of Persia and Great India."

In 345 A.D. the Syrian connection began. The Bishop of Edessa sent four hundred people under Mar Joseph of Uraha to India. They joined the Christians already there (whom they reported to have fallen into a sad state of ignorance) and they obtained an engraved copper plate from King Chereman Perumal, giving them landed rights. Henceforth the Indian Church was called "Syrian," and for many centuries there was coming and going between the Malabar coast and the Middle East.

The extraordinary tolerance of Hinduism is well in evidence here. Not only did Hindu rulers allow this large community of an alien religion to live in their midst, but they gave them tracts of land, they allowed them to build their churches in the near vicinity of Hindu temples, and never at any stage during nineteen hundred years has there been any hint of persecution.

But persecution came to the Christians in due course. Early in the sixteenth century the Portuguese arrived. When they found, to their utter amazement, that there were Christian churches all along the Malabar coast, they called the people together and said, "These churches belong to the Pope."

"Who is the Pope?" the Syrians replied. "We have never heard of him!"

The Portuguese worked slowly. First they started a Franciscan college at Cranganur, but nobody went to it. Then they started a seminary, which taught in Syriac, and the priests of which wore Travancore dress, in an effort to attract the Travancoris. But still it was boycotted. The Indians had their own religion. So then the reigning Syrian bishop, Mar

Joseph, was seized and sent to Rome. There, under duress, he embraced Catholicism, but when he returned to India and recanted, the Portuguese seized him again and put him to death.

The bishop who was sent from Babylon to take his place, Mar Abraham, was also captured by the Portuguese. They tried to send him to Rome, but he escaped on the way and went back to Mosul, which is where he lived.

But in 1595 Menezes came out from Portugal, armed with a Papal Brief. He called Archdeacon George to him (the Archdeacon was acting as head of the church in default of a bishop) and ordered him to embrace the Church of Rome. Archdeacon George replied, "I am sure that the Roman Church has no more to do with the Apostolic Church of St. Thomas than the Apostle had to do with the Church of Rome!" But Menezes pointed to the declaration that he had put before the Archdeacon to sign and said, "Sign it, Father, for it is full time to lay the ax to the root of the tree!" And the Father signed it. The Portuguese then forcibly collected all the Syrian priests and made them sign what has become known as the Ten Articles.

For fifty years the Syrian Church was in subjection, and nearly all the fine old churches were pulled down and replaced by baroque. But in 1653 a bishop named Ahathalla was sent out by the Patriarch of Antioch and was captured by the Portuguese. He managed to smuggle a letter through to the Syrians, however, telling them to appoint one Thomas to the head of the Church. The Portuguese put Ahathalla on a ship, intending to send him to Goa; but when the ship reached Cochin, twenty-five thousand armed Syrians were there to greet it and to demand the release of their bishop. The Portuguese refused, however, and took the bishop out to sea and drowned him. The Syrians thereupon assembled at an ancient cross in Cochin (it is still there for all to see and is called the Coonan Cross), and there they took a vow to return to their old Church and to have no more to do with Rome. Portuguese power was by then declining, and the Syrians were able to hold out. They went back to their old liturgy, which, in fact, they had used secretly right through the Portuguese time, just as they had secretly guarded and propagated Father Philipos's yeast, and they resumed their old customs.

But in the early nineteenth century a new influence affected them. Anglican missionaries came and persuaded them to allow Anglicans to cooperate with them, run a seminary, and reform, to a certain extent, their Church.

This connection went on fairly happily until 1840, when the two churches fell out about some points of doctrine. The great bulk of the Syrians broke away from the Anglican connection and started up on their own again. I heard a rather pathetic story about this. When the great Bishop Gore went to try to convince one of the Syrian dignitaries of the rightness of the Anglican theories about whether the Holy Spirit derived from the Trinity or from God the Father and the Son, after two hours of immense erudition during which the poor Syrian Father was completely lost, the latter suddenly flung his hands up and cried, "What does it matter, what does it matter where the Holy Spirit came from, provided that it exists?"

And so still the Syrians carry on in their own way, chanting their liturgy which they have guarded, every word of it, for perhaps nineteen hundred years! True, the Anglicans persuaded them to translate it from Syriac into Malayalam, so that the people could understand it, and this alteration they have retained.

Father Philipos and I drove out, in a car which he borrowed from a wealthy parishioner, to look at an old church at a place called Chandragore. Parts of this church have been dated as probably earlier than 400 A.D. When was the first existing church in England built? The pre-Portuguese churches were designed very much on the style of Hindu temples, and there are many obviously Hindu features to this one, such as stone lamp standards, pillars carved with Hindu motifs, and magnificently carved wooden doors. In no guidebook to India can I find mention of any of these ancient churches, an omission which it is hard to understand. Surely they are among the most remarkable monuments of Christendom.

I was introduced to most of the leading citizens of Kottayam. The Syrian Christians are nothing if not solid citizens. The banks, big business houses, many big plantations, and most of the industry in Travancore are in their hands. Until recently they were always a strictly caste organization, and did not admit lower-caste people into the fold. Now this is being altered.

I went to a Syrian wedding. Much of the ceremony was Hindu in origin, including the placing of a string around the bride's neck (the string was rendered respectable from a Christian point of view by hanging a tiny cross on it). I had described to me the elaborate prewedding ceremonies—the ritual bathing, ceremonial haircut, prewedding feast, etc. After the wedding we went to the groom's house, but were not allowed inside it until the happy pair arrived with the bishop and entered first. But outside in the street a huge canopy had been erected and for a long way the street had been decorated.

As we entered the front gate, we were showered with scent by small girls, and each given a lime fruit to hold, and a perfumed stick. We then sat down, just the five hundred of us, to an enormous meal of rice and meat. We ate in a *pandal* which had been erected, a temporary structure of bamboo. We should have sat on mats, but this family was modern, and rich, and had long tables and chairs.

But besides the five hundred guests there were another five hundred people round the back of the house—five hundred poor people, who were being given a free meal. A gramophone blared music through a loudspeaker, alternating American jazz and Indian film songs, and there were buns, candies, cigarettes, cigars, fruit of all sorts, and waiters dressed up like maharajahs. The whole party, I was told, had cost over ten thousand rupees, more than two thousand dollars.

But this was a union of two very important commercial families.

As everybody knows, extravagance at weddings is a curse all over India. If a banker will spend three thousand dollars on his son's wedding, a *ryot,* or small cultivator, will spend three hundred. And the man who cleans out the buckets will scrape together about fifty, the most money that he has ever had in his life. In every case the expense is crippling. And really, these vast parties are not much fun. As far as giving real enjoyment goes, it is money down the drain. Even the five hundred poor, who get a free meal, would probably far rather have their share of three thousand dollars! Most Indians nowadays realize the folly of these vast weddings, but nevertheless they still go in for them. They say it is the fault of the women. The women will not be satisfied with less. For months the women of both families prepare for the wedding, and for that period it is the main interest in their lives.

Another pernicious feature of Indian marriage is the dowry system. The father of the bride must hand her over with a large sum of hard cash. It is the custom in Hindu weddings for the priest, at a certain point of the ceremony, to announce the amount of the dowry being given, whereupon everybody applauds the generosity of the giver.

Not only is this system grossly unfair to the wretched man who is blessed with five daughters but no sons, but it is largely responsible for the poor status of women. What couple can rejoice when a daughter arrives, and not a son? A daughter simply means the necessity of finding, at some future date, a really large sum of money. But a son means getting money, for after marriage the son stays in his father's family. Probably he goes on living in his father's house, for the joint family system is still very much the custom in India, particularly in the South. A son, therefore, is a matter for rejoicing; a daughter, for lamentations and condolence. When an Indian friend tells you that his wife has just given birth to a fine girl, it is polite to shake your head and cluck your tongue and say, "Never mind! Next time it will be a boy, if God wills it."

Marriage in India, except in a very few cases among the most highly westernized people, is decided entirely by the parents. The couple getting married have no say in the matter, and it would not occur to them to demand it; they are conditioned from birth to expect this thing to be decided for them. The choice of partners is largely a matter of haggling. The father of a lawyer will demand a much bigger dowry than the father of a clerk. The father of a deputy collector will demand the earth—and the moon thrown in as well! And the couple must not only be of the same caste, but the same subcaste also; so the field for choice is very limited. What is more, an astrologer almost always is consulted, even in highly educated families, and if the horoscopes do not agree, well, the search goes on. This is not only the case among uneducated people; it extends almost to the top.

And there is no doubt whatever that this extreme conservatism concerning marriage is kept up by the women. Many

men would like to change some of the customs, but the
women look upon it as their domain; they had to go through
it all, and they are going to see that their daughters have to
as well!

A strong movement is on now, though, to abolish the dowry
system by law. We had a discussion about it at this Syrian
wedding. One man said that the law would do no good—there
would simply be a black market in dowries. The father of the
girl would go to the prospective groom's father and offer to
give him the money secretly. Anything to marry his daughter
off to a good match. But someone else said that he thought
that eventually the law would have its effect. The law against
sutteeism, or widow suicide, had been bitterly opposed at first
and often defied, but in the end it had worked on public
opinion and achieved its aim. Sutteeism became unrespecta-
ble, and so people ceased to practice it.

There was also at the party an Indian who had spent most
of his life in New York. He had gone there young, married
an American girl, made money in business, and now had
come to visit his old home for the first time in thirty-five
years. He said that he had sworn not to return to India until
India was free. Somebody suggested that it would have been
more patriotic to have come back to fight for freedom, but
the Indo-American waved this aside.

I asked him how he liked India now, and he said he thought
it was a terrible country. A *terrible* country! They were too
slow, they had no drive! He had come to teach them a thing
or two.

"The trouble with this country," he said, "is that they
don't know what business is. They've never even heard of the
easy-payment system. Why, back in the States anybody can
own a car, a television set, a refrigerator, a dozen good suits
—all because he can get them on time. I've come here to try

to show these guys how to act. I'm going to introduce India
to the installment plan!"

Well, well, India has weathered worse storms than installment buying

There was a young man at the wedding who told me that
because of the current labor troubles he now found it necessary to spend at least a few days every month up on the big
tea estate from which his family drew its income. So, to temper somewhat the rigors of this ordeal, he had just spent half
a *lakh* of rupees (more than ten thousand dollars) on a bungalow for himself there. I asked him if it wouldn't have been
better to have spent the half *lakh* of rupees on improving
the labor conditions, and he said he hadn't thought of that.

10

ENGLISH EXILES

J ust when I was preparing to leave Travancore I ran into
a young man whom I shall call Robinson. He was man-
aging a rubber plantation, and very kindly asked me up to
have a look at it.

Early in the last century, when the whole of India had not
yet come under British rule, it was discovered that the jungle-
covered mountains of the Western Ghats were good country
for growing coffee. So the benevolent government of the East
India Company allowed ex-army officers to go up there and
stake out two to three hundred acres of jungle and turn it
into a plantation. Then came the coffee blight, and now if
you get around in the jungle, far from the beaten track, you
can find the remains of old abandoned buildings and machinery, and even coffee bushes still trying to hold their own
against the indigenous bush. Men's lives and hopes buried
in the wilderness.

But many planters survived the coffee blight by scrapping
their coffee and planting tea. Tea grows well higher up in
the mountains. The higher, the better; lower down, the qual-

ity is not so good. And then from South America, via Ceylon
and Malaya, came the rubber tree.

Now the original soldier-settlers had in many cases amal-
gamated their holdings by forming groups, or companies; and
these companies were able to take up large holdings of jungle
country and clear it and plant it with rubber. The estate
Robinson was looking after contained 3,700 acres, over two
thousand of which were planted with rubber, the remainder
being held under jungle as reserve.

When the early planters went up into this tiger- and snake-
infested jungle, they found it fairly easy, in the long run, to
get people to come and work for them. Some of the "Mala-
yalams" (that is, the people from Travancore who speak
Malayalam) went up, but then many more people from the
other side of the mountains began to come from what is now
Madras State. These speak Tamil and are, as one might guess,
called Tamils.

These people had been wretchedly poor back in their villages. They were mostly landless laborers, always the first
people to go hungry in a bad season, and they were willing
to work for the *doris,* as they called the white men, for very
little. They asked little and they received little.

Some of them went back to their villages eventually, to be
replaced by others, but most stayed on. They reared families,
and in a few generations perhaps forgot the old family village
from which they had come. Their only home is now on the
estate: they are "tied" laborers in every sense of the word.
If they lose their jobs, they lose their homes and have nowhere else to go.

At first these coolies, as they were called, lived in grass
shacks, as did their masters. But as the planters became established, they built good bungalows for themselves, and for the
coolies they built "lines." These lines consisted, and still con-

sist, of rows of tiny one- or two-roomed dwellings, with walls of stone or brick, and corrugated iron roofs, usually without windows or chimneys.

Now although these dwellings would be the minimum accommodation that a farmer would give to his pigs, the coolies were quite satisfied with them. They were somewhere dry to sleep and make love and have children. There was work to be done during the day and food to eat during the evening. What more could a man want?

It was an industry of ups and downs. For years sometimes the estates would run at heavy losses, and planter after planter would go bankrupt. But they were a tough breed, and most of them managed to survive; they weathered the bad times, and enjoyed the good times. Some of them died of fever, some took to the bottle, and some got rich and went home to England to retire and live at Maidenhead.

But in honesty one must say that, no matter how good the times became for the planters, they never became any better to the coolies. The *dori* eventually built himself a magnificent bungalow, with electricity, hot water, a garden such as only a millionaire could have in England, and every other possible comfort. Why shouldn't he? He was doing a tough job a long way from home. Why shouldn't he make the best of things? But the lines never altered. Most of them, in spite of endless talk about labor reform, are exactly the same now as they were fifty years ago. I know there are exceptions to this, but not very many.

Nowadays, mark you, the *dori* seldom owns the estate. He is generally a paid manager, for the estates have mostly come into the ownership of large companies. But these companies very rightly look after their supervisors well. And they pay them well. A senior superintendant working for the company for which Robinson works is paid close to $10,000 a year.

And then, you see, there are the shareholders. They have invested money in a risky undertaking, have certainly gone many years without a penny back on it (a rubber tree does not grow in a day), and when at last there *are* some profits, they want them.

So where does the poor old coolie come in?

Well, the government of New India intends to see that he does come in somewhere. One of the leaders of the Planters' Association was heard to say, rather pathetically but quite justly, "The tea industry is the most labor-legislated industry in India!" And he might have added, and indeed I believe he did add, that it is the most heavily taxed.

But all this, strangely enough, does not seem to make the coolie's life any more joyful. (One must not call him a coolie any more nowadays; of course, he is a *worker* now, and about time.)

He still lives in his miserable lines. Now lines are for horses; human beings should have *homes,* not lines.

He still has a bare minimum of food for himself and his family. This is not the planter's fault nowadays, for food is strictly rationed in Travancore. The ration when I was there was one pound of whole wheat, one pound of rice, and one pound of tapioca per day. The workers did not know what to do with the wheat; they hate the stuff anyway. Rice is the only thing they really know how to eat.

A man got, when I was there, about forty-three cents a day, and a woman, nearly twenty-eight cents. And needless to say, prices of commodities are so adjusted that very little can be done with this. The traders in near-by towns and villages run a spy system so that they know the moment that the planters put the wages up, and not even an anna of the increased wage remains to the worker.

The rations, by the way, are paid for by the worker out of

his wages, but at a much cheaper price than that for which he could get them on the market; and this difference in price is made up by the planters by means of a subsidy.

Robinson's car had broken down, so we took a taxi from Kottayam and drove out of that picturesque town toward the hills. As the road got nearer to the wall of the *ghats*, cultivation began to give way to jungle, and eventually we entered the rubber country. Soon rubber closed in around us everywhere, the tall, crooked-stemmed trees covering every yard of the steep hillsides. We came to a sign which pointed to our estate, and there we turned off the public highway; from now on we drove along the estate road.

After several miles of winding track, through the somber and gloomy forests of rubber trees, we arrived at Robinson's bungalow. It was a beautiful single-storied stone house, built on a hill. "When I came here six years ago," Robinson said, as we got out of the car, "I was greeted everywhere by the coolies with *this*." And he held up his hands in the graceful Hindu greeting: both palms together as in the attitude of prayer. "But now all I get is this!" And he made the Communist clenched-fist salute. "They even train the little children to march about in front of my bungalow shouting abuse at me."

This is the sad story of the change that has taken place on the Travancore estates in the last two years.

We went inside, had baths, and settled down to a whisky and soda. Robinson told me how he had been besieged on one occasion for three days and nights in his bungalow by a threatening mob. This has become a common thing. Most planters round about that part of the world have been besieged in their bungalows. The mob holds meetings in the garden, addressed by rabble-rousers through loudspeakers. It says a lot for the nonviolent character of the Indian peasant that, up to the time I was there, no planter had been physically injured.

Now I am quite sure that all this unpleasantness was not Robinson's fault. For one thing, every other British planter in that part of the world has gone through the same thing; for another, Robinson certainly is not the sort of man to antagonize his workers. In fact, I believed him when he told me that when he had first arrived he had become really fond of them, and had been looked upon by them as a friend.

How, then, did this unpleasantness come about?

Well, Travancore, probably because, as we are so often told, there is such a high rate of literacy (unaccompanied by much true learning) has for long been one of the most Communist parts of India. Before Independence, when it was still a princely state, Communism was put down ruthlessly, which of course encouraged it. And so when Independence came along, the Communists decided that their time had arrived. They had fought against the British Raj, they had won, and now they intended to enjoy the fruits of their victory. In fact, of course, the new Congress government did not show itself any more favorable to Communism than the British Raj had done.

But Robinson told me that, when Independence was declared, swarms of young men, most of whom he believed had tried but failed to obtain the bachelor of arts degree, came up into the rubber and tea country and preached Communism to the workers. And so the seeds of trouble had been sown.

Most of the Communists had gone away again. Some, in fact, had been put in jail; but other young men—also, according to Robinson, young men who had tried and failed to obtain that useful scholastic qualification—had come up and started trade unions. There were five such trade unions existing now on this very estate, all trying to cut each other's throats, but all, nevertheless, quite capable of making a lot of trouble for the planters. Most of the young men who formed them, incidentally, had obviously taken no harm by having done so; for every one of them now drove about in a large American car. And now when Robinson went among his workers, he was greeted with scowls instead of smiles.

Next day, after breakfast, we wandered around the estate, climbing up the steep wooded hills, and I saw what Robinson meant about the scowls.

We watched men climbing high into the tall rubber trees, dragging after them nozzles and hoses, while others below labored at hand pumps, pumping some new kind of spray into the foliage, to counteract some new kind of blight. Women and children carried gasoline cans full of the chemical on their heads from the place near a small stream where it was being mixed. The liquid, which contained copper-sulphate, had slopped over onto them and made them blue, and the air under the trees that were being sprayed was full of fine blue mist. I had lived to see the air actually turning blue!

"We're always getting new blights and diseases in the rubber and in tea," said Robinson. "Experiments are being carried out all the time—mostly by the planters themselves. There is very little government research."

Whatever India finally does with her rubber and tea industries, she will always owe a debt of gratitude to the men who developed them, found out by their own good sense and initiative how to cultivate the wild rubber tree, how to grow tea on a commercial scale, and how to combat all the various pests and diseases as they came along. True, they did it for money; but nonetheless, they did it and should be given credit for it.

The boundary of the estate was marked by a stone wall, and beyond this was more rubber. But this was owned by small-holders. A man might own an acre or two of rubber, and by his standards be quite well off. Robinson told me that the previous year fifteen per cent of the rubber produced on the estate he managed had been stolen by the tappers. I asked how they did it, and he said, "Well, look at that wall. Why shouldn't the man over there leave a bucket on his side of it and one of my tappers simply pour some of his latex into it after he's tapped it? We pay the tappers an anna a pound for their latex, and they can get four annas on the black market. Why, they pour it into holes in the ground and then come at night and dig it up. And this year it's far worse; we'll find we've lost about thirty per cent from theft. Very soon this game won't pay any more, and the rubber estates will fold up."

"Why can't you take steps to stop the theft?" I asked.

"What steps can we take? I employ a dozen old ex-policemen to prowl around at night, but so far they've never caught a man. And they wouldn't dare. They'd get beaten up. I'd like to get some Gurkhas down, and when the tappers found a few bodies lying around with no heads on them, they might start to think!"

In the evenings while I stayed with Robinson it was our custom to have our baths and then sit on the porch over a whisky and soda. Robinson used to tell me of his experiences in the war as skipper of a motor torpedo boat. They used to creep out of Ramsgate at night, and lie tied up to buoys in the Channel, waiting for German convoys to pass. When the last ship of the convoy had glided by in the foggy dark, they would slip the buoy, open up their engines, race after the convoy, and spit their tin fish at it! Then a racing turn and back to harbor as hard as they could go, and possibly a gun battle with E-boats on the way. He used to go on the "ball-bearing run" to Stockholm, relying on speed and stealth alone to get him through the German blockade. He spoke of these things with enthusiasm; it was obvious that he had reveled in the life. It was a life of daring, excitement, high purpose, and, above all, companionship. The companionship on these little boats must have been unequaled. Captain and crew lived together, ate together, fought together, and laughed together. They were at war, but their enemies were known and in the open, and they themselves lived among comrades.

It seemed to me as we talked that Robinson now felt that he lived among enemies, but they were enemies that he couldn't fight.

Living on a rubber estate is to me like living down a coal mine. The trees are planted on every available space, and underneath them all is dark, gloomy, and monotonous. And they stretch around you for miles, as far as you can imagine. The climate, too, in rubber country, is warm, damp, and oppressive. Then, of course, for an Englishman, it is extremely lonely. Rightly or wrongly he will not mix socially with others on the estate and probably he has no friend nearer than the next planter, who may be twenty miles away.

But in addition to this, when you get threats and scowls and constant trouble and friction from every single person working under you, to say nothing of outbursts of near violence; when you live among thousands of people who look upon you as an enemy, then even the surrounding all-enveloping rubber trees seem to be threatening you and closing in on you. I could understand why Robinson spoke with nostalgia of the days of glory and excitement in the North Sea and the English Channel.

I asked him why he did not do some counterpropaganda to that of the young men with loudspeakers, and his answer was something like this: "On this estate there are seven hundred workers and two thousand, seven hundred acres of rubber. That means that the Communists can promise each worker over three acres of rubber for his very own if their party gets into power and kicks us out. Now three acres of rubber, as these chaps know perfectly well, would make every one of them, by his own standards, a very rich man. What answer have I got to give to that? Each tapper is simply waiting for the day, which he thinks will be soon, when the Communists will take over and dish him out his three acres of rubber."

"But could he farm it efficiently?" I asked. "Does he think he could control disease and all that?"

"Of course he couldn't," said Robinson. "But that wouldn't matter to him. There are scores of smallholders round here, each with a few trees, and the trees have every imaginable disease under the sun. But it doesn't matter. They still give him some rubber. With three acres, or even one acre, of bad rubber the man would still be far better off than as a tapper on this estate."

I asked him how long he thought his job would last. Like all the other planters in India, he just did not know. "The central government wants the plantation industry to go on," he said. "In the end they would like to see it Indianized, but they realize that we still have a part to play. But from the state government we get nothing but obstruction. Then, of course, nobody knows how long the Congress Party will stay in power. If almost any of the other parties gets in, they'll kick us out. So it's all a matter of just hanging on and seeing what happens. *We* won't leave until we're chucked out. No fear of that. A few private chaps have sold out to Indians, but none of the big firms have. In fact, the tea people are expanding, when they're allowed to. Anyway, I hope to hang on here, by hook or by crook, as long as I can. That's all I can say."

Well, *chacun à son goût!*

I made my way farther up into the mountains, to the tea country—where the planters have a club. This is a beautiful world, about four thousand feet up, with cosmic views over jungle-clad mountain ranges and down to the blue plains below. It was Saturday night, and all the planters and their wives were at the club. Some played bridge, some played billiards, and others sat in the bar and talked.

And they talked of only two things, labor troubles and the shortcomings of the government—chiefly the state government.

They told me the story of the battle of Passamala, which occurred on April 22, 1952, about six weeks previously.

Mr. Jimmy Milner, the superintendant of Passamala estate, a man sixty-five years of age and of all the planters in the district the one who was most popular with his workers, was on that date besieged in his office for twelve hours by a shouting mob. Mr. Cooke, the general manager of his group of estates, heard about the trouble and telephoned the police. Three policemen arrived, reasoned with the mob, and escorted Jimmy Milner to his bungalow. They then went back to fetch the clerks, who were still in the office, but were set upon by the mob and partially undressed. Mr. Cooke heard of this, too, and he telephoned for the Armed Reserve, a branch of the police force. Soon after this a magistrate came in a truck, together with twelve members of the Armed Reserve. The mob attacked the truck, and in the subsequent inquiry a bayonet was produced that had been snatched off a policeman's rifle by a member of the mob; the policeman could not have fixed it on very well. The magistrate ordered the mob to disperse, but they flung stones. The magistrate ordered the police to perform a *lathi* charge, but the mob grappled with them and looked as if it would overpower them. The magistrate thereupon ordered one policeman to fire. The policeman did so and killed, officially, three people and wounded twelve. The mob did not so much disperse as disappear, into thin air. For several days there was not a man to be seen on the estate, although women and children remained. But after a time the men came back and resumed their work as though nothing had happened. Needless to say, it was the *workers* who got hurt; the rabble-rousers who had stirred them up to it had taken themselves away to safety long before the unpleasantness started.

Everyone deplored that such a thing should have happened, but nobody could see how, under the circumstances, the magistrate or the police could have acted in any other way. But in any case the action had achieved one thing from the point of view of the planters: It had shaken the confidence of the workers in their leaders. The leaders had said, "The police will never fire at you." But the police *had* fired. There had been no further trouble on Passamala since the incident, and things had quieted down elsewhere as well.

They were all laughing at the club at the sad story of a young man, straight from Eton, who had arrived a week or two previously to be a *creeper,* or learner, on the estate of a big company. Four days after his arrival he had gone to his boss and announced his determination to go straight home. "It's all been a ghastly mistake!" he cried.

For years, I imagine, the phrase "It's all been a ghastly mistake" will find currency among the planters of Travancore.

I was also told of the case of a doctor, an Indian, who, after distinguished service during the war in the Royal Army Medical Corps, had taken the job of doctor in a big estate hospital.

He had all his life been a great Anglophile, and he deplored the fact that the British had ceased to govern India. He was educated in England, completely westernized, and altogether "as British as the flag," in the words of a well-known advertisement. He applied to join the planters' club. Nothing doing. No natives allowed.

This had so annoyed him that he had relinquished his post, become a labor agitator, and was now the chief thorn in the flesh of the planters! I could not resist saying when I heard this, "Well, it serves you right!"

One large and motherly Scots lady who was there said: "But surely, why shouldn't we have our own club? Indian students in London have their own club, to which Londoners are not allowed. The English in Hollywood have their own club. Americans in England have their own club. Of course, we want to be with our own people at times. We live out on our estates and see Indians all day and every day. At the week ends we want to see our own people!"

"But by your account this doctor *was* one of your own people," I protested.

"We'd have loved to have had him," she said. "But, if we'd taken him, how about other Indians living round here? There are lots of Indian planters now. How could we have refused them? The club down the hill admitted some Indians, and they brought their friends. There are now a majority of Indians there, and we feel out of place and not at home when we go there. They can start *their* club and not let us in if they want. It's all very well for you people who come out to India for a year or two to look around. But when you've got to spend your life here, as we have, you long for the company of your own people. Every other race would do just the same."

What argument is there against this?

I do not think there is any excuse for completely cutting oneself off from all social intercourse with the inhabitants of the country in which one lives, which is what, in fact, these planters do; and this is a charge to which they would all freely admit. I think they deny themselves so much. I know of no people in the world from the society of whom I obtain more pleasure than the Indians' (except of course the people of East Suffolk), and I feel that these planters miss the best of living in this fascinating country. However, they know far more about it than I do: They've lived there for years, and it's their business. Who am I to try to teach my grandmother how to suck eggs?

During the fortnight I spent up in this rubber and tea country I met with hospitality that it would be hard to equal anywhere, and what is more, kindness and friendship. It must seem churlish indeed for me to criticize adversely the people who were my hosts. Yet what is the good of my writing this book at all unless I set down in it what I believe to be the truth?

In discussing the labor trouble they spoke of one particular evil: the rapacious trader from whom the worker has to buy his needs. I asked them why they did not establish cooperative stores on their estates? One of them said that cooperative societies had never worked in India and never would, and the rest agreed. It was impossible to get honest men to run them.

This is, in fact, quite untrue. I have seen cooperative societies of every kind working extremely well in most parts of India, and some which have been working well for very many years. In fact, India might be called a land of cooperative societies; it is not far behind Denmark in this respect. But this unwillingness, or inability, on the part of the planters to start them is symptomatic, I think, of a deeper trouble. And that is their complete inability, at the present time, to come to any sort of an understanding either of the new kind of worker—the union worker—or of the new India.

The worker now believes that India belongs to him, and that the *dori* is an interloper. He will never go back to the old coolie mentality again. The tragedy is that he finds such unsuitable people to lead him in his fight for better things. I met some of these "labor leaders" later on. They had obviously never done a stroke of work in their lives. They didn't know what labor was. Miserable specimens! Either the workers themselves must become more educated, and develop some real leaders, or else some idealistic young men of the educated class must first learn what work is and then go and lead them. I should like to see some youngsters from college get jobs as tappers or tea coolies and stick at that for a few years and *then* engage in union activity. These failed B.A.'s, who come up in their American cars (paid for out of the contributions of the people they are supposed to represent) and who stir up such unpleasantness and then disappear at the first sign of what looks like physical danger to themselves, are not labor leaders at all.

What will happen to the tea and rubber industries depends upon what happens to India. If she goes Communist, then they will be commandeered and the present planters will be replaced by commissars, who will behave in almost exactly the same manner as the planters now behave, except that they won't know much about planting. If the agrarian revolution, which shows signs of already having started in an uncertain sort of way, really gets going, then it may be that the estates will be turned into cooperative societies, and the present owners probably will receive compensation. If this revolution takes another turn, then maybe the estates will be cut up into smallholdings, the holdings farmed by peasant proprietors under close supervision, and the estate factories, only, run as cooperative societies. If the present government remains in power or is replaced by a government with a similar moderate policy, then the industries will be kept on as they are now, perhaps with stricter application of labor legislation, a strengthening of labor unions (and one hopes a more responsible attitude by them), and taxation as heavy as is compatible with keeping the industries alive. The government has no intention of killing the goose that lays the golden eggs, but it intends to see that the supply of eggs is fully maintained. It will be a long time before foreign exchange loses its importance.

Personally, if I were a coolie, I should prefer the third alternative: that the estates should be cut up into smallholdings and that I should be given one of them. If this happened, efficiency would no doubt fall off alarmingly—efficiency at producing tea and rubber. As for efficiency at making people happy, well, that is a horse of another color. But nobody pays much attention to that kind of efficiency nowadays.

11

HINDUS AND JEWS

Jonathan duncan, in his *Remarks on the Coast of Mala-bar,* which he wrote in 1807, says (according to a fasci-nating book written by J. H. Hutton, called *Caste in India*): "A Nayar may approach a Nambudri Brahman, but must not touch him; a Tiyan (toddy tapper) must remain 36 paces off; a Malayan (*i.e.* Panan, exorcist basket-maker) must keep three or four paces further off; a Pulayun (cultivator and untouch-able) must keep 96 paces from a Brahman. A Tiyan must not come within twelve paces of a Nayar, and a Pulayun must keep 96 paces from a Nayar as well as from a Brahman. A Panan may approach but not touch a Tiyan, but a Pulayun may not even approach a Panan. If he wishes to address a man of higher caste he must stand afar off and 'cry aloud.' If a Pulayun touch a Brahman, the Brahman must at once bathe, read 'much of the divine books,' and change his Brahmanical thread."

I quote this, not because there is anything unusual in it, but simply because it is so very typical of the rules and regu-

lations of caste in India, and it happens to apply to the part
of India which I am describing: the Malabar coast.

Not so long ago the temple at Nagercoil had to be pulled
down and reconstructed because it was entered by a Brahman
who had lost caste. This he had done by allowing his daughter, who had been married as a small child and whose husband had died almost immediately, leaving her a virgin, to
marry again.

Travancore is as caste-ridden as any part of India, although
most other places are nearly as bad. But the Travancore caste
system differs in important ways from that of the rest of India,
and is interesting.

For example, the Brahmans—in other places always the
leading caste—have lost caste to some extent in Travancore.
This is due to a very curious thing.

Before the Aryans came from the north of India, the important people in Travancore were called the Nayars. And
they had a matriarchal society. They were a warlike people,
and as the men were often away on raiding expeditions, the
women ran the estates, and it came about that all property
was put in the hands of the women. When a man married, his
wife did not come and live with him, but remained in her
mother's house and her husband came and visited her there.
Such is the incredible conservatism of India that this matriarchal society is still, part of it at least, in existence.

Now when the Aryans came from the north, they presumably conquered the Nayars and imposed on them the caste
system. And in this the Aryan Brahmans were, of course, at
the top. The Nayars were classed as Sudras—the fourth of the
four big castes.

But the Nayars retained their matrilineal society, and a
strange thing happened. A custom was started whereby every
Nayar girl had to have a token marriage to a Brahman before

she was actually married to her real Nayar husband. Whether the Brahmans instituted this custom because they rather liked Nayar girls or whether the Nayars had always had the custom of token marriage to a priest and merely adapted it, there is no way of telling. In recent years this token marriage has not been consummated, and some historians say that it never was; but comparison with similar customs in other parts of the world (where a consummated marriage to a priest was the prelude to real marriage) leads one to suspect that it was.

Now, whether as a result of this custom or not, the custom arose that only the eldest brother in a family of Brahmans could marry properly a Brahman girl (unless this first marriage proved childless, when the second eldest brother was allowed to marry). The younger brothers then had to console themselves as best they could with mistresses drawn from lower castes, and there were a large number of Brahman women who could never marry at all, because, of course, they could not marry into other castes. Because of this and the immorality that naturally resulted from it, the Nambudri Brahmans, as the Brahmans of Travancore were called, fell in the estimation of the other people. They lost the respect that Brahmans normally enjoyed in those days because of their irregular sexual habits, and their caste fell from its position of supremacy.

The Nayars rose and took their place. Nowadays people will tell you that the Nayars are the Brahmans of Travancore. They are not, of course. In fact they are Sudras, but undoubtedly they fill the place that the Brahmans normally fill: that of being the leading community. (As a matter of fact they share this lead with the Syrian Christians, who consider themselves, and are considered by the Nayars, as equal to the Nayars.)

One good result of the matrilinear society of the Nayars

has been that their women have enjoyed high status in the community, and they still, in fact, enjoy this high status. Women generally in Travancore and Cochin are more highly advanced than women in most other parts of India. Education for women is well established and developed in Travancore.

Now the reader who does not know India might suppose that most of the above fantastic ramifications of caste will by this day and age have broken down. Nothing could be further from the truth.

I will not say that caste is as strong in India now as it ever was; perhaps some cracks have begun to appear in its foundations. The distances within which lower-caste people pollute those of higher castes have become shorter, owing to the general use nowadays of the public highway. The day came, some time ago, when lower-caste or outcaste people could no longer be forced off the highway when a Nayar or a Brahman appeared, and so this is now, more or less, waived. I do not think that there are many Brahmans in Travancore, however, or indeed in the whole of India, who do not feel a sense of defilement if an outcaste or untouchable comes too near them.

One still reads frequently in the papers of such things as attacks on Harijans as they are nowadays called (this word was made popular by Gandhiji—the suffix *ji* is a mark of respect—and means "people of God." He popularized it in an attempt to remove the stigma from the untouchables). These attacks are caused sometimes because these people try to send their children to school, and the parents of the other children object to having their offspring in the same classrooms. In many village schools one sees the poor little Harijan children sitting outside, listening to the lessons through a window. Sometimes trouble is caused because a Harijan is caught drawing water from a well used by caste people, or wearing clothing on the upper part of his body, in a district where this is not the custom, or wearing shoes, or carrying an umbrella. Sometimes there is a riot, because Harijans try to insist on their right at law to enter a temple or perhaps a Brahman eating place. To say that caste has broken down in India would be to say something quite untrue.

But there is no doubt that an attempt is being made to break it down, and that broken down it will be. Public opinion—awakened by Gandhi and Nehru—is against it, even though the individual often finds it impossible to ignore it. The significant thing is that the first effective attack on caste and untouchability has been launched by the Hindus themselves. Before Independence it was only the Congress Party that really attacked caste, and since Independence great efforts have been made, and are still being made, to break it down. Caste is a Hindu disease, but now that the Hindus realize it is a disease, its days are numbered. For it is a disease which the Hindus themselves can cure.

A strange thing about India is the manner in which castes or communities manage to keep themselves to themselves, with practically no intermarriage at all, for thousands of years. And an outstanding example of this is the White Jews of Travancore.

When the ancestors of these people came to India is a matter for conjecture. Certainly fleets of merchantmen in King Solomon's time used to trade to the Malabar coast, for that is where they got their peacocks and apes and other knick-knacks. There are many other theories: one that they are the descendants of the Jews taken in captivity to Babylon by Nebuchadnezzar. At all events, it is certainly known that there was an old-established Jewish community there when the Romans used to trade to Cranganore before the time of Christ, and that there still is.

They were there also when the Portuguese arrived in Malabar, and with typical Christian tolerance the great Admiral Albuquerque wrote to the King of Portugal asking His Majesty "whether I may be permitted to exterminate them one by one as I come across them?" It is not known whether or no he waited for an answer, but it is known that he completely destroyed their city at Cranganore, and also sacked the Jewish community in Cochin, burning, among other things, the old synagogue.

When the Dutch ousted the Portuguese, however, the remnants of the community came together again, and enjoyed a period of peace and prosperity which has lasted until this day.

I was prepared to be disappointed by the White Jews. For one thing, I did not expect them to be white. They had lived, with only one or two small influxes of new Jewish blood (mostly from Spain) for well over two thousand years amid a sea of people of a darker color and I thought even if there had only been one or two cases of intermarriage in every century they would certainly by now have been of mixed blood.

So when I went to Cochin I decided to stroll along and have a look at them.

Cochin is a strange town. It is built on a narrow spit, which forms one side of the mouth of the Malabar Backwaters, and it can only be approached by water. The Backwaters form a fine harbor, and here part of the Indian Navy is based. Large merchantmen and tankers come inside and tie up to Willingdon Island, a piece of artificial land built before the war.

At the very end of the promontory on which the city stands, the Dutch built a fort, one of their typical walled towns, such as are to be found in scores of places scattered about the Indian Ocean. There are fine old Dutch buildings in there still, and also some Portuguese remains, including the church in which Vasco da Gama is said to be buried.

I met a man named Mr. S. S. Koder in this town, and he told me the above facts about the White Jews, and told me where to find them. He should know, because he is a White Jew himself. So I followed his directions and made my way through the streets of the busy port.

The road led away from the Dutch town, running parallel to the shore of the Backwaters. It was a narrow road, incredibly congested, and had alleyways running off it at intervals down to wharves on the Backwaters, where *wallams* were loading and unloading cargoes. I found one unloading a cargo of toddy—coconut toddy—and I sat down near by and drank a swig or two before I went on. It was very strong, and not really the stuff to drink during a longish walk under a sweltering hot sun. For Cochin is hot and no mistake.

Rickshaw wallahs plagued me, little boys and girls ran along beside me like pilot fish round a shark, begging for annas, and the teeming population stared at me in the good old Malabari manner. Gentlemen who owned rowboats ran up and explained to me that they were willing to take me on a tour of the harbor for a song, or introduce me to refined young ladies of their acquaintance for little more.

Eventually I came to a yard where women were spreading peppercorns out on canvas, to let them dry in the sun. And behind this yard was a building which I was told was the famous Paradesi Synagogue. It was not very magnificent, and I did not see any White Jews about. A myth, I thought.

But I found my way round behind the synagogue and came to a narrow street, hot and hemmed in with tall old buildings. Airless, suffocating. And there I saw the White Jews.

They are dressed as I suppose Jews were dressed in the Middle Ages, and they were certainly white—a pallid, parchmentlike white, as though the sun and air never got to them. There are only a few hundred of them left there; others are scattered throughout India, mostly in Bombay, and some have gone to Israel.

Their features are most striking. They are the most aristocratic-looking people I have ever seen. There were women sitting in doorways, their legs bare but their feet shod with sandals, and I saw some young people walking about, tall and thin and aloof, and with this striking pallor to their complexions. They certainly had no drop of Indian blood in them. And it struck me that they are possibly the most inbred people in the world.

I tried to walk along inconspicuously, for I hate gaping at people. To a tourist, I suppose, the world is a sort of human zoo, but I try not to be a tourist. I carried my camera inconspicuously and did not use it.

I found the old man, however, who looked after the synagogue. He was delightful. He was fat, had a merry face and a big mustache. He spoke some English and laughed all the time. He made me laugh. He opened the door of the synagogue with an enormous key and let me in. There are some fine tiles on the floor, but the place has no great beauty. The old man showed me some copper plates with writing on them. They were presented to the Jews by a Hindu king named Bhaskara Ravi Varma, and the purport of the writing on them is to cede certain lands to the Jews, and promise them peace and the friendship of the Hindus. Like the Syrian Christians, in thousands of years this little community never suffered a single act of persecution from the Hindu rulers of the country.

I went back to Cochin feeling rather guilty.

When I got back to the Dutch fort, I found a small hotel under some huge and shady trees. From the veranda in front of it you looked over a stretch of green grass to the water's edge where, under the old town wall, men worked the Chinese fishing machines. These, like the *wallams,* the gabled roofs, and the wide straw hats of the Travancoris, were introduced by Chinese sailors many centuries ago. They consist of huge bamboo frames on which nets are slung, so that the nets can be lowered to the bottom of the harbor, left for half an hour, and then whipped up quickly so as to encompass the downfall of any fish that might have been swimming above the net at the time.

While I sat drinking lime juice and water and watching these, two men came in, both young Travancoris. We started talking, and I found that one was a commercial traveler and the other a man who went around advising people who owned machinery what sort of oil to put into it.

I asked the commercial traveler if he liked his job. "I hate it," he said.

"Why do you do it?" I asked.

"My family" (by which he meant the joint family to which he belonged—probably his father's family; he himself was unmarried) "needs the money."

"It does not matter what job you do," said the oil-advising man. "We all have to do some job to get money, but our real lives go on just the same outside that. Have you read the *Bhagavad Gita?*

"Of course I've read the *Bhagavad Gita,*" said the commercial traveler. "But I find that my work interferes with my own life. I can't ignore it. If I could, I would give it all up and take to the road with a begging bowl."

"I knew a millionaire in Bombay who did that," said the

oil adviser. "He gave up his business, left his family, and walked away with a begging bowl. And nobody's ever heard of him since."

"Every Indian has a hankering to do that sort of thing," said the traveler.

"That's what's wrong with India," said the oil man. "That's what we've got to fight against. That's why we're not like America."

"Do you *want* to be like America?" I asked.

"Well, in America every third family owns a car," said the oil man, "and every fourth family, I think it is, owns a television set. There's not *one* television set in India."

"How dreadful," I said.

"And in America nobody starves," he went on.

"I would rather starve than have India like America," said the commercial traveler.

"All you want to do is meditate?" I asked the commercial traveler.

"We are like drops of water," said the commercial traveler, "which have been torn from their mother, the ocean. The ocean is God. The drops of water must strive to return to the ocean. But they have many troubles. They fall on the mountains and are turned to ice. They are held up in small and stagnant lakes. They are absorbed by plants and swallowed by cows. When they are nearly back to their mother the ocean, perhaps they are evaporated again and blown to another continent by the wind. But always they must have that urge—to return to the ocean, to reunite with God. That is what we call meditation. The attempt to reunite ourselves with God. We are each a fragment of God, torn away from the main body. We must strive to reunite. I am wasting my time with this commercial traveling. It is not bringing me any nearer to God."

"I shouldn't think it is," I said. "But it's giving you a living. It's keeping you alive while you meditate in your spare time."

"That is the mistake you make in the West," he said. "And it's the mistake I've allowed myself to fall into."

I cannot remember the words of the conversation that followed well enough to reconstruct it here sufficiently faithfully, so I am not going to try. But one is always having this sort of conversation in India. There is always this hankering to withdraw from the turmoil and sit or wander quietly and think. There is always this great concern with metaphysical things, the things that cannot be measured or ascertained empirically. The things that can only be guessed at, divined, discovered by intuition.

The main difference, it seems to me, between the Western and the Eastern thinker is that, paradoxically, the Westerner is an idealist, and the Easterner is a realist.

Both wish to strive after ultimate truth. But the Easterner, some millenniums ago, decided that the attempt to strive for *material* perfection in which to live while striving for the ultimate was futile, and he gave it up. He abandoned it. He tried to make a short cut: school himself to *ignore* hunger, dirt, disease, poverty, and concentrate entirely on thought, intuition, and mysticism, which he considered were the ultimate, the only worthy, activities of man.

The Westerner, on the other hand, says, in effect, "We cannot sit down to meditate, or to search for truth, in all this confusion and squalor. First let us advance materially, until we have all the material conditions favorable for thought: plenty of food, good houses, good clothes, labor-saving gadgets to free us from drudgery. Then, when we have these things, let us discover as much about nature as we can by scientific observation, so that we have all the data and facts and figures that can be obtained about the universe, and then let us sit down and try to get some sense out of it. *Then* maybe we will have time to sit and think, and to try to put the pieces together and find out if the cosmos does make sense after all.

"In others words, let us put our house in order first, get the drains working and the larder full and the vacuum cleaner going so that none of us need be a drudge but *all* may have a chance to seek salvation; *then* (if there is still time before our short lives are over) let us devote ourselves to the real business of man—the finding out of what it's all about."

The Easterner says: "We cannot waste time over the drains and the larder and the vacuum cleaner. We can, however, school ourselves to ignore the smell and the hunger and the dirt. As far as the larder goes, we'll wait until we're hungry, and then we'll worry about that. If we can afford it, we'll have a sweeper and a servant boy, and we won't waste time feeling sorry for them. We've invented the theory of Karma to take care of them. They are paying, in this life, for sins committed in the last. Also, if they are really superior beings, there is nothing to prevent them from smearing themselves with ashes and taking the road as *sadhus*. They won't starve.

"As for learning more about the universe by science, such knowledge is trivial, and has nothing to do with the purpose. What does it matter how many stars there are? or what they weigh? or what they're made of? Such matters are the concern of immature people. We will not waste our too-short lives over them.

"We will sit down here where we are, on the floor amid the litter and the dirt or under the nearest tree, and, ignoring the beggars and the flies, we will think."

One method, I suppose, is as good as the other, but I am not quite sure where either of them leads. The Indian method has the advantage, however, that so far it has not led to anything like an atomic bomb.

12

MINING, MAHARAJAHS, AND MAHATMA GANDHI

FEW PEOPLE COULD BE less capable than the present writer of seeing the point of digging gold out of one hole in the ground only to bury it in another; but, nevertheless, I have a habit of going down gold mines. Not that I want to get any gold—I just like going down mines.

I do not like large mines in the sense that I approve of them. Small ones can be fun, of course, but life working down a large mine—and I have worked down one or two—is unpleasant, like life working in any large organization. But all the same, there is a fascination about the mines themselves. So when I found myself in Mysore State, not far away from the "deepest mine in the world," I could not resist the temptation to go down it.

Now there are three "deepest mines in the world": one in South Africa, one in South America, and the other in South India. The one in South India is Ooregum Mine in the Kolar Gold fields, and it goes down to slightly better than ten thousand feet. And if the mine in South America goes down to slightly better than ten thousand and one feet, I do not care. Ten thousand feet is far enough for me.

Bangalore is the biggest city in Mysore State, for Mysore City proved to be too far off the trade routes to compete successfully. Bangalore is fast becoming one of the most important commercial and industrial cities of South India, and like all such cities is horrible. Everybody tells you how clean it is. Cleanliness is a negative virtue. To me, Bangalore is ugly and dull.

Mysore State itself is a great rolling tableland, the un-jungled parts of it almost treeless—wide-open sweeping grasslands so much like the high veld of South Africa that I almost thought I was back in that country. The climate suits the country—windy and invigorating, and not too hot.

Over such a world one drives to the Kolar Gold fields, which are on the eastern edge of Mysore State.

There are four mines, but they are all managed by the same firm, and they are all very deep. I went down to a mere seven thousand feet, but even at that depth the rock pressure is so great that I saw steel railway lines twisted like pieces of wire, steel trucks squashed like matchboxes, and granite blocks that had been crushed to powder and then reconsolidated again into rock.

It is dangerous mining at such depths. The rock that one mines is being subjected to such pressures that nobody can be quite sure what it is going to do. On the surface one notices huge piles of squared granite blocks, and finds that these are for being taken down the mine to be packed into the stopes after the ore has been removed, in an effort to keep the walls from coming together again. I climbed down one of the stopes, into which men were busy stacking these blocks.

The stope in question was narrow—about six feet wide I suppose—and nearly vertical. It was a vertical cleft in the rock made by the extraction of the lode of ore. It was being mined by the underhand method; the miners were drilling and blasting beneath their feet, so that the stope was continually getting deeper. But as they mined they had to fill up the space over their heads with these granite blocks. And they had to keep the granite blocks fairly close to their heads too, otherwise they would get what they called a "rock burst" or "pressure burst"—the walls of the cavity they had created would come together very quickly.

So what they did was to jam in timber "stulls"—pit props—horizontally across the stope over their heads, and then stack the granite blocks on these. When they first put them in, the blocks were loose, of course, just resting on one another and on the timber, but after a day or two this was not the case. The blocks were crushed together, the timber stulls were splintered, and the miners knocked them out with crowbars as being of no further use. The granite blocks were now supported by the pressure of the rock, which had started coming together.

It is impressive to stand in the bottom of a narrow stope, down which one has climbed on vertical ladders suspended from the rock, and watch these colossal forces at work—to see the splintered timber above one's head, and even see where the hard granite blocks have begun to crush.

Normally this pressure happens slowly, but sometimes it comes in a hurry. In the twinkling of an eye, the granite blocks are crushed to powder and reconsolidated into rock. I saw a place where there had been one of the pressure bursts, and thought that what I was looking at, at the end of a tunnel that was being driven back into the devastated area, was the white line of ore that had not yet been mined. "That's granite," said my guide. "That's what happens to it." And one can imagine what happens to any miners who happen to be around at the time.

The day before I got there thirty miners had been killed down one of the mines by just such a pressure burst. The rescue squads were busy trying to get survivors out when I was down the sister mine.

No warning is given before a pressure burst occurs. It just happens—*wham!* The sides of the slot that has been cut into old Mother Earth just come together, and it's unfortunate for anybody who happens to be between them when they do.

There had been several bad pressure bursts within a few months. Minor earthquakes occur on the surface when it happens, and most of the buildings on Kolar Gold fields have cracks in their walls from the effects of these.

So many of the accidents had occurred that people in India were getting concerned. Questions were being asked in parliament, and the newspapers were leading off about it. People were saying that men should not be sent down to their deaths to get gold. Now there may be many reasons for not letting people dig for gold, but this is not a good one.

The miners look upon the rock pressure as a challenge. They are constantly seeking a way to control it. They know the risk they run, and they accept it. No one should be prevented from risking his neck if he wants to. I asked the manager of the mine if there was any difficulty in getting men to go underground, and he said there was a waiting list a mile long of people wishing to sign on.

The miner who took me down was a Cornishman. He was a rare man, had risen from the ranks of mining and had the Cornishman's love of underground. These Cornish miners only open up and blossom when they get below the surface. We had plenty of them on the copper belt. This one told me he had a son who was training to be a doctor. "Good thing,

Coming about on S.S. *Deyvadahighi*

Captain Mahomed Aliad (*in front*) and his crew

Weighing the anchor on S.S. *Deyvadahighi*. (The man coiling down the "traveler" on the right of the picture is the cook.)

Mahomed Abdul Cassim, the Captain's son

Malayalam children on the Malabar coast

View from one of the four great *gopurams* of Madura Temple

A gallery of the temple of Minakshi at Madura

Spraying rubber

A *wallam* on the Malabar backwaters

Sri Krishna stealing the *gopis'* clothes

Krishna playing the flute as he watches the *gopis*

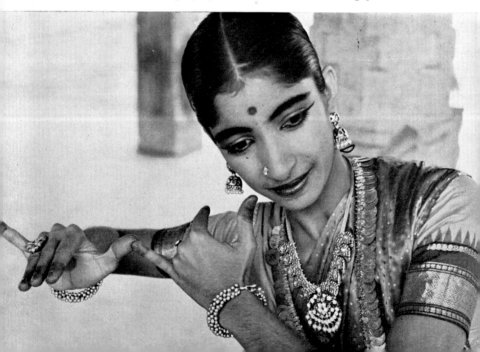

Syrian Orthodox service in the old seminary at Kottayam

His Holiness the Catholicos at the Syrian Church

The women and children standing at the back of the church during the service

Crucifix at the foot of an old stone cross at the Church of Changannor

Cotton spinning on the portable wheel developed by Mahatma Gandhi

Carding cotton, by vibrating the string of a bow in it

Deep-well turbine at the new agricultural station in the Terrai

One of the many sugar mills at Barwasni

Badrachalam Temple with Godavari ruins in background

Brahman priest in Badrachalam Temple

The author at Simla, temporary capital of the Punjab

Meeting of the *Panchayat* or village council in the village of Barwasni, Rohtak District of the Punjab

Nomadic blacksmiths in the Punjab

Punjabi picnic near Simla, in the hills

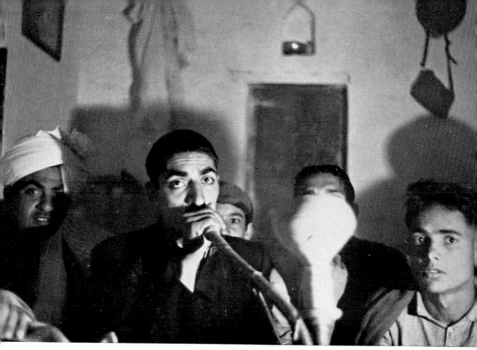

Chaudhri Mohan Dass, my host at Barwasni

Wedding procession in the village next to Barwasni

(*Above, left*) Chaudhri Prabhudayal, the enthusiastic Punjabi schools inspector

(*Above, right*) Sardar Madhusudan Singh, Community Project Officer at Sonepat

(*Left*) Sri Bawaji, Rural Development Officer at Ongole

too," he said. "I never thought he'd be anything but a miner, but he's got more sense. Dirty, filthy, dangerous job, mining. Look at me, I've been at it all my life, and where's it got me?" He obviously gloried in it!

We came to a fault, which cut across the reef through which we were walking in a level. The reef just suddenly stopped, and the way was blocked, as it were, by a wall of barren country rock. "We had to go to look for it again," said the Cornishman, "so we struck off into the footwall." A cross-cut turned at a sharp angle from our level and we walked along it. After about twenty yards we came to another level, which continued again parallel to the old one but offset to it. Men were busy putting timber up in the cross-cut that joined the two levels and it was obvious that the hanging was bad.

"Nasty bit of ground," he said. He was a hulking man, with a deep husky voice and a strong Cornish accent. "Always get nasty ground in these faults. Ground shifts a lot. Can't trust it."

"Why do you follow the fault then?" I asked. "Couldn't you drive along a bit farther and then cross-cut in undisturbed country?"

"Look," he said, stopping to face me and searching for words to explain something to an English foreigner who after all could never really understand things like a Cornishman, "look, if you're fighting a tiger you keep close to him, don't you? You grapple hold of him? You don't let him get at a distance so's he can spring at you? That's why we keep to the fault-line. We can keep ahold of it. We know when it's going to spring!"

That was at a shallow level, where there was not much rock pressure, but lower down all the levels and cross-cuts were lined with short lengths of railway line, which had been bent round into oval shapes so as to fit into the tunnels and support the rock. These steel sets were placed very close together, almost touching. We came to an area where the sets were not made of railway line, but heavy steel angle-girders.

"Useless!" said the miner. "We can't get old railway line nowadays, so we have to use this. It bends like wire. Rails will stand up to a bit of pressure." It gave one to think a little, walking along these steel-lined tunnels in the rock, and knowing and *feeling* that the rock was straining to come in on you, to crush the feeble six-inch steel girders like hairpins, and you too.

"How much deeper do you chaps intend to mine?" I asked him.

"Deeper? We'll go on mining to hell if the price of gold keeps up—and the bloody politicians mind their own business."

"Won't you get worse trouble from pressure and heat?"

"Of course we will. But that's what we're here for. To find a way round trouble. If the gold holds out and the price holds out, we'll beat it all right. We're miners; that's our job."

This man is as much an explorer as Christopher Columbus was. He is going to places where no man has been before and where no man ever thought it possible to go. They can leave the gold where it is, for my part, but I have to admit that there is a glory in this deep mining, this bearding of Pluto in his den. I saw the tedious business of extracting the gold from the rock; I saw the long and dreary rows of huts built for the Indian miners—the "unimproved" quarters and the "improved" quarters. I suppose they were the best that could be provided, but people should not live in "quarters" any more than they should live in "lines." They should live in *homes,* which is quite a different thing.

But this is not the fault of the mining companies of Kolar Gold fields which spend a lot of money on "welfare."

There are over a hundred Britons on the mines, and I met some of them in the mine club. As fast as possible Indians are being trained to take over, for the government has asked that this should be done. I don't think I ever saw better relations either, between British and Indian officials than I did at Kolar. Men cannot work together at such a hazardous and highly technical job as deep mining without getting to respect each other.

A new reef had been struck at Kolar, or rather an old reef that had been thought too poor to be worth mining had been discovered, at a lower depth, to be rich. I walked along the half-mile-long cross-cut underground from the old reef to the new, and saw ore there in which the gold was actually visible.

"We'd want a million pounds to sink another shaft and develop it," the manager told me when I got back to the surface.

"Where?" he said. "Do you think foreign investors are go-

"Can't you raise the money?" I asked.

ing to sink money into an undertaking like this? We don't know from day to day here what the government's going to do. Supposing the Communists get in? Supposing they do another Abadan on us? Where's the security?"

"What about Indian capital?"

"Indians haven't got the habit of investing money in joint stock companies yet. They put it in the family business."

"What about the government?"

"Heaven forbid!" said the manager fervidly. "We are pestered and poisoned with officials and inspectors and forms in triplicate now!"

I have a feeling, though, that the new reef will not lie undisturbed for long.

The men in the club were all talking about the recent disastrous pressure burst.

"What can you do to stop it happening?" I asked.

"Just what we're doing now, I suppose," said a Scots mine agent. "Only a bit more so, perhaps. Keep on stowing with granite, only keep it a bit closer to the face. And hope for the best." He, too, scoffed at the idea that a limit might be reached beyond which it would be unsafe to mine.

Fighting a tiger, that just about describes it.

At Bangalore I fell in with a man named Bartley, a member of the Anglo-Indian community. I went for a long drive with him around the countryside.

Bangalore is a great place for Anglo-Indians, the people of mixed Indian and British descent. They have a big club there, where they play the great game of Lotto, or "Housey-housey," on Saturday nights.

Many of them feel that they have had rather a poor deal out of Independence. But my friend Bartley was not too dissatisfied.

"Our community must accept the fact that India is our country; we must stop talking about 'home' all the time, and wishing we weren't *here*."

"Have the Anglo-Indians been unfairly treated since Independence?" I asked. He did not think so. Such troubles as they had had, he said, they had brought on themselves.

"But we must remember that times have changed," he said. "We must educate ourselves. In the British time Anglo-Indians didn't bother much about education. We left that to the Baniyas and Brahmans. Anglo-Indian boys were sure of jobs on the railways or in the mines. Nearly every engine-driver and stationmaster in India was an Anglo-Indian. Now we must compete with the rest; our favored position is gone. We must go all out for education."

After Independence many Anglo-Indians left India, some to go to England, and many to Australia. But the "White Australia" policy made it difficult for many to go there, particularly if they were dark of complexion, and the ones who got there found life not what they had expected it to be. The men had to do manual work, and the women had to look after their houses without servants. Many of them came back again.

Bartley himself had left his very good job with a big oil company and gone to England. He had even bought a house there, in some inconceivable place in the Midlands. Naturally it was horrible. He had tried hard to get a job but had failed; he thought because he was colored. I hope not, but who can say?

So he had come back to India, and the oil company—very generously—had given him back his old job and not even made him lose any seniority.

Bartley drove me to Mysore City, where we saw the incredible palace of the maharajah. Like other cities with maharajahs in them, Mysore is completely dominated by the palace. Everybody there talks palace gossip, many people draw their livelihood from royal employment, and wherever you look you see the emblems or traces of royalty. I forget how many hundred cars there are in the royal garage, or coaches in the royal coach house, or harnesses with gold or silver fittings in the royal harness rooms. Mysore used to be looked upon as a model state, and, in fact, a lot of money was spent in the old days by the maharajah on good works and public services. But this amount must have been only a fraction of what was spent on the various trappings and appurtenances of royalty. The state army has been disbanded now, all except for about a hundred and sixty men, and there is some dissatisfaction because most of the ex-soldiers are now unemployed. Before, they were unemployed too, of course, but the difference is that then they were paid for it.

We saw the royal elephants, including the animal of which Sabu was mahout before he took to the films.

Bartley deplored the cutting down of the pomp and ceremony since Independence. He said that it added some light and color to life if people could go and see the huge processions through the city, when his highness rode in state. I suppose everybody has his own idea of light and color, and of what he is prepared to pay for it.

We drove up to Rayalaseema, or what used to be called the "ceded districts": territory that was ceded to the British by a former Nizam of Hyderabad after a war. They were having a famine when we arrived, but it was not a bad famine. The government appeared to have it well under control. Numerous public works were being done to give people employment, and, in fact, everybody who wanted work and a wage could get them. Soup kitchens had been opened in places where the people were really hungry, and I think it fairly safe to doubt whether there had been any deaths from hunger in that particular famine. At all events, we spent several days driving round to fairly remote villages and did not see anyone who looked as though he had suffered seriously from lack of food, although many of the poorer villagers looked undernourished. This famine had received quite an amount of publicity, and, in fact, had been written about as being a very bad famine, and I was glad to see that the new India was capable of dealing efficiently with emergencies of this nature. I was in Bengal during 1943 when they were having a famine there, and had the almost unbelievable experience (unbelievable that it should happen to oneself; one never really believes things that one is told about by other people) of stepping over corpses and dying people in the streets of Calcutta.

I remember putting a rupee note into the hand of one man who was still breathing, and seeing him look at it, but show no sign of trying to do anything with it. His wife and children lay dead on each side of him. He was past fighting.

There was nothing remotely like this in Rayalaseema.

In Rayalaseema also I came into contact for the first time with something which afterwards I decided to be of great value, though at that first impression I did not like it at all. And that was Mahatma Gandhi's invention of Basic Education.

Standard education in India has become simply an elaborate competition with clerkhood as the prize. Stuff your memory with a huge collection of unrelated facts about nothing at all that matters, satisfy some examiners that you have done so, and you will get a job as a *clerk* and be able to spend the rest of your life without having to do any real work or having to justify your existence in any practical way. That is the promise of education in all civilized countries, and in India in particular.

Until shortly before Hitler's war Indian education was simply a copy of English education, which was, on the face of it, absurd. Any Indian educated in those days knows more about the dates of the kings and queens of England than he does about the history of his own country. He knows the tale of King Alfred burning the cakes and King Canute demonstrating his inability to control the tides, but nothing at all about the doings of his own forefathers. Indian education is no longer like this; but it is still simply an Indianized version of English education. The schoolchild must work extremely hard at stuffing his head with facts, so that he can have no time to learn anything of real value or interest. I met Indian boys who were curious, as all boys should be, about the universe, but who would never have the time to satisfy their curiosity until they were grown up, when their curiosity would be dead: boys who might have developed a love of literature or music or painting or farming or bird-watching, or all these things and a thousand others, but had no time. They had had time only to scrabble for the dreary facts of the pedants, to stuff and stuff their heads until they were filled with barren rubbish, until the last spark of originality or enthusiasm or generosity in their minds was smothered beneath the great stinking heap of square roots and dates of battles and past participles.

A feature of every Indian town and city nowadays are the "cram shops." These cater to children of all ages, and even to adults. More and more Indian children, when they come home from school in the evening, are then sent straight to the cram shop—*to go through again what they were supposed to have learned at school during the day!* In Madras I visited several of these as I went round with Dr. Sambandam of Ashok Vihar, and often in India one passes the doors of one and hears the maddening chanting of the old-fashioned kind of Indian schooling: the voices in chorus repeating again and again some foolish fact, the parrot chorus.

Gandhi realized the wickedness of all this, and he endeavored to devise a system of education that would stimulate the imagination of children instead of killing it. And he called the system that he devised "Basic Education."

His idea was that young children should be taught everything by way of manual activity, and that they should never be told any fact until their curiosity already had been aroused about it.

One can best explain the method by an example. The children are taught to spin cotton. This activity is fascinating to small children, and they take a great pleasure in it. Now while they are spinning the teacher asks them if they know certain things, and if not he tells them. Where is cotton grown? Geography. Where is it not grown, and what is used instead? More geography. He tells them that it is sometimes spun in big mills. Economics. He tells them that the British are alleged to have tried to kill the Indian hand-loom industry to protect Lancashire. Politics! More economics! Possibly lies, but I do not know enough to argue about it. He makes the little children count, and keep an account of the number of slivers of spun cotton, and work out how many hanks of spun yarn they will make. Elementary arithmetic. He stops the class and makes them work out slightly more complicated arithmetical problems concerning this cotton. More arithmetic. As the children get older he is probably able to drag algebra into it. Algebra.

Some of this may seem a little farfetched perhaps, but in practice it does relate theory to fact in a way that is good. The children can see a *reason* for acquiring the knowledge that is being imparted to them.

And, of course, there are other things besides spinning cotton. Or at least there should be. There should be gardening, and farming, wood- and iron-work, and a dozen trades and manual crafts. And the teacher must be able to use all these for imparting academic education.

There is one weakness about the system in my opinion, and that is that it requires first-class teachers. And, of course, it does not always get them. The Basic teacher had no set rails to run on. He must constantly be using his own intelligence and imagination, he must strive to kindle interest, fan it, and keep it going—*awaken,* in fact, instead of dulling and deadening as is the much easier task of the orthodox schoolteacher. It takes good people. The mediocre teacher can teach nothing by the method except the bare bones of the crafts and trades through which the real teaching is supposed to be imparted.

A great advantage of the method, particularly in a country like India, is its emphasis on manual activity. "Work is Prayer" is the slogan written over the front door of a lot of Basic Education schools, and what is meant is real work, not the form-filling and machine-minding that have come to pass for work in Western countries. And the children themselves have to keep their school clean, cook their own meals, run the farm, and they do all this—as I saw quite clearly with my own eyes later on—with great gusto and pleasure. They are not little drudges of Dotheboys Hall. It is all great fun to them, and they grow up with the idea that manual labor is dignified and, what is more, a good way of passing the time. They do not yearn to be clerks, but are contented to do work that actually makes something useful.

But the Basic School I saw in Rayalaseema did not impress me. It seemed to me that the teachers in it were drawn from human material of far too low a standard for the purpose.

It was a teachers' training school, and young men with a certain (not very high) standard of ordinary education went there to spend eighteen months learning to be teachers in Basic Schools in villages.

I believe that they were devoted young men, for the most part, and genuine followers of Gandhi. They would not have been there otherwise, for the pay was enough for bare subsistence only, and even after training they would never earn much more than a coolie. But there was not sufficient intelligence about the place. Intelligence is not, perhaps, the most important thing in the world, but there are places where it is indispensable.

In his writings on the subject the Mahatma always used cotton processing as his illustration, perhaps because that happened to be his own speciality and pet subject. But he emphasized that other trades should be taught as well.

But these stupid people had got the cotton, and nothing else. Those wretched young men who were learning to be teachers spent six hours a day (the figures were given me by the headmaster) sitting on the floor ginning, carding, slivering, and spinning cotton. The rest of their time was taken up with chores and fatigues: cleaning up and working in the kitchen.

There was no farm there, no garden, no livestock, and no other activity except cotton.

Now I know that this will outrage the followers of Gandhi, but I believe that *spinning is not a fit activity for men.*

> When Adam Delved, and Eve Span,
> Who was then the Gentleman?

A magnificent comment on the social system, but also a sensible division of labor between the sexes.

And these young men at this Basic Training School had not benefited, I believe, by all this spinning. They were weedy. Too much squatting on the ground hunched over the *charkha.* They were mentally dull. Too little variety. Too much repetition of a monotonous and mechanical job. Spinning is difficult, but it is not a craft in the sense that cabinet-making or wrought-iron working are crafts. A piece of furniture or a wrought-iron gate can have individuality; in fact, they can be great works of craftsmanship, if not of art. A length of cotton thread can be well spun or badly spun, but it cannot really be said to have individuality, and it certainly cannot be said to be a work of art.

My sojourn in India converted me wholeheartedly to a belief in the social philosophy of Mahatma Gandhi, who is without any runner-up the greatest prophet and reformer of

our century. But I believe that he and his followers wasted
a lot of time and energy on this spinning cult.

Not that there is anything wrong with hand spinning. It is
definitely right. But it should be done by women who do it
well naturally and like it, just as they do well and like embroidery, or millinery, or knitting; and it should not have
monopolized so much the attention of the Gandhi people.
More attention should have been given to other things.

I should have liked to have seen these learner-teachers out
in the fields for part of the day plowing, and milking cows.
I should have liked to have seen them quarrying and dressing
stone, molding and burning bricks, building houses, cutting
trees and sawing them into planks and making them into
door or window frames and furniture. Doing men's work.

The school premises consisted of three rows of single-story
buildings making three sides of a triangle, with a flagpole in
the middle. There was a big kitchen, an eating room (where
one sat on the floor, of course), several classrooms mostly full
of spinning apparatus, and one weaving shed with some hand
looms in it, but the hand looms had not yet been assembled.
They had only recently arrived from the makers.

I asked the headmaster why the students did not learn to
make their own hand looms, as he told me that they cost a
lot of money and that was why the school had had to wait for
them. He laughed, and said that it was a job that only a professional could do. Now I looked at them, and I am quite
certain that any intelligent boy of fifteen in the carpentry
class at my old school could have knocked one up, with one
hand tied behind his back, in three of our Wednesday afternoon periods.

The dormitories were tiny rooms, meant for two students
but actually occupied by five. The students slept on mats on
the floor, and when I went round they were mostly sitting

on the floor of their dormitories—spinning. They had to spin during most of their spare time, the headmaster told me (in addition to the regular spinning they did during "working hours"), in order to produce the weekly quota of hanks that was demanded of them. The headmaster apologized that they were so overcrowded, but complained that his school was short of buildings. I asked him why he did not set his students onto building some. He said that building was a skilled job, and that he was waiting for the Public Works Department to come and do it. He should have said that he and his assistants had been brought up in the ancient Indian tradition that people such as they could not do coolies' work, and that they had an inborn repugnance to dirtying their hands.

Spinning is a nice clean job.

13

THE VILLAGES OF ANDHRA

BACK TO MADRAS I got on a bus heading north. North
along the coast of Coromandel.

To the Kitsna and Godavari river country.

At Ongole, after a couple of days of busing, I decided to
have a rest.

Ongole is a typical little country town of that part of India:
a haphazard collection of single-storied houses, with large
expanses of dusty, dirty, bare ground in between, but shaded
with trees. The place is a minor government station. There
is a bazaar, a crowded street full of small shops with three- or
four-story buildings over them, and altogether Ongole is not
an attractive place. South Indian towns have not the charm,
architecturally at least, of towns and cities of North India.
The North Indian towns have crammed, winding, narrow
alleyways, overhung by jutting upper stories like the streets
of Elizabethan England. South Indian towns are apt to be
just characterless.

But I decided to stay in Ongole for a day or two, as I

wanted to look at something called the Firka Development Scheme.

Madras State decided soon after Independence to go ahead with the improvement of the rural areas on the lines laid down by Mahatma Gandhi, without waiting for any central government or foreign financial aid.

I got off the bus in the bazaar, and left my luggage in a shop. I always do that, and it's a good idea, if you are traveling through India. You get off a bus, and what are you to do with your luggage? You don't want to carry it about with you. If you take it to a traveler's bungalow, they will expect you to stay there, which will be both dull and expensive, but if you just take it to the first shop you see and ask them to look after it they will do so and enjoy doing it, for being a foreigner you are an object of interest to them.

The shops in the bazaar were small and hot and dark, and in them fat merchants sat cross-legged on low platforms, clad in white cotton, waiting for business. In the street people sat on the pavement offering goods for sale: sweetmeats and sticky cakes.

In India good intention is often taken to mean as much as effective action. A woman squats on the pavement behind a tray of some food that she is trying to sell, and you cannot see what sort of food it is because it is so closely covered with flies. But the woman knows as well as you or I do that flies on food are undesirable. And her intentions in respect to the flies are good. So once a minute—or oftener, perhaps, if her intentions are very good—she passes her hand across the food and for the interval of a second the flies are airborne. Then they settle on the food again and the woman rests, honor satisfied and good intentions displayed.

I walked out of the bazaar and along the road to where the government offices are, intending to look for whomever was

in charge of this Firka Development business. At the foot of
a rocky hill, under some big trees, I found a house—a rather
ramshackle, corrugated-iron-roofed house—in front of which
a man was taking a motorcycle to pieces. I asked him if he
knew where the Firka Development officer lived. "I am the
Firka Development officer," he said.

Within five minutes I was sitting on the veranda drinking
coffee, and a servant had gone to fetch my luggage from the
shop.

Mr. Bawaji, for that was the gentleman's name, was a
stoutish man about thirty-three, and a typical ex-army warrant officer. He had been taken prisoner of war in Singapore
and had spent three years in a prison camp, and had then
returned and found this development job. "Do you like the
job?" I asked him.

"I do now," he said, "I've got really interested in it. But
at first it was just a job. Now I love it."

"Did you join the I.N.A.?" I asked. The I.N.A. was the
Indian National Army, the body formed of Indian prisoners
of war who repudiated their oath and joined the Japanese.

This of course was a tricky question.

The late Subhas Chandra Bose, "Netaji" to his admirers,
is considered to be a great hero by many Indians. It was he,
of course, who formed the I.N.A., and came to his end, people
think (although there seems to be some doubt about the matter), in an air crash in a Japanese airplane. There are a few
Indians, however, who are not so fervid in their admiration
of this controversial man.

Personally I find no difficulty whatever in making up my
mind about him. Before the war I was all for Indian national
aspirations, and was a staunch admirer of Congress and of
Gandhi. I still am. It infuriates me, however, to see, as one
often does, next to the statue of the great Mahatma another

statue of a pompous, pot-bellied, comic-opera warrior with a huge sword which he wouldn't have known how to use, dressed in a Japanese officer's uniform: an imitation Mussolini, put up beside the great man of peace. Bose did nothing effective whatever for Indian Independence, and was perhaps history's most persistent backer of wrong horses.

But Bawaji was not to be drawn into the subject. He answered me with great dignity: "I did not join the I.N.A. I remained a prisoner of war. None of my battalion went over to the enemy because we had faith in our C.O. and he told us to stick to our oaths. He was a fine officer, and he stayed with us right through and put up with everything we had to put up with."

Bawaji took me to see his grandfather's tomb, which was at the foot of the rocky hill, not far from the house. Near it was an old *choultry,* broken down now and no longer used.

A *choultry* is a building put up to shelter pilgrims or other travelers, and is generally built by someone who can afford it as an act of charity. There are *choultries* all over South India. This one, Bawaji told me, had been built by his grandfather, but now that there was bus service people no longer required it. For they no longer had to walk to where they wanted to go.

Not far from the *choultry* was a *puttu,* or old termite (white ant) hill, and therein dwelt a snake. A cobra. A wall had recently been built around the *puttu* and a small shrine erected on top of it.

"Three months ago," said Bawaji, "we had a circus here, and the manager of the circus came and sat under this tree and worshiped the *puttu,* because, you know, to us cobras are holy. And while he was worshiping, the cobra came out and extended his hood—and that is a thing that doesn't often happen. The circus manager was so pleased at this that he gave me money to have this shrine built, and this wall and a small statue of Sai Baba to put in the shrine."

"Who is Sai Baba?" I asked. Sai Baba, I was told, was (as all the world should know) a saint whose spirit is always to be found where cobras live in *puttus* under *magosa* trees. (Sai Baba in the flesh lived at Siridi, near Ahamednagar, and died in 1921.)

"Does the snake often come out?" I asked, backing away perhaps a little.

"Every day people come here and put milk for it," said Bawaji. "And at night it comes and drinks. I see it sometimes in the night. It crawls around outside here. But in the day-time it doesn't often come out. When it does, it's a good omen."

"What would you do if a snake came into your house?" I asked.

"Give it milk," said Bawaji. "And then put kerosene near it perhaps to make it go away."

"Supposing you thought it would be a danger to your children, would you kill it?" I asked.

"No Hindu would kill a snake," said Bawaji.

We went back to the house and sat on the floor of the veranda and ate rice and hot curry. Ongole is in the Andhra country, the part of India where the people speak Telugu, and where they eat the hottest curry. The pepper water was like fire, and yet I found myself taking great gulps of it to cool my mouth after the far hotter curry. Anyone should be able to chew up handfuls of the ordinary red chillies that one buys in London, but in India there are chillies which are far hotter than those. There are some tiny little black ones that even Bawaji would boggle at, I imagine. Just what effect this chilli eating has on the digestive system I do not know, but I am told that, except where the people chew *pan* (betel leaf, lime and areca nut) with tobacco in it, the incidence of gastric ulcer is very low. I always feel particularly healthy when I am living on hot curry.

I was introduced to Bawaji's father, who was a retired cloth merchant, and who spent most of his life—like a lot of other Indian grandfathers—dandling his grandchildren. The pleasure that old Indian men and women get out of their grandchildren is enormous. Bawaji's father was a little doubtful about the wisdom of having a foreigner staying in the house (they were Mudaliars, the same caste as Kutti), but Bawaji had his way, and after I had been there a few days I was on good terms with the old man. With such an old gentleman, though, one must be very careful not to transgress any caste customs.

I dropped a colossal brick one day. I wanted to wash my face after I had been shaving at the well, and I dipped my cupped hands into the well bucket to do this. And to my horror I looked up and saw Bawaji senior looking at me— and to his horror too, for he rushed up shouting in Telugu in complete dismay.

For, of course, by rights the bucket should have been thrown away after this. For *anyone* to put any part of his person into it meant complete pollution. I should have tipped the bucket over and poured the water into one hand and splashed my face with that.

No one else saw this outrage though, and I believe Bawaji's father decided to keep quiet about it, for the bucket was not removed. On the theory, I suppose, that what the eye doesn't see the heart doesn't grieve over, for I am certain that if any other orthodox Hindu had been watching something or other would have had to be done.

At Bawaji's I ate off banana-leaf plates, which were then thrown away. The glass from which I drank was presumably discarded after I had gone. The Hindu, when drinking in another person's home, pours the liquid from the glass into his cupped hand and drinks from that, thus avoiding contaminating the glass with his lips. Bawaji told me that if his own uncle came to the house he would be given his food on banana-leaf plates, but a brother would be allowed to use the family crockery. Bawaji himself, when he ate with me, used banana leaves out of politeness, to keep me company as it were, but when he ate in the bosom of his family he used brass plates. China or earthenware is not much used in Hindu homes; it is considered unclean, and brass or copper are preferred.

Now Hindus, if they see that you are well disposed towards them and not apt to act the *pukha sahib,* will go to great lengths to avoid giving offense to you about their customs. I believe that it was a real wrench for Bawaji's father to let me go near the well at all—after all there were very few of his own Hindu neighbors who were allowed to use it—but he did so simply because he knew that, as a foreigner, I could not be expected to appreciate Hindu scruples, and as a guest I must not be offended. He himself never dined with me, though, and not once did I clap eyes on Mrs. Bawaji, who Bawaji told me was very orthodox. Bawaji himself, having been a warrant officer in the army, was broad-minded, but even he, I believe, found it difficult to throw aside all his caste scruples. No doubt, though, his own children will grow up to be even more free and easy about things than he is. For it is evident that the more tiresome of the Hindu customs and restrictions are on the way out.

There was one bed in the Bawaji household, an ordinary *charpoy,* or string cot. I slept on it, out on the veranda, while Bawaji and his old father slept on mats on the veranda floor. This was not selfish of me, for both of them assured me, and

I had good reason to believe them, that they never did sleep on the bed. The floor was healthier and more comfortable, they said. The bed was for occasional lounging during the heat of the day. Early in the morning we got up, and it was the work of a moment to roll the mats up, lean the bed against the wall, and the veranda was tidy.

After breakfast the next day I got on the back of Bawaji's motorcycle, which, I may say, had no form of rear springing, and we rattled away along one of the bumpier roads. During the next few days I spent a lot of time on the back of Bawaji's motorcycle, and felt like the cavalry trooper who complained in the song to his sergeant that a certain part of his anatomy was not made of wood. We rattled round to the villages which Bawaji, as Firka Development officer, was responsible for developing.

Among many others we went to the village of Jammula-palem.

Jammulapalem is in fertile country, on what is known as "black cotton soil," to the south of the Kistna delta. The chief crop grown nowadays is tobacco, and a British tobacco company has a depot at Ongole to which tobacco is brought. Virginia-type tobacco is grown, and experts say that it is just as good as Virginian Virginia, provided that it is properly flue-cured, which nowadays it is. The farmers around Jammulapalem are good farmers, and they own comparatively large holdings of land, up to a hundred acres being not unknown, and fifty being common. They have the finest cattle in India. The Ongole breed of cattle is renowned not only in India, but abroad also. Ongole bulls have been taken as far as Africa and South America to improve the local stock.

You approach the village by a long straight road that runs over the open fields, and the village itself is composed of several hundred one-storied mud-brick houses, with sloping tile roofs, jumbled fairly closely together, many of them even touching. Roads run here and there in the village, just earth roads, and they become very muddy in the rainy time. There is a sizable temple, a school and now another building: a Grama Seva Sangham. As we drove noisily into the village and drew up, in a cloud of dust, in front of the Grama Seva Sangham, every able-bodied man, woman, and child who was not out in the fields rushed out to welcome us.

Chairs were rushed out in front of the Grama Seva Sangham building, glasses of milk were brought, everybody crowded round. Wherever Bawaji went on his shocking old motor-bike I found he was welcome.

The secretary of the Grama Seva Sangham was a keen young man named Sri A. V. Subaya. (*Sri* was originally a word meaning almost the equivalent of *Lord*, but now is employed throughout India as the equivalent to our *Mister*, and is just as meaningless. Why we cannot just call each other by our names is something that I never could understand.)

There was a charming girl in the village called Kanselia Devi, and she was introduced to me as the women's welfare officer. (Devi is the feminine equivalent of *Sri*—it really means *Goddess* and was always applied to Brahman women but is now put after the names of all women. I like it.)

Well, Kanselia, Subaya, and Bawaji started explaining to me what a Grama Seva Sangham is. It is a village council for improving the life of the village. (The words are Sanskrit for Village Service Society.)

At Jammulapalem the Sangham had, with Bawaji's aid and advice and a small amount of government money, done the following things:

Built several miles of road (with voluntary labor but government help with culverts).

Built a new school building.

Built a reading room and fitted it with a radio set and some
books.

Trained a village midwife.

Dug a new well and built up the walls in three old ones.

Built a village washing place.

Started a *khadi* (home cloth production) improvement
center, which was obviously very successful.

Bought a stud bull.

Bought a stud buffalo bull.

Bullied everybody into digging compost pits for turning
vegetable rubbish into manure, digging refuse pits for keeping the village clean, sweeping the streets regularly, keeping
their houses cleaner than they had done before.

It had also attempted, so far with complete lack of success,
to make people use latrines, and to break down the caste
barriers.

And numerous other things, which it would be tedious to
mention. But it had achieved enough, during the six years
since the Firka Development Scheme had been going, to alter
very radically the life of the village.

Kanselia Devi was fighting an uphill battle, I felt. We went
to her house, in which were held the meetings of the equivalent of a Women's Institute, and she showed me what she
was doing. She held literacy classes for the village women,
taught them hygiene, cottage industries, child care, and all
the rest of it, and I felt that she really knew what she was
talking about on these subjects, and that she approached her
job with enthusiasm and ability. But alas, she was up against
the Demon Untouchability.

For she insisted on admitting Harijan women into her
sessions, and that kept the caste women away. When, once
or twice, she had managed to inveigle some caste women into
her classroom, a Harijan lady had come in the front door and

the entire class had disappeared out of the back. It was an insuperable difficulty, and it seemed that only the Harijans could benefit from her activities, and they made up less than twenty per cent of the village.

Bawaji took me to the Harijan-cherri (*cherri* means village) which was the quarter where the village Harijans, or people of "exterior castes," lived. The Harijan-cherri was set at a short distance from the main village. The houses in it were very small, mere shacks, but I was surprised how clean the place was kept. Normally the Harijan-cherri are fairly dirty; but Bawaji told me that now the Harijans were becoming class-conscious about their community, and were becoming determined to show the world that they were as good as anybody else, and better than most.

The weaving industry was centered in the Harijan-cherri, and the clack-clack of looms could be heard from most of the houses, and people were busy preparing their yarn for weaving, threading it through the comb to form the warps, and dyeing it, or bleaching the finished cloth. I went inside one house and found it almost pitch-dark in there. The weaver sat at his loom in a corner, and all the light he had was from a tiny window in the mud wall the size of a dinner plate. I asked him why he didn't have a larger window. First he said that he was afraid of burglars, and then he said that a smaller window kept it cooler, and then he said that darkness kept the flies away. So you can pay your penny and take your choice. Anyway, I suppose the size of his window was his business.

We went into a shoemaker's house, and saw extremely good sandals being made, and cowhides being tanned in the yard to make the leather.

"A village like this is completely self-supporting," said Bawaji. "The women spin the cotton which the men grow, they bring the yarn to these weavers, the weavers make it into cloth and take it back, and the women make the clothes. The wheelwright goes out and cuts down a *pipal* tree and makes a plow with it; he makes our carts, every part of them; the carpenter makes doors or window frames, spinning wheels for the women, looms for the weavers; a potter makes pots—there are very few things which the village has to get from outside. And every kind of food that a man can want is grown here, nothing in the way of food is bought." And I had a lot of meals in villages such as Jammulapalem, and can vouch for it that the food is satisfying enough.

Back at the Sangham building we had a discussion about untouchability.

"The thirtieth of every month was set aside by Gandhiji as Harijan Day," said Bawaji, "and then we hold meetings and processions to try and break down untouchability."

He told me that they had held such a procession in Jammulapalem. First there had been a meal, and the Harijans had sat down to eat with caste members of the village. Most of the younger caste men had joined in. (When I asked one why he did so, he said, "Our Gandhiji told us to.") Then had come a procession through the village to the gate of the temple. The intention had been that the procession should enter the temple, and that the people should worship. But this had not happened.

"The priests and the temple guardian had stood by the gate," said Subaya, who spoke good English, "and they would have let us in, with reluctance. But the Harijans would not go. They refused."

"Why?" I asked.

"They had intended to go in," said Bawaji, "but when it came to it their nerve left them. This generally happens."

"But the law now says that any man may enter a Hindu temple," I said.

"The law is one thing," said Bawaji, "but thousands of years of custom and habit are another. The Harijans in these villages just cannot bring themselves to enter a temple. Of course, most of them work for the caste people, you see, and no doubt they are afraid of losing their jobs."

"We must break down caste," said Subaya, "our country cannot go forward until we do. But you do not know our difficulties. It is hard for us. The young people in this village say, 'We want to free ourselves from caste, but our old people won't let us! Wait until the old people die, and then we will do it. We cannot move the old people.' And you know, we Indians are obedient to our old people above everything. We cannot go against the wishes of our parents."

"But don't the old people agree with Gandhi that caste must go?" I asked.

"They say, 'We agree but we are too old to change. We cannot bring ourselves to do it. Our habits are too strong. You must wait until we die, and then you can do what you like. We are too old to alter.' "

"But another thing people say," said Bawaji, "is that the Harijans have castes among themselves. You saw that Harijan-cherri. Well, there there are two main communities of Harijans: the *Malas,* or weavers, and the *Madigas,* or shoemakers. Now each of these castes thinks that the other is unclean. They have two wells, and when the Malas' well ran dry the other year they took water from the Madigas' well, and there was a free fight and the Madigas wouldn't use their well any more because they said it was polluted. So the caste people here say, 'Why should you expect us to accept the Harijans when they won't even forget caste themselves, they are even untouchable to each other?' "

"Will caste never die?" I asked.

"In time it will die," said another man who lived in the village, and who spoke English. "We are determined to kill it. We believe in what Gandhiji said about it. He was our Father. But it will be long, it is difficult. Even when ourselves we denounce caste, we find we cannot uproot it. I am all against caste—I fight caste—and yet I cannot bring myself to take food from the hands of an untouchable. I *cannot*. I try to force myself, but I cannot!"

"Is it because you think that he is physically dirty?" I asked.

They all spoke at once. "No, no, no!" they cried. "It's nothing to do with physical cleanliness," said Bawaji. "You saw how clean these Harijans here are, and some, of course, are scrupulously clean. As you know, many of our first citizens now are Harijans. It is something which one can't explain to a non-Hindu. It is far deeper. It goes back into the past. I was in the army, I am westernized. I don't believe in caste. And yet, I feel it too. It will take generations to root it right out."

As a matter of interest, in Jammulapalem, which was a fairly typical large village in Andhra country, there were about three thousand people. The caste members of the village—the people who were not Harijans or untouchables—are divided up as follows:

Kammas, Yadavas, and *Reddis.* These are all farmers, although the Reddis are more in the moneylending line.

One family of *Moslems,* and they keep a *tonga,* that is, a small horse-trap for taking people about.

Dhobies, or washermen, who collect dirty clothes each morning (each man collecting from about thirty houses) and wash them by beating them on stones in a pond. This pond is outside the village, and one sees perhaps twenty or thirty men at a time standing knee-deep in it, sedulously swinging white cotton garments and bashing them down on large stones (to knock the dirt out of the clothes, not break the stones). Incidentally the dhobies, like everybody else in the village who renders a service, are never paid in cash. They are retained to do a family's washing for a year by a payment of rice at harvest time.

The *Mangalis,* or barbers. These shave and cut hair, and also run a brass band, which musters for weddings or on other auspicious occasions. The barbers' wives are traditionally the midwives of the village.

Two families of *Brahmans,* who fill their traditional role of priests.

Several families of *Vaisyas,* who are traders and money-lenders—rogues to a man, I was told.

Four families of *Yenadis*: hereditary watchmen. They sleep during the day, but roam around the village with spears during the night; and I was told they would run a mile if they saw a burglar.

Kamsala Battulu, several families. These are combined blacksmith-carpenter-wheelwrights, and are also paid by the *ryots,* or farmers, with a share of the harvest.

Telegas and *Naidus,* who are house servants and field laborers of one sort or another.

Another caste who, surprisingly, live in the caste part of the village, are the *Wedaras*: diggers and pig-keepers; but I imagine that they are actually treated as untouchable.

And that is the lot.

I was taken round the houses to watch the women spinning, for this was part of the great *khadi* drive: the production of cloth at home so as to free the people from the millionaires. I was introduced to one lady who, although elderly, was still extremely beautiful, and she carried herself like a queen. The women of Andhra are tall and stately, and beautiful in an aristocratic sort of way. This one was the wife of a rich farmer, and herself, I was told, owned several *lakhs* (hundred thousands) of rupees. She was the richest woman in the village.

But what pleased me was that later on I saw her walk by with a basket on her head, and the basket was half-full of cow dung, and she still looked like a queen, and she paused wherever she came to where a cow had eased herself and stooped down to retrieve the valuable manure, to put in her compost pit or to burn on her fire.

Bawaji saw me looking at her. "She is rich, but she's still a village woman," he said. "At heart, we Indians are simple people. I think it's good that we should stay simple."

And I think so too.

14

THE NEW WAY OF LIFE

IN THE ONGOLE FIRKA (a *firka* is a subdivision of country) there are forty-eight villages, twenty-eight of them big ones like Jammulapalem. Twenty-eight such firkas, up to that time, had been selected by the government of Madras for development under the Firka Development Scheme, and this number was to be increased as finances, manpower, and experience permitted, until the whole State of Madras was covered.

Bawaji had a colleague, Sri Satyaranarayana, a Brahman, who did exactly the same work as Bawaji did, but in the other half of the firka. After I had gone around with Bawaji for a few days this gentleman invited me to go and look at his part of the world, and we set off one morning in an old taxicab, which was hired for the occasion.

Madras' Firka Development is being done cheaply, as regards money at least. Each firka being developed has an appropriation of only sixty thousand rupees or $12,600 per year. Hence the old taxicabs and motor-bikes. Later I was to see another development scheme in India which was costing

enormous sums. There were jeeps and lorries galore, in fact;
but I could not find that it was being done more effectively
than the Madras scheme.

Satyaranarayana was a tall, lean, handsome man, and he
dressed in rough gray *khadi*. He was an almost fanatical be-
liever in Gandhian economics. He was one of these lean and
ardent types, who force the more easygoing of us into activity.
Above all he was a patriotic Indian, and I believe that he had
to overcome a certain prejudice against me because I was an
Englishman. He had been put in jail by Englishmen for
Congress activities.

But he was determined that I should see India Resurgent;
and he rattled me around his half of the firka in a most un-
relenting manner. I insisted, as I do on such occasions, that
I should choose the villages that we looked at. Some of them
at least, because otherwise it is too easy for one's guide to give
one an unbalanced picture of what is going on. And I must
say that I was impressed.

In every village that we looked at a substantial amount of
work had been done by the villagers, egged on and helped by
the Firka Development officers. We drove along a road—
nearly fifteen miles of good, macadamized road where no
road had been before—which had been built by village cooperative societies for an expenditure by the government of
twenty-five thousand rupees. Later I saw a written estimate
by a P.W.D. (Public Works Department) engineer for making
this same road in the usual manner (with contractors), and
the estimate was *two hundred* thousand rupees! This is
forty-two thousand dollars, which is about what such a job
normally costs the government in that part of the world.

And herein lies a tale.

Sri Rajagopalachari, the First Minister of Madras, has allowed himself to be placed on record as saying: "If the Com-

munists are my public enemy number one, the Public Works Department is my public enemy number two."

I sat one evening in a traveler's bungalow in Mysore among a party of P.W.D. road engineers. One of them was leaving the district, and the others were throwing a party for him. One of them got up and said, in English, "Let's have the good old P.W.D. toast: 'Two inches for the road, two inches for the engineer, and two inches for the contractor!' "

When I inquired what this meant I was told that if six inches of ballast were ordered to be applied to a road, two inches actually went on the road, the money value of two inches went into the pocket of the engineer, and that of the other two inches into the pocket of the contractor.

The Indian P.W.D. has done some great works, and no doubt it has had some honest servants; but the system is such that only a very good man could remain honest for long under it. As for contractors, there *could* not be an honest contractor, for he would never get a single contract. Why should an engineer give him a contract without being bribed, when there are a hundred other contractors waiting to try to outbid each other in bribes just outside the door?

The result is that jobs done by the government in India are apt to cost enormously more than can be accounted for by material and labor only. And many jobs are scamped.

This P.W.D. problem is India's toughest at the moment. On whether it is solved or not will depend whether India becomes a decent country to live in, or no place for honest men.

A war was going on in Madras while I was there, and the road which I saw, which had been built under the Firka Development Plan, had been a battle in that war, and a battle won, I am glad to say, by the right side.

This road had been built under the supervision of a P.W.D. engineer, and by a contractor; but the contractor had been not an individual but a village *sangham,* or service council. This, under the guidance of my friend Satyaranarayana, had tendered for the contract of building the road and had done so at a small fraction of the cost that an orthodox contractor would have charged. The sangham valued the labor of its members at so much per man per day, they all went out and worked hard, there were no bribes to pay, no large profits to make, the road was built honestly and well, and the money received was shared out among the members of the sangham who had earned it in the sweat of their brows.

Now there is no reason why all the work done by the P.W.D. in India should not be done in this way. There *can* be no venery or corruption with this system; the whole thing is too public. Every member of the village can come to the meetings of the sangham and have his say. The money paid out by the government goes to where it is needed: into the pockets of the villagers who do the work. The work costs a fraction of what it would in the old way.

But if anybody rules India it is the contractors. The contractor has always been a great factor in Indian economy, and the British, unfortunately, looked upon him as a necessary evil and made use of him and let him have his pickings more or less without interference. And the contractors' lobby, in Madras and in every other state government, and in the central government too, is one of the strongest factors. Why shouldn't it be? These men are the richest, the most unscrupulous, the wiliest, the most worldly, the most aggressive men in India. They are not going to sit quietly back and see their world fall about their ears. And they are not doing so. First, they managed to get an order made in Madras, that village societies should not be allowed to do public works "because they are not competent." Just what competence it needs to carry broken stone and put it on a road, or dump earth on

a dam under the supervision of a trained engineer, it is hard
to see. But because of the direct intervention of the First
Minister, this rule was rescinded, and it was then ruled that
sanghams *could* undertake "works of a nontechnical nature."
But who is to decide what is nontechnical? Why, our old
friend the P.W.D. engineer, of course. And is he going to
desert his blood brother the contractor? Not on your life, not
while his blood brother is waving a thousand-rupee note under his nose.

Satyaranarayana was very proud of some buildings which
were being put up, one in each large village. These were village centers, *cum* reading rooms, *cum* theaters. There were
to be performances in them of the old mythological Indian
plays, and also new plays, and a renaissance of the Indian
theater was to start there. The reading rooms were stocked
with newspapers and a small selection of books, but reading
matter was a great difficulty. The people of Andhra speak, and
read, Telegu, and there is not a big literature in that language. A great literacy drive is going on in the country, but
what is the use of teaching a person to read, if he then has
nothing to exercise his new knowledge on?

There were Tamil, Hindi, and English papers and books
as well as Telegu, including a lot of American propaganda
in all these languages. The latter can be got, in any quantity,
for nothing; and it is too great a temptation for the centers
not to have it. But this American propaganda is almost unbelievably inept. Its purport is largely to show what a rich
country America is, how everyone there has cars, television
sets, scrumptious food out of cans, five or six suits, etc. Anything less likely to impress the real Indian villager it would
be hard to imagine. Another type of propaganda is the political comic (or tragic—as it should be called), the luridly
colored strip cartoon.

I saw one publication that showed a "native" village somewhere (there exists, in the cartoonist's mind, a sort of universal native, like the universal foreign spy, aryan-hero-who-only-fights-with-his-fists-and-whose-shoulders-are-always-threatening-to-burst-his-jacket, and various other stock characters).

Now the sophisticated, ultra-civilized Indian *ryot,* with his millenniums of high culture behind him, and his cynical, mordant sense of humor, is offered this little illustrated story about these simple "natives" who are under the domination of one of their number, Lopez by name, who is—guess what— a *Communist!* But alas, they are stricken down with smallpox. Immediately a broad-shouldered young American, who obviously uses a well-known brand of sticky matter to keep his wavy hair in place, together with an American girl who manages to combine sizzling sex appeal with a sort of Nurse Cavell look on her face, appear and start making speeches about Democracy, and the Brotherhood of Man. Lopez ups and makes a counterspeech. The natives back Lopez and refuse to be vaccinated against smallpox. Providentially, though, Lopez falls a victim to the fell disease himself, and is carried in to our young hero and heroine covered with spots. He is vaccinated—the natives are too—Lopez becomes converted to the American way of life, and the couple drive away from the village with the happy natives waving to them as they go. It is noteworthy, incidentally, that their short visit has not only cured the smallpox, but has also fattened the family of pigs which in the first picture lay emaciated and filthy by the road, has repaired the native huts which in the first part of the strip were shown half in ruins and has caused beautiful flower-gardens to grow where none were growing before. And the effect of the vaccine has filled out the natives miraculously. One can hardly recognize them from the miserable specimens that one saw in the first few pictures.

Satyaranarayana showed me this particular piece of literature with great amusement, and the village people who were in the room laughed heartily about it. What sort of idea, they asked, did the Americans have of the mental condition of the Indian villager?

Later, in New Delhi, I met a member of the U.S.A. Information Service, and he asked me, quite seriously and because he was genuinely concerned about his job, what was wrong with U.S. propaganda in India? Why was it so completely ineffective? What answer could I give him?

These reading rooms, by the way, are substantial stone buildings and were being put up at a cost of 12,000 rupees (nearly three thousand dollars) of which the government paid only 2,000 rupees. The rest was contributed voluntarily by the villagers who would benefit by the building, their payment being mostly in stone, cartage, and unskilled labor.

I saw a tractor that had been bought by three *ryots* in a village called Santanotalapod. The three owners owned fifty acres of tobacco land each, had tried tractor plowing for three years by hiring a government tractor, had liked it, and so had now bought this machine.

"Do they quarrel when each one is to have the tractor?" I asked Satya, and he said no. "They will," I said, perhaps too cynically.

We saw a lot of motor-driven pump sets, set up on the banks of a river to pump water out of it onto the land. Most of these had been established by small village cooperatives. In every village were several cooperative societies, for one purpose or another. Cooperation has caught on in India for good. We visited a village multipurpose society which showed a profit of 120,000 rupees (over twenty-five thousand dollars) for the four years since it had been founded, and it only had seven hundred members. This society supplied almost all the commercial requirements of its members. It bought their produce, sold them what they wanted, established them in small industries, lent them agricultural instruments, supplied improved seed and fertilizer. And in spite of the fact that it had managed to make this large profit, it was still able to pay better prices to its members for produce, and sell them retail goods cheaper, than were the private traders, with whom the members were perfectly free to trade if they wanted.

We went to another Basic Training School for teachers at a place called Minampore, but here I was much better impressed than with the first establishment of the kind that I had seen. The headmaster was a man of intelligence and of great enthusiasm.

"We will extend Basic Education all over India," he said. "At present we are laughed at. We are laughed at because when we go back to our towns or villages we insist on sweeping the streets, for people in India sweep their houses, but sweep the dirt out into the streets and nobody sweeps them. But we followers of Gandhi go around with brooms and sweep the streets, and for this we are laughed at. But it is right that we should set an example of civic cleanliness. For if we don't, who will?"

Here was a farm, small but being increased, and what there was of it was well run, and besides *khadi* there were other activities, although not as many as I should have liked to have seen. But the school was new. At any rate there was great enthusiasm there. One young chap said, when I asked him if he believed in Basic Education: "We believe in the principles of Gandhiji, the Father of our Nation!" He struck me as being rather a prig in fact, but he was very young.

And for enthusiasm—there was enthusiasm wherever we

went in the firka. There is a real resurgence in these villages.
I was convinced that the villagers have been won over to this
development idea. They like it. They feel that it is not something just imposed by the government, something the politicians are doing to make themselves popular. The pity is that
the firkas so far chosen for development cover such a small
area of country. Let us hope the area will soon be expanded.
For here is work for every educated Indian of goodwill to do.
There is shocking unemployment among graduates and lit-
erate people in India, and yet there is need for such people
in the villages. The villagers must help themselves; but they
also need the help of educated men. Most Indian graduates,
unfortunately, would not take work out in the remote villages. Their tradition is against it. Gandhi tried hard to break
this tradition down.

In spite of his lack of humor and his air of fanaticism, his
lean and hungry look, I liked Satyaranarayana. He is the sort
of man who can do things in India.

He was deeply ashamed of the nepotism and corruption
that is India's inheritance from the past, and was anxious to
see an end to it, and he was convinced—I think quite rightly
—that an end could be put to it by an extension of village
cooperation.

"Look at these big irrigation schemes our government is
doing," he said. "Contractors from Delhi send lorries and
machinery a thousand miles to do the work, while *lakhs* of
villagers look on, idle and without sufficient food. Our villagers could contract to move earth in their ox carts at a
fraction of the cost that the machines take to move it. The
job would be slower, but the country would not be ruined by
this enormous expenditure. Every one of these great schemes
has cost many times what was estimated. Let our villagers do
the work, in their traditional manner, and get the pay for it,

and then enjoy the result of their labor in the knowledge that it was *their* labor, and they are beholden to nobody. We are selling our country to foreigners, for no reason. We got our country back from the British, now we are letting the Americans in instead. Let us only do schemes that we can do ourselves, with our own labor, for labor is the one thing we have plenty of."

Before I left Angole, my friend Bawaji asked me if I would like to meet his mother. That lady, he said, had expressed a wish to see me.

Naturally I said yes, but Bawaji took me, not as I had expected into the back of the house where the women lurked, but up the rocky hill behind the house. We walked past the ruined *choultry,* and the tomb of Bawaji's grandfather, and the place where the snake lived, and then started climbing the steep hillside.

Near the top of the hill, in a very craggy and secluded spot, we saw a white flag flying on top of a pole, and under it a small shrine, or tomb, built of rock and not much bigger than a fair-sized dinner table. In the door of the tomb, for such it turned out to be, sat an old lady. "That's my mother," said Bawaji.

I went up and gave her a *namasté,* holding my hands in front of my face in the attitude of prayer, and she did the same to me, and got up and dabbed some saffron on my forehead and put an orange in my hand. She did not speak English, and her son interpreted the small amount of conversation that we had. But we did not say much to each other. We waived the small-talk. She saw what I was like, and I saw what she was like, without the need for a lot of conversation. To have got to know each other better would have taken more talk than we were likely to have time for.

After we had taken our leave and had started walking down the hill again, Bawaji told me about her.

When Bawaji had been taken prisoner of war he had been reported missing, and his mother had lost all interest in life. Three times she had tried to kill herself by throwing herself down wells, but had been taken off eventually to an *ashram,* or place for learning and contemplation, and put in the care of a holy man.

When Bawaji had been reported alive she had elected to remain in the *ashram,* but when her son returned from the wars she came home and lived quite normally and happily for a while. But one day she just announced that she was going to retire from the world.

"That tomb she lives in is the grave of my grandfather's *guruji,*" said Bawaji. (A *guru* is a teacher, or spiritual leader.) "The *guru* was buried alive in it, sitting in the position of meditation. He left instructions that the grave should be opened after six months, he should be examined, and then the grave should be filled again and after that never opened."

"What did they find when they opened the grave?" I asked, expecting wonders.

"The *guruji* was dead," said Bawaji. "But now my mother lives up there where you saw her, and she hasn't come down for six years. She seldom lets men go and see her—you are the first for a long time. But some of the women from the town go and sit at her feet, and she talks of starting an *ashram* for women up there."

"What does she live on?" I asked.

"Coffee and oranges, which children take up to her. And we send her water."

In India one ceases to be surprised. Bawaji certainly finds nothing abnormal in his mother's behavior, and he is a very normal young man. He intends to set his three younger brothers up in a garage and workshop, where they will repair the tractors and automobiles which he feels sure will soon be disturbing the peace of the countryside.

"Does your father go and see her?" I asked.

"He went once, about a year after she went up there," he said. "But she told him to go away. She said she had renounced the flesh and didn't want to see him again. And, of course, he respects her wish."

She seemed to be quite healthy on her diet of coffee and oranges, although I daresay there was more to it than that; and one thing I would like to stress is that she is perfectly normal. She is sane. One glance into that old woman's eyes is enough to let you know that if she isn't mentally healthy, then all the rest of us are as crazy as foxes.

15

THE GODAVARI RIVER

THE ROAD over the Kistna River was flooded, so I had to go on by train. I bought a ticket to a place called Vizagapatam, where the new Indian shipbuilding industry has been started. But fate was against me. I was not to go there.

As the train rumbled across the wide Godavari, I looked below and saw sailing ships and small motor launches navigating the waters of the river. I looked upstream and saw where the great brown flood came through a gap in the mountains—mountains crowned with lowering rain clouds, cold and forbidding and very mysterious. As the train drew into the Godavari station, just beyond the bridge, I found myself looking hastily at my map. I asked a fellow passenger how far those little motor launches went. He said for three or four days, but no gentleman could go on one; they were for pilgrims. As the train started my bedroll was halfway out of the window. As it gathered speed, the bedroll had hit the platform and my odds and ends—including my shoes, which had been removed for coolness—were following it. And I jumped out myself just before the engine had achieved a dangerous speed. I had decided to go on one of the motor launches.

But I had to wait a day or two, I found, before a launch was going. I fell in with a man named Venkataraju who lived at a place called Samulkot and he asked me to go and stay with some friends of his there. The friends were large *ryots* or farmers. A typical joint family, they owned about fifty acres of delta land. This is the equivalent of several hundred acres of most other land, for the Godavari delta is extremely fertile, and produces three good crops of rice per year on the same field.

The farmers lived in a very large house which they had just built in the middle of Samulkot, which is quite a substantial town. The old father had designed the building himself, and built it with the help of bricklayers, and although it is extremely solid and suitable for its purpose, it is not beautiful. The reasons for the ugliness of most contemporary Indian architecture is this otherwise excellent propensity of Indians to build their own houses. It is a pity that they do not consult architects first; but, of course, there are no architects. Indian architecture is in a very poor state at the moment.

This building had a ground floor devoted to shops, and these were let out for rent. The second floor was used by the family to live in, and the roof had been left unfinished so that a further floor could be added as the family increased and as funds allowed.

That delta country has a picturesqueness. Canals lead everywhere, and boats navigate them, sailing when they can with lateen sails, or otherwise being poled, or pulled by the crew walking along the bank. These boats are of a distinctive type, designed for use on the wide and swift and dangerous Godavari, and also on these narrow and shallow canals. The land, nearly all of it irrigated, is unbelievably fertile, for it can be flooded many times a year from the Godavari, the water being raised to the requisite level by a great *anicut* or weir which has two and three-quarter miles of masonry and another mile and a half of earth bank. It was designed by Sir Arthur Cotton in 1852.

My friends in Samulkot took me to see what they called "the agricultural farm." By this they meant a government agricultural research station. There are many of these in India, mostly started during the last fifty years, and some of them have done extraordinary work in raising the yield of crops on the land. But, of course, as the population always keeps up just behind the food supply, it is doubtful if any efforts to produce more food make people happier if unaccompanied by other efforts to keep the population stationary. Paradoxically, in the end, more food just means more hungry people.

This particular farm has been particularly successful. It was in charge of a man of remarkable enthusiasm and intelligence, and he nearly killed me dragging me around it and showing me all that he was doing. He was experimenting vigorously with different kinds of green manure, for when you take three "white straw" crops a year off land you must do something pretty effective to keep up the humus supply. There were some beautiful, feathery-leaved leguminous trees which had been planted along the *bunds,* the little mudbanks that divide the paddyfields. These trees have very soft branches—they grow extremely quickly—and it is possible to cut the branches off once a year and throw them into the mud of the paddyfields where they quickly rot and act as manure. The manager also told me of the improved seed-multiplication scheme, which is fairly widespread now throughout India, whereby seed is improved by crossing and selection at the agricultural research stations, and then sent out to private farmers to be multiplied and distributed finally to the whole district. Seventy-five per cent of the land in the delta, the manager reckoned, is now being sown with improved seed.

We had a discussion about plowing. The manager said that the attempt to encourage the use of mold-board or breast plows—the sort that turn the furrow over—is not meeting with a lot of success in India. The *ryots* are doubtful about them. They plow deeper than the *dési* plows *(dési* means local, or country), but many of the *ryots* are doubtful about the advisability of deep plowing in their climate. We were talking about plowing dry land, by the way—not irrigated paddyfields. Some of the *ryots* say that there would be more erosion if they plowed deeper, and others fear bringing up too much of the barren and sometimes even toxic subsoil. Others say that there is so little humus in their land, anyway, that it is of no advantage to bury it deeper and mix it with an even greater proportion of barren soil. And the final argument used is that their cattle cannot pull the mold-board plows anyway.

No one in India apparently has ever though of yoking more than one pair of oxen to anything. I once told an Indian farmer that I had plowed in South Africa with no less than twenty oxen in a span and, although he was very polite, it was quite obvious that he did not believe me. But in fact one pair of oxen *can* pull the little mold-board plows that the agricultural department is prepared to supply cheaply. It is simply a matter of adjusting your plow to take a narrower slice. So, if it is indeed an advantage to use a furrow-turning plow, there is no reason why one should not be used. The *dési* plow is just an iron-shod pointed stick, set at an angle to a horizontal pole the other end of which rests on the yoke between the two oxen. The pointed share merely scratches into the earth for perhaps four or five inches, and it does not turn it. It is hard for a person used to Western farming to appreciate this kind of plowing. We are so used to seeing a good deep furrow plowed out and turned over and all the weeds and rubbish on the surface properly buried. But it does not do to underestimate the knowledgeableness of the Indian farmer about his job. He may be wrong in this instance, and possibly too conservative; but on the other hand he may be right. The *ryots* have been very quick to adopt other methods and improvements in their farming, when they were convinced that these were good.

There was a cattle expert at the "agricultural farm"; he was there on a visit, and we had a discussion about cattle in India.

Of course, there are too many of them.

I asked the expert why the cattle that I had seen at Ongole were so good; almost without exception they had been fine cattle. Now the reason why it is strange that they should have been fine cattle is the Hindu reluctance to kill cattle. Cattle, like humans, if left alone, breed faster than they die off, and therefore as time goes on they increase in numbers. And like humans they increase in numbers until they reach the limit of the food supply, and then they begin to starve.

Before they were domesticated, cattle had natural enemies which used to keep their numbers down by killing some of them. After they were domesticated, man himself kept their numbers down, also by killing some of them. But the Hindus refuse to kill any of them.

This would not matter so much if the Hindus would also not let them breed too rapidly, but of course they do let them breed. They keep them for milk, and to give milk a cow must first have a calf.

Wherever I had been in India before I had reached Ongole I had seen the most miserable-looking cattle imaginable. Any

Western farmer would be ashamed to own such half-starved, scrawny animals. It was quite obvious in fact that their numbers were being controlled by starvation and nothing else. But at Ongole it was different.

The cattle expert said that this was because the Ongole farmers sell some of their cows to dealers, who take them down to Madras and keep them there for milking. The dealers buy cows and calves, kill the calves, milk the cows until they are dry, and then the cows mysteriously disappear. There are quite a number of Moslems and Christians and Harijans and other communities in Madras city who have no scruples about eating beef. And there is always plenty of beef for them to eat, though of very poor quality.

The Ongole cattle are in good condition because their numbers are kept within reasonable limits and have therefore enough food.

Shortly after this conversation with the cattle expert I saw this in a newspaper:

MARTYRDOM FOR BAN ON COW SLAUGHTER

Hazaribagh, July 31. Pandit Ramchandra Sharma 'Veer,' who had undertaken a 65 days' fast to press his demand for banning cow slaughter in Bihar died at 3.30 p.m. here today.

Today was the 25th day of his fast.

Declining requests of his friends to end his fast as he had grown very weak he said last night that it pained him to find lack of veneration for cows in India nowadays. He preferred to die if it helped reviving love for cows, he said. . . .

True, the next day the paper said that the Pandit had not died after all, and a few days afterwards it published a picture of him looking hale and hearty—not to say well-fed. But there it is. If the Jan Sangh, of the Hindu Mahasabha, or any other right-wing extremist political party, wants to find a stick to beat the Congress government, it merely has to raise this issue of cow-slaughter. It is already illegal to kill cattle in some states, and in fact public opinion is so strongly against it in all of them that it is actually impossible to do so in most places. But so far Pandit Nehru has refused to let himself be badgered into passing a central government law about it.

Cows are our mothers, the Hindus say. But they do not worship cows as Westerners sometimes think they do, any more than they worship monkeys. True, the bull is said to be the vehicle of Siva, just as Hanuman, the monkey-god, is said to have been the ally of Rama; but that does not make all bulls or all monkeys objects of worship. Hindu pantheism holds that *all* life is sacred, and many Hindus would not, if they could avoid it, kill anything.

But their love of cows—*veneration* is not too strong a word for it—is very strong, and is not only religious in nature.

In an Indian village home the cattle live in the living room, and the children are brought up with them, and as the family probably owns only a few, the cattle almost become members of the family.

There is a lot of genuine humanity behind this reluctance on the part of Hindus to kill animals.

You will say that Indians are often cruel to their cattle, and beat them with sticks. If any man has to drive oxen for long he beats them with sticks, or with a whip. There is just no other way of driving them. If you say to a Hindu: "You love cattle, and yet you let them starve," he will answer: "If the cattle could talk do you think they would say, 'Kill us rather than let us be hungry'?"

But my expert friend said that his countrymen must overcome their reluctance to kill cattle. Neither the cattle nor the people could flourish without some limitation to the numbers of the former. I asked him if he was a Hindu, and he said: "Yes, certainly. And I used to be very orthodox. It took me forty years to stop being orthodox. But my work with cattle convinced me that the numbers of cattle must be limited. There is no other way. We will always have to be ashamed of our cattle in India until we learn this." Then he went on with a lot of figures showing that India had more cattle per acre than any other country in the world, and that they were worse cattle, and that they gave less milk, and did less work, and were of less use either to themselves or anyone else. "If ever you see good cattle in India," he said, "you can be sure that there's an outlet for surplus stock, like there is at Ongole. But prejudice will break down. Even now, *ryots* take surplus cattle to *shandies* (markets) and sell them to dealers, and they don't ask many questions as to what happens to them after that."

The son of my host, the farmer, by the way, wanted to go to England to study mechanical engineering. He wished one day to start up a workshop and tractor repair shop in Samulkot. He had already enrolled at Sunderland Engineering College, and—as I write this—there he is. For when I got back to England a letter from him was waiting for me, and I hope shortly to see him. He and his family asked me about a hundred questions concerning Sunderland, all of which I was unable to answer (not being quite certain even whether that city was in Scotland or England) except that I did say that it would be extremely cold there, not to say foggy, and that landladies certainly would not know how to cook rice.

Back at Rajamundry, on the Godavari, I boarded my motor launch at midnight. The vessel was to leave at three in the morning.

She was long and narrow, and powered with a hefty British diesel. Amidships, next to the engine room, was a tiny compartment, with two wooden athwartship benches in it of a narrowness that made it extremely difficult to lie on them. I had been persuaded to buy a first-class ticket, and this entitled me to perch on one of these benches. Fore and aft the body of the ship was filled with pilgrims going up the river. Over our heads was a deck of corrugated iron, and such pilgrims as did not mind getting *corrugated*, and occasionally rained on, slept up there.

Three o'clock was optimistic, of course; but we got away about six, and chugged against the very strong current under the enormous railway bridge that spans the Godavari at that point.

Later on in the morning I left my cubbyhole and went up on the corrugated iron. There I met a man, a pilgrim, who spoke voluble, slangy, and occasionally ungrammatical English. I later found that his home was in Bangalore, where he kept a cloth shop, and so had possibly come in contact with British soldiers, and thereby learned his English slang.

He was of a vegetarian Vaishya caste, and very orthodox. He would eat no food unless it had been prepared by a member of his own caste.

"I am very orthodox," he said, "and my friends are amazed that, even with this orthodoxy, I have travel so far. I have my wife and little boy below, and we have been to all the holy places in North India, even to Kashmir. In spite of our great orthodoxy. Even *with* this orthodoxy we have gone so far. My friends are amazed when I get back."

"Where are you going now?" I asked.

"Bhadrachalam, of course," he said. "Where Rama wept when he found that his wife Sita had been stolen from him. But then I want to go to the holy places of South India. Before I return home I want to have seen all the holy places of India. For I never get another chance in my lifetime of traveling in India. After this, I have to stay in Bangalore only, and mind my shop."

His little boy joined us, and said to his father that he was hungry.

"We are all hungry," said the pilgrim. "How can we eat? We will not eat grub unless we cook it ourselves. My wife is tired out, she is exhausted. This trip has been terrible for her. Because there is no rest, she must prepare all our food. We cannot use a restaurant or lunch home. I will go nine days, ten days, without food rather than eat food which is not right for me!" Indeed both the father and son looked undernourished and haggard, and the poor wife, whom I later met and who was extremely pleasant to me, looked worn out. But it was worth it to see the holy places.

The scenery was magnificent.

The Godavari flows through a gap in the Eastern Ghats, and through this gap we went. Steep and wooded mountains rose up on both sides of us, and the wide river flowed fast and muddy and brown. Although our engine labored, we moved past the bank very slowly. We had to weave from side to side to find slacker water and also to keep in the deeper channels. For the river was shallow, and I was told that for several months in the year it was too shallow to navigate.

There were plenty of motor launches like our own, carrying passengers and goods, and also a large number of the graceful Godavari sailing barges, sailing upstream with the wind or coming down on the current. When both wind and current were against them they were pulled by the crew who walked along the bank.

Frequently we stopped at a village, and people got on or off; and sometimes we stopped long enough to go ashore and have a meal. I stayed with my pilgrim friends, and it was painful for me to sit and eat a good meal at a restaurant (for

I am *not* orthodox) and watch them eyeing me hungrily, although no doubt it was even more painful for them. As we were walking up the main street of one fly-blown little place, the little boy stopped and looked longingly at some sweets in a shop. He then came and said something to his father, and his father said to me, "He say that even if it is given him, even one rupee's worth of that stuff, he won't eat it, even though he is hungry. But he won't eat it because it not be prepared by people of our caste."

I found him very amusing to talk to. "I love the English," he said. "And I think I must be English in a former life. You know why? Well, I so much love potatoes. I always like eat potatoes. Also you see, my father he is born on twenty-sixth December."

"What's that got to do with it?" I asked.

"Why, that's your English Boxing Day, isn't it? You see, I know. And my love of potatoes is quite famous. In a former life I am English."

He said that when his son was a little older he would send him to me in England and I could make him a doctor, or a lawyer, or an engineer.

There was a Department of Fisheries official on board, a Brahman, and he annoyed me. He was a decent man himself, but he annoyed me because like all officials he quietly accepted things that were wrong.

"We are going to stop the fishing here, except for people with licenses," he said. He went on to explain that until then anyone could catch a fish for his breakfast in the river, and there had always been enough fish for everybody. "But now we are going to stop all that," he said.

"Why?" I asked.

"Why, because all things must be properly regulated," he said. "Now we will sell licenses. We will auction the license to fish a certain stretch of the river, and we are now recruiting river police to patrol the banks to see that people without licenses do not fish."

"Well I hope your filthy policemen will all fall into the river and drown themselves and you, too," I said.

I hate this sort of thing! What on earth is the good of it? For twenty thousand years people have been catching fish out of the Godavari, in peace and comfort, and eating them for their breakfasts. Who the blazes has the right to come and interfere with them now? Who put the fish there, anyway? Whose fish are they? And what will be the practical result of the policy? Simply that there will be more officials and inspectors and others living parasitically on the men who work. More people to bribe. Men will still catch fish in the Godavari—but they will have to do it by stealth; and when they are caught themselves by the precious river police they will have to bribe them. That is all.

Must every country fall into this mania for regulating everything? A license for everything. Licenses and permits, and more and more people sitting in stuffy offices to issue them, and fewer and fewer out on the land or on the water working for food. The time will come when the last one of us becomes an official, and then we shall all starve, unless we find that we can eat permits and licenses and forms-in-triplicate. And meanwhile, good luck to the noble army of poachers and smugglers and illicit toddy tappers and backyard chicken-keepers who defy these silly and wicked regulations!

The mountains passed, we came into a flatter land, well forested but rather dry. Parts of the jungle had been cleared, and here people had built villages and were growing crops. Tobacco was a common one. The history of the Godavari has been altered considerably by the introduction of the motor launch.

Up until then the jungle along the banks of the river had been the home of the Koys, a wild, pagan jungle tribe who occasionally indulged in human sacrifice. But with the opening up of the Godavari to commerce, Hindus began to arrive from the Madras Presidency to grab land from the Koys and settle along the banks of the river. Now a sensible government has ordained that the Koys shall no longer be allowed to part with their land; so perhaps this change for the worse will not go any further.

For in spite of an alleged occasional human sacrifice, the Koys are likable and happy people. They scratch a good and simple living from patches of land which they have cleared from the forest, and also by killing animals with their bows and arrows. As there is plenty of forest, they have unlimited land and can always move on and clear some more when they exhaust the bit they are using. Their lives are simple and carefree, they do not suffer from overpopulation and consequent famine like more civilized people, and they do not periodically try to annihilate their neighbors with ever more barbarous and ferocious weapons. What is an occasional human sacrifice compared with that sort of thing?

We spent the night tied up against the bank at a village, and started early next morning at the battle against the current. All that day also we chugged, slept a second night tied to the bank, and before midday of the third day of our voyage reached Bhadrachalam.

Bhadrachalam where Rama wept.

16

THE PLACE WHERE RAMA WEPT

OWING TO THE HOLINESS of the spot, there has for a long time been a settlement at Bhadrachalam, and now there is a considerable temple there. We landed on the dirty bank of the river, were met by children and old women who offered to carry our luggage, and my pilgrim friends asked me to stay with them at a *choultry,* or pilgrims' rest-house. This proved to be a large building, built around a shady quadrangle, not far from the river. It was double-storied, and for a few annas you could have a room which you could padlock.

Now this *choultry* had been built by a pious Vaishya, and was for the use of Vaishyas only. But the old, bearded caretaker was called, and was persuaded by my pilgrim friends to let me stay there. But it was not to be.

For one of the shipmates we had had on board had been a Moslem working for the tobacco company. Just as negotiations had been successfully concluded for me to remain at the *choultry,* this man turned up, with a team of old women carrying a lot of shiny luggage, and demanded a room also.

Now for a strange bird from another continent to be given a room in the *choultry* was one thing; but for a *Moslem* to be allowed to enter was another. It was unthinkable. So the Moslem gentleman was refused and he said: "Why do you allow this *firangi* in, then? He is also not a Hindu. If you allow him, you must allow me!"

So neither of us was allowed in. We had to go to the traveler's bungalow. which must be the worst traveler's bungalow in India.

In the afternoon my pilgrim came to see me and asked me if I would do him the honor of going to the temple with him. I would indeed, and we walked through the parklike country to the town, and through the narrow and very picturesque streets of the town to the temple.

At a shop outside the temple we bought some offerings for the gods: a coconut each, some flowers, a little packet of sugar, one of saffron, some spices, some incense. We entered the temple by a large gate, left our shoes with one of the temple guards (a man dressed as a policeman, and armed with a rather dirty short magazine Lee-Enfield rifle) and we paid the temple secretary the sum of one anna each for the privilege of having our coconuts broken—for which sum we were given receipts.

It is not an ancient temple. It contains no fine architecture or sculpture. It has no great mysterious galleries or corridors like Madura or Rameswaram. It is just a temple. There are ten Brahmans, learned in the scriptures, who live in Bhadrachalam and carry on various businesses, and who take it in turns to do duty at the temple, two at a time. There are also perhaps a dozen temple servants of various kinds, half a dozen temple guards, and a few officials: the secretary, the temple manager, and some others.

We were shown the wealth of the temple: fabulous animals

and minor gods of wood with gold and silver fittings on them, and two large vaults full of gold, silver and jewels. There must be many thousands of dollars' worth of jewelry and precious metals there, all donated at various times by worshipers.

The temple manager told me the story of the temple.

All this is Rama country. The God Rama was banished into the jungle by his father, who was King of Oudh, in favor of a half-brother, whom the king made his heir instead. Rama and his wife Sita went into the jungle to spend the allotted term of ten years' banishment with a hermit named Valmiki. During this time the king died, and Rama's half-brother invited Rama back to be king, as he was the elder, but Rama declined the offer, saying that his father had ordered him to stay in the jungle for ten years and for ten years he would stay, for above all things a Hindu must obey his father.

But during the time of the banishment, Ravana, the king of Ceylon, urged on by his sister whom Rama had passed over in favor of Sita, came and stole Sita away. Now Bhadrachalam was the place where Rama crossed the Godavari, as he started on his journey to Lanka in search of his wife, and he sat down there before crossing the river and wept for her.

As a matter of interest, after a great war in which the monkey god Hanuman fought for Rama as an ally, and incidentally built a bridge of stones over the Straits of Mannar so that Rama could get to Ceylon, Rama defeated Ravana and got Sita back. But such is Hindu morality that, although Sita had steadfastly remained faithful to him while she was in durance, he would not take her again as a wife.

The temple of Bhadrachalam itself also has a miraculous story attached to it. Sometime in the eighteenth century the prime minister of Hyderabad, who was a Hindu, decided that it was fitting that there should be a temple on the bank of the Godavari where Rama wept, and so he had one built. To do this he used a large sum of money which he had embezzled from the Nizam's treasury for the purpose.

Unfortunately he was found out, and the Nizam, who was a Moslem, cast the prime minister into jail; saying that he would not be released until the money was refunded. For ten years the prime minister lay in prison, and fasted and underwent penances; and at the end of that time had a dream in which the God Rama came to him and handed him a bag of gold.

But it was more than a dream, for when he awoke the gold was still there, and he paid the Nizam what he owed him and was forthwith released from prison. And the Nizam was so impressed by this miracle wrought by a Hindu god that he generously endowed the temple, and the Moslem Nizam of Hyderabad pays an annual grant to the temple authorities to this day.

Well, after having heard about all this from the temple secretary and been shown the treasure, we walked up some wide stone steps, through a gate, up some more steps onto a large stone platform. From here we had a fine view over a great sweep of the Godavari, with the green jungle on either side, and at the back of us and below us the roofs of the crowded town. On a clear space between the town and the river were some stone pillars, and there, I was told, a *pandal*, or canopy, is erected once a year, and under this is enacted the marriage of Rama and Sita; the idols of the gods themselves being carried in a great procession to their wedding.

"At that time there are lakhs of people here," said the temple manager. "Lakhs and lakhs of them. They come from all over India, and bathe in the Godavari. There are twelve holy rivers in India, you know, besides the Ganges, and one of them is the Godavari. And once every twelve years we think that the waters of the Ganges flow into each one of these rivers by turn. And the year that they flow into the Godavari there are lakhs and lakhs of people here, for this place is very holy, as holy as Mother Ganges."

I was shown a room into which had been thrown some tons of paper, old exercise books and suchlike. The priest who was with us pulled some out and showed us that all this paper was closely covered with writing, and the writing only said one thing: SRI RAMA. Lord Rama.

"People write this and send it here," he said, "and they have to send us an offering for every lakh of times they've written *Sri Rama,* and once a year we tear all this paper up and throw it into the Godavari."

"How many times do most of them write *Sri Rama?*" I asked.

"Look at my fingers!" said my pilgrim friend, and indeed the first and second fingers on his right hand were heavily calloused. "I am writing *Sri Rama* for eight hours every day, when I'm at home. And I not reached a crore yet." (A *crore* is ten million.) "It is hard to reach a crore. It take many years."

"What is the idea?" I asked.

"We acquire merit by it," said the pilgrim. "It is our sacrifice."

"Some people bring the paper," said the priest, "but others send it by registered mail." And he told me that people often also sent money orders by mail, and asked for *pujas* to be performed for them at the temple.

Much of the platform on which we stood was taken up by a roof supported on pillars, and at one end of this roof was an *adyta,* or shrine of the gods. Normally non-Hindus are not allowed to approach this in this particular temple, but owing to my friendship with the pilgrims, and the fact that I seemed well disposed, I was allowed to have *puja* performed for me like the others. In fact, during my stay at Bhadrachalam I was treated just like one of the other pilgrims.

The officiating priest took our offerings, one of us after the other, and broke our coconuts in front of the gods and let the milk run away into a drain. Then he showed our little bags of sugar and the rest of it to the idols and put them away in a safe place, then threw our flowers on the laps of the gods, and returned us one each to keep.

There were six idols altogether. Three of them were of stone and were fixed to the place, and the other three were of wood. The three stone ones had appeared miraculously, but the wooden ones had been carved in the ordinary manner by men and were used as tokens for the stone ones, as the latter were not mobile.

The three gods represented were Rama, Sita and Lakshmana, the latter Rama's brother who went into exile with him. The wooden effigies were about three feet high, and the stone ones, which sat behind, perhaps four feet. They were all lavishly garlanded, and had various offerings of food, and small coins, on their laps. To my eyes they were extremely ugly, and not less so because enormous cockroaches—attracted by the food and suffered to remain by Hindu tolerance of lesser creatures—crawled about on them.

The priest said some Sanskrit prayers for us, and put red ochre on our foreheads and anointed our heads with oil, and gave us some sweet stuff to eat, and for this *puja,* or sacrifice, we were expected to pay a few annas. There was none of the rapacity in this temple that one saw at Madura. I simply gave what the other pilgrims gave, and if I had given nothing I am quite sure that no exception would have been taken.

As each one of us had our *puja,* the bystanders crowded around to get, as it were, the backwash of sanctity from it.

You went up, handed over your gifts, had the *puja* performed, and crowding around behind you were a dozen other people perhaps, men, women and children, all trying to see what was happening and hoping that they would be lucky and the priest would dab something on *their* heads too, and give them a little of the sweetmeat that had been offered to the gods to eat.

After we had all had our *puja*, we sat around on the floor in groups, talking and waiting for the main service of the day to take place: the putting of the gods to bed.

There were some ladies sitting near us, peasant women I should think, and they started talking to me in a friendly sort of way, using my pilgrim friend as an interpreter. But he was an unwilling one. I could not get him to carry on a decent conversation with the ladies. He said, "They are nothing. They shouldn't talk to you. They are inquisitive, take no notice of them." So all I could do was to smile at them and give it up. They were not young ladies, I might be advised to add.

After perhaps forty people had come in, the ceremony was started. A table was brought out and put in the middle of the sheltered part of the platform, and a mirror on a stand, the sort of thing you used to see in servant girls' bedrooms twenty years ago in England, was placed not far away from it. It is strange, this juxtaposition of fabulous wealth with utter junk in Hindu temples, and I have noticed it in mosques also. There was all that silver and gold in the vaults downstairs, and quite a lot around about us too, and yet this scandalously old chipped and cracked mirror was used for the gods to see themselves in as they had their toilets performed for them.

A filthy old curtain hanging on a string was pulled so as to hide the mirror from the table, and then the priests went

into the *adyta* and brought out the three portable wooden
gods and placed them on the table.

One of the priests then took his place in front of the idols,
and performed a great deal of *puja* with coconut oil, holy
water, and flowers. He would hold up a spoonful of oil to the
mouth of one of the idols—muttering in Sanskrit the while—
then throw the oil into a receptacle on the ground into which
everything was thrown after it had been offered to the gods.

While this was going on, a man stood on one side of the
three gods, and a woman on the other, and they fanned the
idols with big feather fans. And everybody sang; in fact, they
were led by a choir of youths who sang loudly but extremely
well. The singing was pleasant; I should have liked to have
heard more of it. The songs were vigorous and sung with
gusto, and an old man clacked small castanets with skill.

People took turns with the fans. I think that this fanning
was a privilege for which you paid a little. One old man, I
noticed, was particularly ardent, both with fanning and with
singing. He was a grand old chap, a *ryot* from Hyderabad I
was told, and I took a great liking to him. He had such character in his face, and he took such obvious delight in what
was happening. He sang with tremendous energy, clapped
his hands to the music all the time, nodded his head in approval whenever one of the priests did or said something
which he considered particularly apt, and gently repri-
manded a boy (by signs and shakings of the head) when the
lad stuck a flower that had been given him behind his ear,
instead of holding it reverently in his hand.

Near the curtain stood two dirty old men, very thin, holding flaming torches in their hands. The torches were wads of
cloth on the ends of sticks, and from time to time coconut oil
was squirted onto them from an ordinary railway-engine
oil can. As there was only one oil can, but two old men, the

oil can had to be passed back and forth, but often one old man would stick to it for too long, when his colleague would make frantic signs at him and, after the can had been passed across, scold him, silently, with frowns and lip movements. They were testy old men, and a joy to watch. As a certain stage of the ceremony the two old men withdrew the curtain, so that the gods could behold themselves in the mirror. My friend whispered in my ear: "Look at the gods in the looking glass, that is very holy!" I did so.

The song that was being sung, I was told, related how the gods were washing their mouths and hands before eating, how they were putting on clean robes before the meal, how scent was being applied to them. And the priests offered them betel leaf to chew, and then brought the betel leaves around for us to chew instead. We also came in for a share of scent and oil to put on our heads, and holy water, poured with a spoon into our cupped hands, to drink.

Eventually, the gods were ready for their meal, and they were carried away into the *adyta* to have it. This was to be behind closed doors, with the two priests in there only, while we sat and waited outside. I know it is irreverent, and I should not allow myself to have such thoughts, but when the priests retire like this and do things *in camera,* I often wonder if they aren't simply taking an opportunity for a smoke and a yarn! I had this naughty feeling during the ceremony of the Syrian Church, too, when a curtain was drawn between the altar and the congregation.

At all events, whatever goes on in there was concluded, the doors of the *adyta* flung open, and the gods carried out, taken around at the head of a procession, and then carried into another chamber in which hung a hammock. The *adyta* and this bedchamber, by the way, and other parts of the temple also, were illuminated by electricity, with colored bulbs, for some rich man had made an offering of a generator to the temple.

After the three gods had been put down in the bed, we crowded around to look at them, and a song was sung to them. And it was a holy thing to do to rock their cradle. The women, particularly, jostled to get a turn at this. On the hammock were Rama's sandals, in case he should need them in the night, and they were of solid gold. One of the priests picked one up—one noticed the great weight of it as he did so—and touched each one of us on the forehead with it. His brother cleric came out from the *adyta* with a large basin of rice cooked in oil, and proceeded to portion this out. To obtain some of this was evidently very auspicious, for it was the actual food of the gods, and people crowded around, eager not to be left out. Thinking, perhaps, that here was a new convert to be encouraged, the priest dumped onto me a huge double handful of the stuff, and I wandered around unhappily for the next half-hour wondering what on earth to do with it. I swallowed as much as I could, but I had already had a large meal, and really it was too much. To have popped it behind one of the lesser idols that stood about would have been unthinkable, but where else could I put it?

My pilgrim friend's little boy came up while I was trying to solve this problem, and eyed the stuff greedily, for I believe he had been missed out on the cooked rice. But I was afraid to offer him any, for I feared that he would be forced to refuse, not being able to take food from a man of another caste; and refusing, he would feel perhaps that he had offended me and would be embarrassed. So I just winked at him, and turned away. But I saw from his face at the moment that I turned that in fact he *would* have taken the rice, and that he was hurt that I did not offer it to him, but then for some reason it had seemed too late for me to alter my decision. I know this sounds very trivial, but it worried me considerably at the time, and is an example of the difficulties one gets into sometimes in strange countries.

After this we dispersed, and I met the fishery official, who was also staying at the traveler's bungalow, and we went to the cinema together, in a large tent. We saw quite the worst film that I have ever seen in my life. We then went to bed, but before we dropped off to sleep the fishery man, who shared my veranda, treated me to a long lecture on the dowry system, which he disliked.

"It ought to be abolished by law," was what he thought about it. "But if it was," he added sensibly, "they would simply start a black market in dowries."

"They would indeed," I answered. "Good night!"

17

THE LARGE MAN IN THE TRAIN

I N BHADRACHALAM I met a white man on a bicycle. Living-
stone could not have been more surprised at seeing Stan-
ley.

If he had been another Englishman, we would probably
have pretended not to notice each other, for fear of breaking
in on one another's privacy or, worse, getting mixed up with
someone of a different social class. After all, you can't be too
careful, can you?

But he was an Australian, and therefore he hailed me, and
we asked each other questions. He was a missionary, his name
was Pullen, and he kindly invited me to go with him to Dummaguden, where he lived with his wife. He was quite a young
chap, had been in the army, and had now spent some six
years at Dummaguden. He was a priest of the Church of
South India, and his parish covered many hundreds of square
miles of jungle. And he and his wife must have been at least
a hundred miles away, over very difficult country, from the
nearest Europeans.

After I had taken leave of the pilgrims, with loud protestations of eternal friendship on both sides, we caught another launch from Bhadrachalam, and in a few hours we had reached Dummaguden.

Dummaguden means "Village of Dust." The village is built on some flat land on the bank of the Godavari, and this land was formed by the dust knocked off a mountain on the opposite side of the river by the wheel of Ravana's chariot, as the wicked king of Lanka drove away with the stolen Sita in his arms. The mark of the chariot wheel still runs along the top of the mountain there, for all to see; in fact, I saw it myself with my own eyes. Some quibbling geologist of course might say that it was nothing but a *kranze,* or outcrop of rock.

That country has a rather steamy and tropical climate, and there is plenty of green vegetation. After we landed we were greeted by children from a school that Pullen runs, and were lent bicycles to ride to Pullen's house.

I mean no disrespect when I refer to my new friend as Pullen, instead of the Reverend Pullen. He was such a pleasant, natural, normal young man that I cannot think of him as *reverend*. I mean no disrespect to reverends either when I say that because a man is pleasant and natural I cannot think of him as a reverend. Many people who are natural reverends are also pleasant and natural, but in quite a different way from Pullen. He was not a muscular Christian either. He was just a very decent young man doing a difficult job in a strange country.

His house was set among big trees, in green lawns, as we often imagine English country houses to be set, and as in fact a few of them are. The house itself was roughly built of timber, brick, and thatch, and had a certain charm about it.

It was old, I found. It had been built as a residence by some Scots engineers who had come to Dummaguden about eighty years ago to build a weir across the Godavari. One of the engineers had been a God-fearing man who had liked Dummaguden, had decided to give up engineering and stay on there to convert the Koys. Thus had the mission started.

Mrs. Pullen was also Australian, a farmer's daughter, as pleasant and natural as her husband. She loved Dumma-guden, as he did. They had both learned to speak Telegu, and were, I think, popular with the people living around them.

After a meal (they had English-style food, which I found a pleasant change) we went for a walk down to the river, and were ferried in a canoe across a canal to an island. The island was perfectly beautiful, the sort of place that makes you long to settle down. Three-quarters of it was magnificent wood-land, humming with bees, birds, and other life; and the rest had been cleared for a tobacco farm.

Here was demonstrated what is—to a farmer, at least—a serious defect in the Indian system of living.

In England, because there is primogeniture, such an island would have been the property of one man, who would have cared for it and developed it in the knowledge that one day he would pass it on to his eldest son. Probably he would have lived on it; it would have been his permanent home.

But in India, land is either farmed by villagers (as by far the greater part of the land is), in which case when a land-owner dies his land is split up equally between his sons, or else, as in the case of this island, the land is farmed as a com-mercial proposition by a rich man.

But the rich man does not live on it. He lives far away, in a town. He may never have seen it. He farms it through an agent. There is no tradition that he should look upon it as a family seat and care for it so that it will be a beautiful place for many generations. It is just something to invest some money in, to exploit for what it is worth for a few years, and then to sell again when the market happens to be good.

One could see that this had happened to this island.

We met the young man who was farming it at the time. He had taken a lease of it from an uncle. He had built himself a rough shack of sticks and thatch and another building to shelter his coolies, and he was busy plowing the land—about a hundred acres—with hired cattle. He was investing in some pumps also, to pump water from the river to irrigate the tobacco.

He looked upon the thing solely as a commercial proposition. He was prepared to live there so long as he had to make money, that was all. He was a decent young man, intelligent and enterprising.

But, of course, land does not benefit by being treated in this manner. Whatever one may think of the British settler—and God knows one may think many strange things—he does go all out to make a *home* from his piece of land, and to improve it so that when he hands it on it will be a better place than it was when he acquired it, whether he acquired it by fair means or foul.

This hundred acres of tobacco land was just an exhausted stretch of light, sandy soil, with no improvements on it whatever. What a paradise one could have made of it!

But we walked across it, and through the steamy, green jungle to the other side of the island, and there we saw the great masonry *anicut* which the old Scots engineers had built across the river so many years ago. This weir was not like the one down in the delta, which was for irrigation. This was built to assist navigation on the river in the days before railways and road transport were very common. In fact, a few rafts of timber do still go through, and an occasional barge up or down, but on the whole the thing has never justified itself. The weir must be close to a mile long, and it struck me as being pretty much of a white elephant; one of the queerer things perpetrated by our Victorian ancestors, hidden away and lost there as it is in the green jungle, unapproachable by road.

Swarms of transparent shrimps were trying to swim upstream against the strong current that was flowing around the abutment of the weir on which we stood. In the water they could not make it, but some of them had the sense to leave the water and crawl around the masonry in the air. If these did not drop off again and get carried back, they achieved their object, entered the river higher up, and continued their journey to who knows where? They seemed to be in a devil of a hurry.

Back at the mission house Mrs. Pullen showed me the girls' dormitory, where small girls from outlying villages live in order to be able to go to school. They were pretty little girls. They did some strange dances for us, curious hornpipelike affairs, and they sang children's songs. They also showed me how to prepare *cholam,* the local brand of millet, by winnowing and cleaning it by throwing it up in the air with a basket scoop. They had a motherly lady in charge of them, and I thought that they seemed happy. I also saw the boys' dormitory, but the boys, I thought, seemed a little forlorn. Children need a grown-up to take a close personal interest in them, but these boys were more or less just left to their own devices.

Only one or two of these children were Koys, for the Koys have not taken much to Christianity. The rest were ex-Hindus of the lower castes, mostly outcastes or Harijans.

Pullen told me that before Independence the Christian missionaries had made most of their converts from untouchables, because these people were getting such bad treatment from Hinduism that they were glad to be able to enhance their prestige a little, perhaps, by becoming Christians. In those days there had been considerable mass conversions.

This had its disadvantages from the point of view of the missionaries, because it gave the idea that Christianity was only for lower-caste people, and people of good caste would not embrace it.

But now, with Independence, and with the drive that is going on in India for the improvement of the lot of the depressed castes, Harijans are not so ready to become converted. In fact quite large numbers who had previously been converted are renouncing Christianity again. You see, if a man wants to get his son into a university, he has a much bigger chance of succeeding if he is a Harijan. For many seats are reserved for Harijans only. But if he is a Christian, he does not count as a Harijan. Before, as a Christian, he might have felt that he had some slight advantage in a country governed by nominally Christian people. Now that advantage has gone.

I asked Pullen what he thought then would be the future of the Christian churches in India, and he said that he hoped that, in time, Indians of the more educated classes would begin to come in, not for any practical advantage, but because they had become convinced that Christianity was right. But at the moment, this does not seem to be happening very much. The Christian churches are losing, instead of gaining, adherents. (Except the Syrian Church, which hardly loses any, or obtains any, because it has become a caste just as rigid as any of the Hindu castes, and you are either born into it or you are not.)

One of the Pullens' predecessors had started a local industry. An elderly lady missionary, apparently on her way back to Dummaguden after a furlough, had seen women doing embroidery in Ceylon. She had learned how to do this (the Ceylonese had learned it in the first place from the Dutch), and had taught her women Christians to do it at Dummaguden. Now the women round about there clamor to do this work, and Mrs. Pullen has to work hard at supplying them with the calico or whatever it is, and the colored yarnstuff, and collecting the finished product, and posting it to various parts of the world where it is sold. The demand for it is good; the bottleneck is the supply of colored yarn, from England. This is kept out by customs regulations.

Pullen and I bicycled about the jungle and saw some Koys. These were rather smallish men, who wore few clothes, but who lived semisettled existences on the edge of the forest. They have degenerated somewhat in contact with a higher civilization. They see the baubles, the paraffin lanterns, and the colored prints and all the rest of it, but they do not see the price one pays for these things: poverty and riches, hunger, and fatty degeneration of the liver, gastric ulcers, greed and hatred, war and boredom.

We had a snake scare at the Pullens'. One night a girl came from the dormitory and said that there was a snake there, and we rushed over to find all the girls standing on their beds with their nighties around their knees, like maiden aunts when they see a mouse! We tracked the snake to the top of the wall, under the eaves, and I managed to clout it with a stick, but I couldn't get a good swing at it and it got away. Snakes are ten a penny there, and it's my secret belief that those girls were not half as frightened as they made out! But life gets dull in a dormitory, I have no doubt, and it's fun to have queer people rushing around in the night with torches and walking sticks and funny hats. It is a change.

They are much troubled by tigers. One killed fifty people, round about Dummaguden, and was killed itself only a month or two before I got there. A Koy shot it with a muzzle loader.

I wanted to go up the river, but the rains really had set in by then; there were no boats going and all the paths would be impossible. After making careful inquiries I decided that they would be impossible enough for me not to want to go to the trouble of going along them. For the last couple of months or so I had been suffering on and off, mostly on, from dysentery, and had been meaning all along to see a doctor and have it treated. But I had not done so. The result was that my energy was low. I was content to drift along quietly, and not to do anything physically strenuous.

So I crossed the river, to where there was a road the other side, and there I was able to catch a bus. This was in Hyderabad, the Nizam's dominions.

I went down a coal mine in Hyderabad, but will spare the reader the details, and eventually I got on a train, intending to go north to Delhi. I was anxious to see my mail, which I had not received for several months, and also I wished to get myself treated for the dysentery. I know now, but did not know then, that there is a new drug that you just take yourself, and rest for a couple of days, and the dysentery, if it is only bacillary, will be gone.

So I got on a train, for Nagpur, the capital of Madhya Pradesh, or what used to be called Central Provinces. But I was not to get there. At least not on that train.

For at a small siding by the way an enormous man got in, accompanied by half a dozen normal-sized ones. The big man had evidently been conducting some sort of an inquiry, for he talked in a loud voice to these other people, and they talked back, and they went over again for the fiftieth time the things that they had already said. He was the sort of man who is destined always to be in the center of an uproar; quiet never descends upon him. He is talking, you are talking, people are shouting to be heard; there is a sense of urgency, of big things happening, not to say of panic.

It is very easy to describe the look of this large man, for, facially at least, he was simply a brown version of the late Marshal Stalin, though his mustaches were bigger. He recognized this himself, and pointed it out to me afterwards when I got to know him.

He was dressed in a most curious striped tunic and pajamas, of his own design and probably of his own making, made of very coarse gray *khadi*. I must say it became him, and looked distinctive.

As the train began to move from the station the uproar between this man and his henchmen increased to a crescendo, the latter jumped off one by one, last-minute orders and questions and answers were bellowed from the window as the train got under way, and that was that. The inquiry was temporarily suspended.

The big man looked at me, I thought, with a scowl, flung his umbrella up on one upper berth, and heaved his huge bulk up on the other. Seeing that no uproar was possible at the moment, he had decided to go to sleep.

The country we were passing through was flattish, jungled, dry and barren, sparsely inhabited, and every now and then we passed a coal mine. This was near the middle of India, and it made me realize that India is not all paddyfields and dense population. Enormous areas of it are dry and infertile, and there is quite enough trackless jungle to disappear into for the rest of your life if you want to.

But my large man woke up. He descended on us. I thought that I would find him a little too much at first, but he endeared himself to me when the train stopped at a station and some peasants tried to get into our compartment.

In Indian railway stations you sometimes get large numbers of peasants from backward areas, who have quite possibly never seen a railway before. They are going, perhaps, on a pilgrimage. They are very nervous of the whole strange business of getting on a train, and, among other things, they are terrified that the train will go without them.

Now the third-class carriages are always packed, and it is with great difficulty that anybody gets into them. So these ignorant fellows run backward and forward along the platform, shouting to their wives and children, who run screaming after them, and their aunts. They all work themselves up into a panic, and they try to get in anywhere (after all they cannot read)—first, second and third class mean nothing to them.

But when they try to enter an upper-class compartment, as they often do in their ignorance, the upper-class passengers show their lower-class manners by shouting rudely at them. There were some other people in our compartment besides the large man and myself, inferior people who shouted at some wretched peasants who, harried and terrified, were trying to board us. "Oxen!" they shouted, in English. "Buffaloes!" They used English because the peasants were sure to be impressed by this language of the ruling classes, which they couldn't understand.

Suddenly, though, the large man turned to these people and said, "Shut up!" to them in such a manner that they shut up. He then turned to the peasants and, addressing one of them as *Bapu,* which means Dad, and is a pleasant way of addressing an old man, told him in a kindly way that he must get into a third-class compartment. The man and his family thereupon went away quietly and sensibly, and with looks of gratitude that here was someone who treated them as human beings.

The large man then turned to me, and smiled—he had a delightful fat smile—and said, "Poor people! Where will you find people so ignorant? But anyone must feel sympathy for them, anyone!"

I found I liked the man. He started telling me about himself. He was a Brahman, a minor official on the railways getting four hundred rupees (eighty-four dollars) a month, a follower of Gandhi. His wife, who was his second, was living with her parents ("we agree well, but so it is better"), he had a humble job because he had failed to matriculate, but this was because he had had to try to study while at the same time running the family paper-manufacturing business, his father being ill. In consequence he had contracted tuberculosis, but had cured himself by *yoga,* and was now as fit as a fiddle. And so he was. I never saw a man so bubbling over, just like a boiling pot, with life and fun and enthusiasm. As I write this, I can hear his roar of laughter when anything amused him, as many things did.

"I live with my mother," he said. "She doesn't cook. My sister lives with us and she cooks. My mother has the Portfolio of the Interior. Ho, ho, ho!"

Gandhi, he told me, had to be shot. "People of such power cannot die the ordinary way. They have great spiritual power, and cannot leave this earth. When their destined time comes they must go violently. No disease or old age can kill them.

"I am a Brahman, as I told you," he said. "But I am modern-minded. I am orthodox though, not because I *have* to be, but because I like it! It suits me. I only eat the orthodox food, and I am a vegetarian. My food must be clean and it must be just right. If not, I lose my temper! I lose my temper terribly and shout!"

When I told him I was going on to Nagpur he shouted, "What? Not stop at Wardha? And I live at Wardha! Not

honor my humble abode? You have seen Sevagram, of course.
I needn't ask!"

"What is Sevagram?" I asked him.

"Sevagram! Sevagram! The *ashram* of our Mahatma?
Where our Mahatma lived before he died? And his house is
there! His own house, kept just as he lived in it, with an
English copy of the *Bhagavad Gita* and the Bible and the
Three Wise Monkeys, one who can see no evil, one who can
hear no evil, and one who can smell no evil? Not see Sevagram?"

"Well, I haven't got time," I said. "I must get on to Delhi."

"Have you ever stopped at Wardha and seen Sevagram?"
he asked.

"No," I said.

"Well, you're stopping there now!" he said. "You stop
there and honor my humble abode and see Gandhi's *ashram*.
I would not let you go on. I will pull you bodily off the train,
bodily. No, no, I will not let you!"

Well, what can you do?

So at Wardha, off I got, and walked off with my captor (his
name by the way was Chaubby) to go to honor his humble
abode.

18

THE HEART OF INDIA

YOU WILL NOT SLEEP HERE," said Chaubby Sahib. "My house is too small, and too many people. Not good enough for your honor. But I will put you in the rest-house. I get you a special room there. My sister lives here. Her husband is in Bombay, but she prefers here because, although my abode is humble, we have all benefits of residence. All benefits. All benefits whatever. Electric light and water we have, a tap just outside. All benefits of residence in my humble cottage, which belongs to the railway. I am a railway officer class three, you see, and I am entitled . . ." and on he went.

We had arrived at the Burra Sahib's house (I nicknamed him the Burra Sahib) and entered that humble abode. Inside was confusion a thousand times confounded! Not a horizontal surface but was covered with junk of every sort—books and papers, and astrologers' charts, and advertisements, and old pots, tin cans, and bric-a-brac of all kinds—all heavily covered with dust.

I was introduced to Burra Sahib's mother: "Meet the Min-

— 233 —

ister of the Interior!" and his sister: "She goes now to cook
you a magnificent Indian meal. You shall see what a magnificent Indian meal, cooked by Brahmans, can be!"

He showed me his books: books by H. G. Wells and Have-
lock Ellis, books—bogus and otherwise—on "Yogi" and "Eastern Mysticism," all the works of, and about, Mahatma Gandhi.
The house and the books were a true reflection of the Burra
Sahib's mind—rich confusion.

The meal was eventually prepared and brought in on a
tray, and a space was ruthlessly cleared on a roll-top desk.
"You are an Englishman; you are unskilled in the art of sitting on the floor. You can take your meal in comfort on the
table, in your own way. Everything for your comfort we
will have ready for you!"

The meal was excellent. Really excellent.

"Now we will go and find you a room," said the Burra
Sahib, and we walked, through the rain I remember, to the
municipal rest-house. There were already two young men
there, a chap named Frank, and another named Peter.

Peter was a Malabari, and a Roman Catholic. His home
was in Mangalore. Small and very dark, like many Malabaris,
he was a first-class type of fellow. One could tell on meeting
him that he would be utterly reliable. Before the war he told
me that he had started cycling round the world, had got as
far as Burma when the war had broken out, and so had got a
job there with the Army, and had come back to India after
Burma had fallen.

Frank was an Anglo-Indian, a pleasure-loving man, full of
amours of the past. But he was married, very strangely, to
an Indian girl. It is most unusual for an Anglo-Indian to
marry a pure-blooded Indian. Maybe more of them will, now
that racial differences are being forgotten in India. It would

be the long-term solution to their problem. Frank, at least, was very happy.

These two youngish men were on some government job, away from their homes, and during the four or five days I stayed at Wardha we had an amusing time together.

Every evening the Burra Sahib came and joined us, sometimes with one or two of his friends, mature and mellowed men like himself, and we would talk into the night.

Wardha is a prohibition area, which meant that in honor bound one had to drink. Fortunately we found a man of the sweeper caste in the town, who, for a small remuneration, used to bring us some *mawa*, a spirit distilled from the fermented juice of the flowers of a certain tree. "Hold your nose when you drink it!" advised Frank, and the advice was not unneeded.

Of course, Burra Sahib would not touch the *mawa*, and indeed we could never persuade him to have a cup of tea with us. "Why don't you?" said Frank. "You are modern-minded. You are a follower of Gandhi, you know he was against orthodoxy in those things."

"Oh, I know all these things are changing, you see," said Burra Sahib. "I know these things. And our Gandhiji was quite against these things, you see. But *still* I am orthodox! *Still* I am orthodox, in spite of what our Gandhiji said. My people prepare me such good food. I am strictly vegetarian, you see, not even taking onions—onions inflame the passions, you see, onions and garlic. I am not even eating these things, you see."

"But what's wrong with having a cup of tea with us?"

"But that boy who is bringing it is a Moslem, you see. I know maybe he is a clean boy, he is a human being, we are all brothers and children of God like our Gandhiji taught, you see, but *still* I am not sure that that cup was properly washed, you see, and supposing the boy might have touched meat, you see, or the cup washed up in water that has touched meat, and I am strict vegetarian."

We talked of England. "I want to go to foreign places!" exclaimed Burra Sahib. "Always I am wanting to go to England. In spite of that I was a Congressman, and I fought the English, still I love them and I am wanting to go to England."

"What'll you eat?" I asked.

"Ah, when I cross the water I am losing my orthodoxy, you see," he said. "I am losing my orthodoxy. Of course I realize that when I go to Europe and England I am having to *conform*, you see. But *still* I am remaining vegetarian; that is possible, no? It is possible to remain vegetarian and yet go to England? Our Gandhiji did it. He lived in England and remained vegetarian. And beer, they say it is necessary to drink beer because of the climate, but that is wrong, no? I can go there without drinking beer?"

And indeed, I thought it just as well that the Burra Sahib did not drink beer. For he starts about six pints ahead of the rest of us, in elation, as it is. What he would be like if he added the effects of alcohol to his natural exuberance I hardly like to think.

"I played Hamlet once," he startled us by saying. "I was Hamlet. This television is a great thing. I think I should be on television! There are so many things I could do, I have so much to say, I am full of things, my life would never be long enough to do all the things I am wanting to do——"

"Tell us about when you played Hamlet," said Peter.

"I played it in Urdu. In an Urdu play. Of course, I am not a native of C.P. I am not from these parts. I have already told you, I am a native of U.P. In Urdu I play Hamlet. I will recite you some Hamlet in Urdu—'To be or not to be . . .'" and he recited.

"But when I come to England you must make them put me on television," said the Burra Sahib.

They spoke of the drama: the old drama of India, now killed by the cinema. "In every village," said Burra Sahib, "we had frequent dramas, monthly, weekly even. Frequent dramas. The old tales, you know, from Ramayana and Mahabharata and the life of Krishna. These old tales were acted. But now people go to the cinema. Never, you see, the old drama."

One evening he brought a friend named Setpal with him, a Punjabi. Setpal told me that he had killed seventeen Moslems with a spear.

"Why?" I asked. It seemed such a lot of trouble to go to.

He said that he had been in the West Punjab at the time of Partition. He had sent his family out, but had remained behind himself to look after his business. But one day his peon, or messenger, who was himself a Moslem, had come to him and warned him to get away while he could. The riots had started. "Leave everything!" said the peon. "Don't try to take anything. There is no time. Just come with me!" At that moment people began to bang on his door, and so he and the peon slipped off out the back, and got away to the station.

"I got on a train," he said, "and we got away. But they stopped the train. The Moslems stopped the train. And only because I am lying on the luggage rack and they missed me I am here today. They kill every other Hindu on the train. But they missed me. The floor of the compartment was deep in blood."

So when he at last got to the Indian side and he had got a spear, and joined a gang of Hindus, he had got his revenge. "We surrounded a Moslem village," he said, "and killed everyone in it, men, women, and children."

"Are you glad you did it?" I asked.

"I lie awake at nights regretting it," he said. "I will regret it until I die."

The Burra Sahib said one of the very wise things that often came from him, mixed up with the rest of it: "The thing that is shocking to me, John Sahib," he said, "is not that people were killed. That is nothing; they would have died anyway. It is that men should have killed them. That our religion should have turned us into brutes."

I was coming into the refugee country, the limit reached by the waves of Sindhi and Punjabi refugees. I was coming into a country with a shadow over it, the shadow of men who had seen things and done things that they will never be able to forget.

But never, in India, did I meet a man who blamed anybody for these massacres. I never heard a Hindu try to put the blame on the Moslems. There was always a complete acceptance that both sides were equally to blame. One has the impression that it was a strange madness which came over people, like the dancing madness of the Middle Ages. Men were seized by some rage or choler outside their control.

We talked of snakes.

A fat balloon manufacturer, who was also a refugee from Pakistan, had joined us, and someone asked him, because we were arguing about Hindu beliefs, what he would do if a snake attacked him, and the only way he could save himself from being bitten was to kill the snake.

"I would not kill it," he said. He went on to tell us of a friend of his who was bitten by a cobra, and a certain *rishi*, or holy man, who lived in Calcutta, was contacted on the telephone and asked to recite some *mantrams*, or sacred texts, to save the man from dying. The *rishi* did so, but it was ineffective.

Burra Sahib then told us that it was the custom to apply the rump of a hen to a snakebite, and the hen would die but the man would recover. "I knew a man," said the balloon manufacturer, "who did this, and they put ten hens to him, and all the hens died."

"What happened to the man?" asked Frank.

"He died, too," said the balloon manufacturer.

Frank told us of the perfidy of women, particularly Anglo-Indian ones. "They are bitches," he said. "I know. That's why I married an Indian girl. They are faithful."

I asked him how he knew that Anglo-Indian women were the way he said they were, and he said "I've tried 'em. I've never found an Anglo-Indian wife I couldn't seduce. All they want is gambling and boozing and dancing and fornicating."

We talked of singing. The balloon man sang a song, a film song from one of the Indian films that was going about. Burra Sahib said, "Nowadays people prefer cinema, you see. But I like scientific. You see, John Sahib, we have cinema singing and scientific. Of course, if you want to hear scientific, that's very different. Very different. If you like, I will sing you scientific."

"Oh yes," said the balloon man, "scientific, that's very different. You sing us some scientific, Chaubby Sahib, so our friend can hear." And, for a long time, the Burra Sahib sang us scientific. By which he meant Indian classical music, and very well he sang it too.

We talked of retiring.

"My astrologer says I am to retire at fifty-three," said Burra Sahib.

"When does the railway say?" I asked.

"Fifty-five. But I will go by the astrologer. He says fifty-three. I am retiring then, for so I have planned my life, you see. I have planned my life. Then for eight years I shall en-

gage in business, you see. You will fix me up in business in
England, John, I think? Get me some good contact or agency,
you see, for eight years I shall engage in business. So I have
planned my life. Then, after that, I will retire and meditate.
I will devote the rest of my life to meditation, as an Indian
should. I will be quiet and meditate."

The Burra Sahib—quiet!

The next day the balloon manufacturer took me to see his
factory. Three brothers ran it, and they employed two work-
men. They were all refugees.

The process was extremely simple. There was a tray of
latex, kept liquid by the addition of a chemical. "It comes
straight from the tree like that and they put this chemical
in," said the balloon manufacturer. "We get it sent up from
Travancore, from a rubber plantation." There were dozens
of little boards studded with bulb-shaped wooden pegs. You
picked up a board, turned it so that the pegs pointed down-
wards, dipped the pegs into the latex, took them out and
dipped them in another tray containing some acid which
caused the latex to set, then turned them upside down, and
placed the boards on a shelf to dry. When the latex was partially dry you turned the lip of the balloons up and left them
like that. Then, next day perhaps, you pulled the completed
balloons off the pegs. Other things besides balloons could be
manufactured, which might be of great use in India's attempt
to control the growth of her population.

Setpal, the man who had killed seventeen people with a
spear, took me on a tour of the town.

We went to a temple built by a rich man at Gandhi's command, in order to try to break down the prejudice against
Harijans' entering Hindu temples. Everybody was allowed in
this one.

Like most modern Hindu temples it was garish and ugly.

The colors were bright and shiny, but crude. The carving and the coloring were the same sort of thing that one sees on the animals of a carrousel: interesting, good, healthy folk art, but a bit garish.

"I am not an idolator," said Setpal. "I am a Hindu, yes, but not an idolator. Idolatry is dying quickly in India. All this, *lingams* and figures of gods and idols, it's for old people now. Old and stupid people. I believe in one universal God; I am not an idolator."

An old man, a Harijan, sat on the floor working a *charkha,* or spinning wheel. "So he earns his living," said Setpal. I asked the old man if indeed he earned his living like this, and he said yes. He was quite happy sitting there spinning most of the day, and it earned him enough to buy his food.

Next we visited a Jain temple.

This was a small building, small and in good taste, with statues of the twenty-four Tirthankaras, all looking exactly alike, around the wall, and a dome overhead, painted blue to represent the sky. Outside was a charming little garden, with a well in it. The Jains generally have a garden attached to their temples, in which they spend a lot of time meditating, possibly about ways of making money, because many of them are rich. A young man who was in the garden, and who spoke some English, came and told me that the Jain religion simply consisted of nonviolence and truth.

We passed a Naga shrine outside, where the cobra is worshiped. There was no cobra there, although there might have been at one time, for the shrine was under a great tree, but the little building had pictures of cobras painted on it, with women's heads on them. "All nonsense!" said Setpal. "Only old men and fools think of such things. I am a Hindu, I believe in God, but not such things!"

Poor Setpal had lost everything in Partition. His flourish-

ing timber business had been left behind, with all his belong-
ings, and now he was just a clerk in a lumber yard belonging
to somebody else.

I borrowed a bicycle and cycled out to Sevagram. The
Burra Sahib saw to it that I did so.

Sevagram has grown to be quite a large settlement. There
is a big school of weaving there, besides Gandhiji's old *ashram*.

Gandhi's house is exactly as he left it. It is a three-roomed
hut, the walls and floor of mud and cow dung, thatched-
roofed, and with practically no furniture. There is the Mahatma's bed, which was simply a raised mud platform with a
grass mat on it, a pillow, and a clean piece of cotton cloth.
Beside the platform is a tiny bookcase with perhaps a dozen
books on it, including the famous copy of *Bhagavad Gita* in
English, and an English Bible. On top of the case sit the
Three Wise Monkeys. Someone gave them to Gandhi and
they amused him.

The Mahatma believed in reading, but he did not see that
it was necessary to *own* a book to enjoy it. One can borrow
books. By the bed, of course, was Gandhi's spinning wheel.

On the scrupulously clean floor (which almost to the last
the Mahatma swept himself) were his sandals; simple pieces
of wood with pegs on the top of them to be grabbed between
two toes. In the corner was the famous staff. I cannot remember that there was anything else in that room at all.

Then there was the bathroom, with a latrine installed by
some American engineer who visited the Mahatma and built
him this as a service! It was just a lavatory seat built over a
cesspit, and was flushed by pouring water into it with a
bucket.

Gandhi was very concerned about sewage disposal. He
wrote and talked about it a lot, and finally developed what
is now known as the Wardha-type latrine, which is being

generally adopted in Indian villages. (This is a mobile hut, which straddles a three-foot-deep trench, and is moved along as the trench fills up. Grass or leaves are put in the trench as it is used, a few inches of earth on top, and after six weeks the trench can be opened up and the contents, now a sweet-smelling and valuable fertilizer, taken away to be put on the fields.)

The reason for this preoccupation with the lavatory was twofold. Firstly, the insanitary habits of many of Gandhi's countrymen with regard to sewage disposal. Secondly, the un-fairness, in Gandhi's opinion, of making some people respon-sible for doing a dirty job that all should do. Such things led to untouchability. Gandhi wrote that one's lavatory should be kept as clean as if it were a temple, and that (put briefly) one should do one's own dirty work.

So here was this beautiful lavatory, installed by an Ameri-can engineer, that the Mahatma himself could keep as clean as a temple.

Next door to it was a room with some curious boxes and frames in it, on which I was informd that Gandhi used to do physical exercises. He was always trying out new and strange health theories. He said of himself, "I am a born crank!" He was, and he gloried in it.

Now, when I thought about the matter, I realized that here, between these muds walls and under this thatched roof, were all the material things that a man could want. Being used to it, Gandhi slept as well on that mud platform as I do in my comfortable bunk. During the day he sat on the same platform, in perfect comfort, for he was used to sitting cross-legged. When he went out he had his sandals to keep his feet from the stones, and he used to walk thirty miles a day in those sandals, for hundreds of miles, and with that staff. He had two dhoties and two shawls, one each of which he wore while he washed the other. Would he have been happier and more comfortable had he cluttered his hut up with vacuum cleaners and washing machines and can openers and electric lights and a thousand and one other things? What could he have done that was worth doing that he could not do with the dozen or so articles, which were all that he possessed?

There is a large Basic Teacher's Training School at Sevagram, presided over when I was there by a Yorkshire woman, Marjory Sykes. She was one of the few Englishwomen who have adopted Indian dress whom I did not feel to be a trifle phony. There is nothing affected about Marjory Sykes. She is as hard-headed and sensible as any Yorkshire person who has never left Yorkshire. She is an authority on Basic Education and has written some books about it.

She took me into the dining hall, and we sat down together and had a meal.

The day happened to be the Brother and Sister Festival, the day when Hindu girls tie bracelets of flowers on the wrists of their brothers, and the brothers in return give them small presents. "Generally we all eat together," said Marjory to me. "We have no sex segregation here. But today the idea is that the girls are to wait on the boys, and then the boys are to wait on the girls. But it looks to me as if now that the boys have had their meal they've gone! The girls will have to wait on themselves."

Such appeared to be the case.

Anyway, we girls (for I had, willy-nilly, to join them, and I cannot say that I was reluctant) sat down both sides of a long hut, on wooden seats perhaps three inches high, and were served by some of our number with a large vegetarian meal, on banana-leaf plates. "We have food cooked in the style of all parts of India here," said Marjory, "because our students come from every part. There's not a corner of India that isn't represented here."

I was very much impressed by this training school. I feel that if there is a solution to India's educational problems, it is here, at Sevagram. And where else should it be, but at the home of the Father of the Nation?

But here was Basic Education as it should be, conducted with intelligence as well as enthusiasm. A large school for children was being run there—children, I suppose, up to the age of about twelve—and if ever I saw children who were having the best in them encouraged, children with the light of enthusiasm and intelligence and fun and love in their eyes, it was those children. As for the pupil-teachers, it seemed to me that they were the cream of young India.

I had never read very much of Gandhi's writings up to my visit to Sevagram. I did not know very much about his theories. I have always admired him as a politician, as a fighter for free India. I have considered for years that he was the greatest statesman of our century. But as a philosopher, and an economist, no! The Gandhian way of life seemed impossible and undesirable to me, what little I knew about it.

But my day at Sevagram made me determined to find out something more about it.

There was more to it than just crankiness, I decided.

Meanwhile, I cycled back to Wardha, and said good-by to my friends there.

Burra Sahib took me aside before I left, and said: "We will meet again. You see, we will meet again!"

"I certainly hope so," I said, and I meant it.

"What I think is," said Burra Sahib, "you and I meeting like this, quite by chance, and we are wanting nothing from each other. That is true friendship. I want nothing from you, and you from me. And yet we love each other! That is true friendship!"

Bubbling over with life and fun and good fellowship; to me, Burra Sahib stands for a lot that is good in India.

19

⁓

THE LAND OF POETS

AT DELHI a monkey ran away with my spectacles. Arriving there in the middle of the night, and not knowing where to go, I asked a taxi driver to take me to a hotel. He took me to a very good one, the Coronation, right in the middle of the old city.

There are in existence two Delhis, and they are quite distinct. There is New Delhi, which is an enormous garden suburb, designed by British architects and inhabited mostly by foreigners and government servants, and there is Delhi itself, which is an ancient city surrounded by a wall.

The latter is a typical North Indian city of the old type.

It resembles one's idea of cities in Europe during the first Elizabethan age: narrow, winding streets often ending in blind alleys, upper stories of houses jutting out so that you can lean across the road and pull your neighbor's nose.

The Coronation Hotel was run on the lines of a first-class Indian hotel. There were large rooms, very clean, each room with a shower and a lavatory (the latter of the squatting type), electric light, and fans (a pigeon flew into my electric fan and ended bloodily on the floor). In a restaurant downstairs you could get good Indian food or bad "European-style" food. Servants cleaned your room for a small extra charge. Such hotels are not cheap, but far better value than European-style hotels, which are extremely expensive as a rule and ostentatiously uncomfortable.

I woke up at six in the morning with the feeling that there was something in the room.

There was.

A monkey was sitting on the table beside my bed trying on my spectacles. I let out a bellow and made a grab at him, but he flew out of the door, taking my spectacles with him, and half a dozen other monkeys who were having a good look around followed him. I followed him too. I had been wearing a sarong in bed—which is a chancy garment at the best of times—and as I ran I had to keep clutching at it to prevent its falling about my ankles. I rushed along the veranda shouting at the monkeys and clutching my sarong, and occasionally tripping over it, until I heard a peal of silvery laughter coming from over the road. I saw two ladies, taking the early morning air, standing on the roof of the house opposite. Something appeared to be amusing them.

The last I saw of my spectacles was when the monkey waved them at me derisively before disappearing round the corner of the building. I hope they suit his particular kind of vision.

After I had obtained some more, I wandered about in the narrow, crowded streets of Delhi. I believe that all cities in Asia and Europe were like this, once. They grew up with a minimum of town planning and were congested and jammed together, the roads being just narrow crevices left, perforce, by the citizens so that they could get to and from their dwellings and businesses.

What a mystery is there, but like all mystery it recedes as

you approach it. As you look along a winding alleyway, you feel that it must hide some strange quality that modern men have forgotten. But when you enter the alley you find there is nothing there. Ah, you feel, but what is in the houses? Supposing you could penetrate one of those high, overhanging façades with the big closed, brass-embossed teak doors? What mystery? But, when you do, what mystery is there? You enter a dark and dirty hallway, climb some rickety wooden stairs, arrive at a tumble-down room with nothing in it but some dusty junk-yard furniture and Messrs. Mukerjee & Sons' last year's calendar hung up on the wall.

The mystery has receded, yet you still feel that it is there somewhere, perhaps in the next alleyway, or in that bigger and more pretentious house over there, or that smaller and less pretentious one with the beautiful latticework over the windows? Is that a lovely girl peering at you through the latticework? Quite likely, but *you* won't get a closer look at her!

Certainly life is lived in such places with intensity. The citizens are all alive-oh. The merchants sitting cross-legged on carpets in their little cubbyholes of shops look out at the passing world with unflagging interest and never miss a thing. The hawkers crying their wares, the beggars in the gutter, the citizens out shopping, determined not to part with a pice more than they have to if it takes all day to find what they want at their own price, the idlers sitting in cafés or standing at street corners, they are all wide awake, sharp; they miss nothing.

Looking through open doors into dark interiors, you sometimes see the prettiest women, and everywhere, children, sometimes disturbingly beautiful, playing or working, but always nearly bursting with life and fun.

Age-old trades are carried on in the bazaars by men and

boys working in tiny shops. You see the gold beaters flicking over the pages of their books of tissue paper, placing between each two pages a sheet of gold so thin that if you sneezed ten yards away, it would be gone. You see men drawing silver wire out so that five rupees' worth of it would stretch a thousand yards. You see the wood and ivory turners at work, their lathes simple gadgets to hold the object being cut while it is turned by the string of a bow. You can stroll along and watch blacksmiths, coppersmiths, gold- and silversmiths, gem cutters, makers of elaborate jewelry, enamelers, inlayers in metal and in wood, potters, weavers who weave with gold and silver threads, carpetmakers, embroiderers, woodcarvers, and carpenters.

All these craftsmen surprise one by their skill. To watch them is like watching a skilful juggler or an acrobat—you realize that the human body is theoretically capable of being made to do the things they do, but you find it impossible to understand how the human mind can direct such intricate operations. The answer, of course, is practice from early childhood. Every one of these craftsmen was born into his trade, for it is his caste, and he started work with his father as early as he could toddle. It is inconceivable to him that he should ever do any other work, or that his own sons should not be brought up in the same trade, and should not draw their wives from families also engaged in it.

These people enjoy their work. There is no doubt about that. You have only to watch them at it to convince yourself of that. Their hours are long and their remuneration is not always lavish. It would be better if they could have more spare time. But even as it is they are happier than machine-minders in big factories, even though the latter have motorcycles on which they can ride off every week end to visit their girls.

I sat on a low platform in a quiet alleyway for a long time.

watching two men playing chess. One of them beat the other,
and challenged me and beat me also, in due course. There
are two slight differences in the rules of chess as played in the
back streets of India, just enough to prove disconcerting to
one not used to them. A pawn cannot move two spaces when
it moves for the first time, and there is no such thing as
castling.

Watching us was a dignified elderly man, dressed in dhoti
and *giba,* who proved to be the headmaster of a local school.
He took me off after the game to a café, where we sat at small
tables and drank milk.

Delhi, he told me, was growing out of all reason. Far too
many people had come to it; it was fantastically overcrowded.
Why, there must be nearly a million people in it, but before
the war it had been a comparatively small town.

When asked the reason for this expansion, he said that
firstly, many of the refugees from the West Punjab had come
there, and secondly, there were plenty of jobs and pay was
high. But rents were impossible; you paid forty rupees a
month for one small room, and were lucky to have that, and
food was terribly dear.

The headmaster told me that he was an old native of Delhi,
and that the old Delhi people were very put out with the
refugees from the Punjab. "They have captured all the trade
and business," he said. I asked him how they had done this
and he said, "By hard work and industry. Have you ever seen
a Punjabi beggar?" I had to admit that I had not. "No. There
you are. Even though millions of Punjabis lost everything
they possessed with Partition you will not see a single one of
them begging. I saw a Sikh beggar once in my life," he went
on. "I was driving in a car with another Sikh and we saw a
Sikh begging by the side of the road. My friend stopped the
car and got out and knocked the beggar into the gutter! I

thought he was going to kill him. Sikhs do not allow each other to beg. You must admire the Punjabis, but at the same time we get fed up with them. They disrupt our old quiet way of life here. We wish they had stayed in the Punjab."

A Punjabi Hindu friend of the headmaster joined us, with a friend of his who was a Bengali. They were both refugees. The Bengali had had to leave his home in East Bengal, which of course had gone to Pakistan also. But the Punjabi (who was a lawyer) had no great admiration for Bengalis. We went on discussing the initiative and industry of the Punjabi refugees, and the Punjabi said: "It's been very different in your part of the world. Bengali refugees have just sat around waiting for the government to help them, I think."

This was hardly a tactful thing to say, and it started off a most acrimonious argument.

"The trouble was," said the Bengali, "that in Bengal the riots started later, not until 1950. And by then there was no place for refugees to go and everyone was fed up with the refugee problem. When the Punjab riots came, everyone helped the refugees. Us they did not help, they were by then fed up with it all. And the Punjabis had grabbed all the best jobs."

"You should have done what we did—chase the Moslems out of West Bengal," said the Punjabi. "We chased all the Moslems out of our side of the Punjab, and then we had room to settle. We could settle on their land. You allowed yourselves to get kicked out of Pakistan, but you didn't reply by kicking the Moslems out of India."

"That's just what Gandhiji and Nehru didn't want!" said the Bengali. "They stood on the principle that India is a secular state. Two wrongs don't make a right. The Moslems are just as much citizens of India as the Hindus. Gandhi died to support that belief."

"The trouble is that the Bengalis are a soft race!" said the Punjabi, warming up to the discussion. "You're not a martial race. We Punjabis are martial. Look, the Moslems were killing your men and raping your women and children in East Bengal; why didn't you do the same to them in West Bengal?"

"We don't fight against women and children," said the Bengali. "It's all nonsense, this stuff about martial races. It's stuff the British put about."

"Why wouldn't the British take you in their army?" asked the Punjabi.

"I was in the army," said the other, "but I was a clerk. The British wanted to keep us as clerks. And why? Because they knew we were fighters for Independence! They were afraid of us. Do you know, the British would not let Bengalis have physical-training schools? They wanted to keep them weak!" (The last statement struck me as being an arrant piece of nonsense!)

An elderly Sihk had come in and joined us. "The British wouldn't have Bengalis in their army because they were not loyal!" he said.

"Of *course* we were not loyal!" cried the Bengali. "Why should we be? We were fighters for Independence. Without the Bengalis there would have been no *swaraj*! Bengalis were fighting for Free India! They would not fight for their oppressors!"

"They wait only that the government is helping them!" rumbled the old Sikh, into his beard. "That is for what they wait. We Punjabis help ourselves. Bengalis will not leave Bengal to look for land and work; we Punjabis have spread all over India!"

The Bengali said that they would leave Bengal if they could all go together.

"Why can't you go alone, like the Punjabis?" asked the lawyer.

"Only our men work in our Bengali families," said the hard-pressed Bengali. "Our women and children do not work like in your Punjab families. We do not like to see our women do rough work. That is why we cannot go along with you. And our people are cultivators. They are not artisans, like Punjabis. They must have land, and the government is not giving land! The government keeps them in camps, and they are being given a few annas a week to live. But even that they are not getting!"

"The officials are getting," said the lawyer.

"The *Congress* are getting, you should say!" rumbled the Sikh. They were all three anti-Congress, and forgot their internecine quarrel to join in abusing the government. If there is free speech in any country in the world, it is in India.

Later I saw something of New Delhi, because I stayed there for some weeks with an English family I met. I found it an oddly unsatisfying town. I used to argue with my host about it. He liked it, and thought that if you had to live in a city, New Delhi was a good kind of city to live in.

Most of New Delhi is open space. Every house is set in a large garden. There are wide strips of grass on either side of the roads, and at the road intersections (the road plan consists of a number of intersecting cobwebs) is often an extensive park, encircled by a traffic circle. If you do not have a car, it is an impossible place. There are enormous stretches of dreary hot tar between every two points you are likely to want to get between. The city seems to have no center, no focal point, no possibility of any corporate life. A person living there could never feel that he was a *citizen;* he merely feels that he is temporarily residing in New Delhi. I enjoyed my stay there because I met such pleasant people; but as a city, I think, the place is a complete failure. I cannot imagine any really vital and lively intellectual or artistic or social life growing up there, although perhaps in New Delhi now is concentrated a large proportion of the intellectuals of India. Somehow the place has no soul. It has no sense of unity, or atmosphere, and I do not see how it ever can have. A city must be a city, and if it is an Indian city, well, then it must be Indian. New Delhi has nothing of India in it. It is a sprawling, emasculated, gutless, invertebrate sort of animal. As a place to live, if you have a car and plenty of money and like life to be an incessant round of dreary "duty" cocktail parties, well, then New Delhi may be just what you want.

A town with far more life and character, strangely, is Simla. Strangely because Simla, like New Delhi, is not really Indian; but was built in the heyday of the British *Raj* as the hill capital.

It has life and character, not because of this, but because it has become, temporarily, the capital of the Punjab, and the stopping place of many of the Hindu and Sikh refugees from Lahore.

Lahore, lost to Pakistan, was once a very special city. It contained the liveliest cultural life of any place in India. This was dispersed at Partition, but some of it has lodged, temporarily, seven thousand feet up in the Himalayas at Simla.

I went there because I was told by a doctor to go to the hills. I spent nearly six weeks there, and met more intelligent, erudite, lively, and likable people than I have ever met before in one place in my life—too sophisticated perhaps, not sufficiently Indian, too dependent on Paris and London for their ideas, not sure enough of their own culture, but they will grow out of all these things.

I did not go to Bengal during this trip to India, or to "Bombay side," and therefore I did not see what was happen-

ing there. But I did spend some time in the Punjab; and the
impression I got there was that, intellectually and culturally,
the Punjab will be one of the great countries of the future.

There is an earthy vigor about Punjabi intellectualism.
Your Punjabi is quite ready to read the works of Monsieur
Jean-Paul Sartre, and quite capable of understanding them;
but he is not at all likely to accept the ideas in them, or the
ideas in anybody else's writings, if his earthy good sense, his
farmer's logic, tells him that they are all boloney. Wherever
his head is, the man from the Punjab always has at least one
foot on the ground.

One of the *Gurus*, or leaders, of the Sikhs, went to bathe
in the Ganges. The other bathers around him were facing the
East as they offered water up in their hands to the Gods. The
Guru faced the West and went through the same actions.

"What are you doing?" they asked him. "Why do you face
the wrong way when you offer up water in your hands? Why
do you turn your back on the East where the Gods dwell?"

"I turn towards my fields in the Punjab," said the *Guru*.
"We are having a drought there. I send the water up to water
my fields."

"Fool!" they said. "What chance do you think you have of
throwing that water all the way to the Punjab? Your fields
are a thousand miles away!"

"My fields are at least on this earth!" said the *Guru*. "Which
is more than your Gods are. If I cannot throw this water to
a place on this earth, what chance do you think *you* have of
throwing it to Heaven?"

The people of the Uttar Pradesh, the state of the North
which used to be the United Provinces, are poetical, sensitive,
and delicate. If a lady from U.P. treads on a peppercorn, she
will sneeze. When a wife from that country wakes her husband in the chill hour before dawn, and he asks her how she

knows that it is time for them to rise, she says, "Husband, I sense that the buds of the lotus flowers are preparing to open!"

The women farther west are less poetical. When a lady of Delhi wakes her husband, and he asks her how she knows that it is time, she says, "Husband, the bangles on my arm are cold. They are chilled by the cool breeze of the early dawn!"

When a Punjabi woman wakes her husband and is asked the same question she says, "I want to go to the lavatory."

The people of the Punjab are supposed to be inartistic and unmusical. It is related that a certain Sikh determined to disprove this, and so he went to the South of India and approached a famous teacher of singing and asked if he could be taught to sing.

The teacher took some persuading, but eventually agreed to attempt the apparently hopeless task, and for twenty years the Sikh labored at the art of music. Then, fully trained at last, he returned to his village in the Punjab.

"I have come to bring music to my people," he said, and he asked that all in the village should come and hear him sing. They gathered around, he sat down on a mat, closed his eyes, and sang. . . .

When he opened his eyes again he found that there was nobody there, except one man. The rest of the audience had faded away.

"Ah!" he cried. "At least there is one man of the Punjab with a soul! At least you, my friend, appreciate divine music!"

"Divine music be damned!" cried the other man. "I'm waiting for my mat!"

But the people of the Punjab do love music; although perhaps, by and large, they are not too enamored of the stylized and highly conventional music of certain other parts of India.

But their own folk music, to my ears at least, is the best in India.

The complete disruption that has followed Partition of the Punjab is perhaps a good thing. It has shaken people out of complacency, awakened them. Strangely, it has taught the Punjabi Hindus and Sikhs to appreciate the Punjabi Moslems.

"They are Punjabis!" says the Punjabis. "We realize now that we had more in common with Punjabi Moslems than we have with Hindus of the rest of India. We spoke the same language, had the same customs, laughed at the same jokes."

"The Punjab must become one again!" is a statement that one constantly hears. Partition is impossible. And, also strangely, bitterness against the Moslems is very seldom found. In spite of the horror of Partition (hardly a person but has his tales of terror to tell)—in spite of this, the Moslems are not held to blame. "We did the same."

"My friend Faiz," said one Punjabi to me. He was one of those who are rather anti-British. (The Punjabis as a whole were the least anti-British of the Indians, but this man had been soured, perhaps, by having been excluded from ice skating on the rink at Simla because he was an Indian!) "My friend Faiz," he said, "he was the finest poet we had, and he was a Moslem. The first poet in Urdu. Urdu is the language of poets. And for two years now he has been in jail. The Pakistan government has thrown him into jail because they say he is against the government."

"Ah, Faiz!" cried another who was there, and who also had just been having a sly dig at the benighted country to which I happen to belong. "Faiz! Indeed the greatest of our poets! He who wrote the lines, during the imperialist days: 'Let me die, striving for liberty, rather than live my life in a cage!' "

"Was he—er—in prison when he—er—wrote that?" I asked

humbly, knowing perfectly well, of course, that he was not. And you could have heard them laughing a mile away!

Poetry is a living thing in India, in a way that it has ceased to be in the West. I went to a *mushara*, or gathering of poets, held in a small town at the house of a rajah. Some twenty poets had been invited, and large numbers of the public came to hear them recite. They played a sort of game.

One poet would recite a verse, and the poet on his left would have to recite another when he had finished, starting it with the same letter that the first one had ended on. And they were not to pause. I was not clear whether they could extemporize a verse of their own, or whether they had to use an existing verse, but I believe that they could do either. At any rate, as they warmed up to it, they obviously became quite inspired, because the verses followed each other like lightning, the onlookers roared with laughter or shouted their admiration, and one felt the intense enthusiasm. They were like people who become eloquent as the evening wears on and they become a little drunker. But these people were not drinking.

Urdu poets do drink, however, or at least some of them do, and not a few of them have rather peculiar morals. The "beloved" to whom much of Urdu poetry is addressed is often of the same sex as the poet. A man who was with me at this *mushara* pointed to one wild-looking fellow and said, "It's the custom at a *mushara* for the host to give the poets anything they ask for. That fellow, when they asked him what he wanted, said, 'Two bottles of rum and a boy!'"

I do not understand Urdu, but I was told by a man who did that the poets at this gathering were pretty earthy poets. Their verse was rough stuff. But it appealed to the ordinary villager and townsman, and both of the latter were enthusiastic about poetry.

Urdu, of course, is the language formed from a mixture of Persian and Hindi, when Persian soldiers began to impinge on Indian people during the Mogul times, and before. It is a rich and poetical language with a big literature, and many North Indians have a great affection for it. The people of the Punjab have their own vernacular, Punjabi; but when they leave home they generally speak Urdu. If ever you see a man reading a vernacular paper in the Punjab, you are likely to find that it is written in Urdu, not Hindi. The people of a great part of Uttar Pradesh also speak Urdu.

Now they are supposed to forget it and learn Hindi. Actually there is little difference in the spoken language, except where Hindi has been artificially altered to expunge Persian words from it and to replace them by Sanskrit. The script, of course, is quite different. Urdu uses the Arabic script.

Urdu is in disfavor because it was brought by the Moslem invaders. Following the same line of thought, we should get to work on English at expunging every word derived from the Germanic tongues, because such words were brought by the Germanic invaders.

I made a journey through the Punjab with a Punjabi friend of mine, a young writer in English called Rambir Vora. We gave a lift to a Sikh whom we found walking along the road, and he immediately started trying to convert us to a new religion that he had just founded. He told us that he had recently addressed a meeting of twenty thousand converts.

God, he told us, was ultramicroscopic. That is how He is everywhere, and yet we cannot see him. We had difficulty in getting rid of the prophet when we arrived at our destination.

Later we were sitting in Rambir's garden, in the city of Ambala, when an old man came along selling fruit. He was a scruffy, unprepossessing-looking old man, and rather derisively I said to Rambir, "I suppose this chap has started a new religion, too?"

Rambir turned on me fiercely. I had been baiting him a little, perhaps. "I don't know whether he has started a new religion or not," said Rambir. "But I do know this: He has a philosophy. And it's his own. He didn't get it ready-made!"

I realized that he could have said this with equal truth about any of the man's several hundred million fellow countrymen.

20

NEW DEAL FOR INDIA

Two days after I arrived in Delhi I went to a party, one of the large and tedious parties that go on all the time there, for everybody has to return hospitality they have received from other people. At this party there were about fifty people, all in evening dress except for one man in a rather disgraceful pair of slacks and a khaki shirt, and we stood around uncomfortably and tried to make conversation, drinking whiskies and sodas which were brought round on trays by flunkeys and which we might as well have thrown down the drain, for all the good we derived from them.

A man was introduced to me, and he asked me if I'd like to go to a place called Nilokherri with him in the morning. I said yes, wondering vaguely whether Nilokherri was a ruin, a temple, or an irrigation dam, and shuffled off to a position more in the path of the flunkeys as they came from the bar, so that I could practice a technique I was developing of darting an empty glass onto a swiftly moving tray, and whipping off a full one in return.

But next morning, at six o'clock, I found myself standing

at the Kashmir Gate, waiting for the man to pick me up. He was right on time, and soon I found myself being driven north along the Grand Trunk Road at a high speed.

Nilokherri proved to be a new refugee township. It had been started by an individual welfare worker, a man of very strong character but rather fanatical views, and it aimed at being a self-contained township, with sufficient industries to support its inhabitants without help from the government. Whether it will ultimately be successful or not I do not know, nor did I take a great deal of interest in it, for the township itself was not what we had come to see. We had come to see a school that was being run there.

This was not a school for children, but for adults. It was being run to administer some training to the officers who were going to take charge of the community projects in India's famous new Community Project Scheme.

The pupils at the school (some seventy of them, for there were to be seventy-odd community projects) were drawn mostly from the junior branches of the civil service. They were young men, mostly with promising futures in the administration. My friend had come to give a talk to them, which he did, and then he drove home to Delhi. I was talking to some of the students in one of their dormitories, and one of them said, "Why don't you stay on here until the term ends? We break up in four days' time. There's a spare bed; why not take it?" I liked the idea, and so for the next four days I found myself enrolled as a sort of honorary student-project officer.

We got up very early in the morning, crowded into the backs of lorries, and were driven off by Sikh drivers to near-by villages. Arrived at our particular village we were greeted by a crowd of small boys with cries of *"Jai Hind!"* ("Victory to India!")

We then jumped off our lorry, unloaded some picks and shovels and those iron trays for carrying dirt on your head, and started work. Whether the villagers liked it or not, we did good works to them. We repaired their wells, dug drains down their village streets, and generally did the jobs which one wonders why they had not done for themselves during the five or six thousand years since the village had been founded.

My fellow toilers were drawn from the most educated class in India. The height of a young Indian's ambition is to enter the civil service, and I think I am fairly safe in saying that not one of them, until he had come to this school, had ever laid his hand on any kind of a working tool before. But they entered into this labor with a right good will. They loved it. They were like kids at a picnic. The whole thing reminded me very much of the more amusing sort of "course" that one went to in the army.

Whatever the villagers thought of the good works we were doing, they loved watching us do them! We were a source of endless amusement to them. After an hour or so's work we would leave them, though, and return to Nilokherri.

There we would suffer ourselves to be lectured to. I never heard so many lectures delivered so pompously in such a short time.

My fellows had had a month of this lecturing, and they were just about sick of it. I should not have liked to have had to lecture to them! They must have been the most unreceptive audience that any lecturer ever had. They had heard it all before. And there was so much uplift. So much exhortation. So many quotations from *Bhagavad Gita* and other works.

After work, our real education began. Then we sat in the dormitories and talked. First we tore, anew, the day's lecturers to shreds. Then we talked about what was going to happen in India.

Now the idea of the Community Project Scheme is just the same as the idea of the Madras Firka Development Scheme, that I have described at such length in Chapters Thirteen and Fourteen. The difference is that the central government is supplying a lot of money for it, and the Americans are helping, too. True, American help has been steadily scaled down since the scheme's inception from a promised fifty per cent to an actual ten per cent of the total cost, but it represents hard currency, which has to be spent, in fact, in the United States.

But those conversations in the evenings, dog-tired as we all were after our hard day's work, were extremely stimulating. We had people from every part of India with us: from Travancoris from Cape Comorin to hillmen from Himachayal Pradesh to slant-eyed, yellow-faced little men from the jungles of Assam, to say nothing of one young and extremely beautiful girl, the only female, from Bengal. India was concentrated in our dormitory, and one heard about the problems of every part of it.

I do not suppose anyone learned much at that school from the lectures, but I think it did good for all those men to come together, and it certainly did them good to bend their backs in manual labor together. It convinced me of one thing: that India will not lack the right kind of men to lead her.

There were all sorts at Nilokherri, from British-trained officers of the I.C.S., who had probably been educated at Oxford or Cambridge, to wild young men who had worn Gandhi caps and been put in jail.

My dormitory captain was such a wild man.

He was a short, stocky, fat-faced fellow with a small mustache. If I had met him without knowing about him, I should have said that he was a merchant of some type, out chiefly to make money. But he was not this. He had been a militant member of Congress in the old days, had been jailed by the British, and since Independence had worked as a volunteer under Gandhi.

Someone else who knew him described to me how he, with a few others, had stood unarmed for two days, barring the way along the roads which led to the Jami Masjid in Delhi.

The Jami Masjid is the greatest mosque in Delhi, if not in the world. At that time in history the post-Partition riots were just beginning to spread to Delhi. Bands of Hindu refugees were coming in from Pakistan, telling of horror and bloodshed, showing their wounds, bewailing the loss of their wives and children.

The Delhi mob was active, and all Delhi's Moslem population had taken refuge in the great mosque. India's army was fully extended. There were no troops to protect the Moslems, but Gandhi and Nehru and the other leaders of the new nation had asked that no Moslem be hurt.

A handful of young men, wearing their Congress caps and their *khadi,* completely unarmed, had stood between the roaring mob and the thousands of cringing refugees inside the compound of the mosque. "You can come if you like, but you will have to kill us first!" they said. They fought the way Gandhi had taught them to fight. For two days and nights they stood there, not eating or drinking or sitting down or experiencing a moment's relaxation from the nearly unbearable nervous tension of forcing their will on a hostile multitude—until Gandhi himself arrived, from the other side of India, and, skinny little old man that he was, turned the mob into human beings again, and sent them crawling to their homes like whipped curs.

There was another man there who had been with Gandhi at this period, going with the Mahatma as he flew from one side of India to another like a shuttlecock, rushing to wherever the riots were worst, stopping the bloodshed wherever he arrived—only to have it, perhaps, break out behind his back again when he had gone.

Nilokherri is near Kurukshetra, the great battlefield on which the battle between right and wrong was fought as described in the Hindu epic *Mahabharata*.

There is a town not far from here where Gandhi said, "If you kill the Moslems here I will kill myself!" Good and Evil had fought here before, and Gandhi was determined to see that they fought here again. Seven times he flew to this town near Kurukshetra. Each time he harangued and stormed at the citizens, and threatened them with his own death, and imposed his will on them. Each time he made the leading citizens of the town sign a solemn declaration that they would not allow the Moslems to be molested. Each time he personally went from house to house, throwing the usurpers out if the house had been occupied by a Hindu refugee after the rightful Moslem owner had been turned out, and each time he went to where the Moslems were taking refuge in a camp —guarded by police and soldiers from the mob—and persuaded them to return to their houses.

But in the end Gandhi had lost. Wave after wave of Hindu refugees came from Pakistan, and the Moslems of that town had lost their nerve and fled. Probably most of them had been slaughtered. But the tide flowed no farther. Kurukshetra was the high-water mark. The forces of Evil may have won the battle, but they lost the war.

We were taken on a conducted tour of Kurukshetra.

There are several old temples there, and a sacred tank, and

other things. There have been cities on that flat plain, and one still sees the mounds that they made.

Our guide was not a sympathetic one. He was one of our fellow students, a Sikh named Madhusudan Singh, an older man, perhaps, than the average among us. He knew the lay-out of Kurukshetra, because he had worked in that district. He was a large man, tall and broad and, like all Sikhs, bearded. His voice was deep and powerful, and he used it to express the most iconoclastic ideas.

"That's where Bishma was supposed to have been shot so full of arrows that his body couldn't touch the ground," he rumbled. "If you can believe that, you can believe anything!"

The Hindus among us smiled tolerantly at this sacrilege.

"That temple over there is where Krishna is supposed to have told the *Bhagavad Gita* to Arjuna," he said, "although, as the *Bhagavad Gita* is three hundred pages of close print, and as the two of them were traveling in a chariot at the time, it's hard to see why it should be just here!"

We trooped along behind him.

"We'll go in and see the old *sanyasi* if you like," boomed Madhusudan Singh when we got just outside the door of the little temple, "but for God's sake don't let him start talking! Because if you do he'll never stop!"

We went in, and the *sanyasi* did start talking.

He was an unusual *sanyasi,* or holy man. In the first place he wore a pair of blue striped socks. No shoes, of course; that would have been unthinkable. But blue striped socks.

He wore the saffron robe in the usual manner, but he had a gramophone and a radio beside him, and among his books, which were all in English, were some very profane ones. Do I remember seeing a P. G. Wodehouse?

He had been a member of the Indian civil service before

he had turned *sanyasi*, and, in spite of his yellow robe, he looked it.

"This spot has never had a temple before," he told us in English, "and as it is traditionally the spot where the most enlightening and intelligent of our sacred books emanated, a book that must eventually influence the entire world—the *Bhagavad Gita*—I felt that there should be a temple here, and that pilgrims should come from all parts of India to do it homage. So, after I retired from my official duties, I raised some money and built this temple."

"Do pilgrims come here?" asked one of us.

"Very few. It has not appealed yet to the imagination of the masses," he said. I could not help wondering if those blue striped socks had something to do with it.

He thereupon shut his eyes and quoted a score or so of verses from the *Bhagavad Gita* to us—in English. He quoted them very well. We then put our shoes on again and went out. When we got outside the door, our guide and mentor said, in a voice that could be heard by every *sanyasi* within seven miles, "We're lucky. He generally keeps you there hours, you know!"

This Madhusudan Singh was a man I immediately took to. He seemed to embody all that earthy good sense that the bearded Sikhs are noted for. Whenever we had a lecture and the lecturer gave off a lot of platitudes, as lecturers will, Madhusudan would stand up and bellow some question at him or some piece of factual information, which would crumple the man up like a shot rabbit.

He said to me, "If you want to see India, you want to go and live in a village, you know. In the Punjab. That's the real India. I've got a house I'm not using, up in Jullunder District. You can live there. You'll see what life in a real Punjab village is like."

I told him that I might take him up on this. Eventually I did; but I did not go to Madhusudan's own village, but to a village in the Community Project Area of which he became project officer, much farther south.

When I left India it was still too early to assess the effectiveness of the Community Projects scheme. My own opinion is that it will not be as effective as the Madras Firka Development, or the Rural Development Movement in Ceylon.

The Ceylon Rural Development has started practically spontaneously among the villagers themselves. It has not been imposed from above. It is costing the government practically nothing, and it has already achieved wonders. It is revolutionizing the countryside, and doing so for the better.

The Community Project scheme is costing too much. It is too much a thing imposed from above. It is too much associated, in the minds of the Indians, with the foreigner.

There was a great deal of opposition to the part the Americans were playing, at Nilokherri. "We got rid of the 'sahibs'," I heard one fellow say, "and now we're letting the 'guys' in!" Several Americans came and gave us talks at Nilokherri, and I must say I liked them. They seemed very sensible, reasonable, forthright young men; but no doubt there was a hint of patronization in what they said. They cannot help this. They take so completely for granted that their way of life is better than anybody else's, just as the English did in Victorian times. It would be inconceivable to them that some Indians, perhaps, prefer the Indian way of life. What, not want hot and cold water? Not want refrigerators? Not want television sets? Impossible! You *must* want these things, and we're the guys to show you how to get them!

Several months later I decided that the Scheme was far too centralized. I was present at an unofficial meeting of half a dozen project officers—all graduates of Nilokherri—in a coffee-house in New Delhi. They had come in to see their boss, and I ran into them.

They were beside themselves with frustration.

"I ordered coal for burning bricks six months ago," said one. "I promised my villagers it would be there. And it's not. I made a special trip to the head office to see what had happened about it, and found some damned office-wallah sitting on it! *Everything* gets held up in the head office! The villagers are just laughing at me!"

"I asked for a book on how to build a children's playground," said another. "I was informed that my letter had been forwarded to the education department. The education department informed me that they had forwarded it to the health department. The health department must have had it now three months, and they've still got it. I wonder where they will pass it to?"

"I have nothing but trouble with my collector," said another. "He reckons he's the boss in his district and he was against the projects from the start. He does everything he can to thwart me. I complain to my chief, but he can do nothing!"

"Huge organizations like our government," said the fourth, "can do one of two things. They can get things done, like the army did in wartime, but only at the expense of colossal waste. Waste and bribery, and corruption all around. Or else they can act like governments act in peacetime, not so much waste, strict safeguards against corruption, but nothing done! Nothing done at all! I've worked like the devil in my area, and I can't see the difference. Everything I promise my villagers gets held up at head office and never arrives!"

This was an indignation meeting, of course, and they were probably exaggerating somewhat. They had come into Delhi for the express purpose of complaining to their boss. But it struck me that here was the weakness—centralization. The huge organization works so well in theory. Such flexibility, such possible concentration of force, such small overhead! But in practice it never works, because the *theory* never takes into account the various frailties of human nature.

The man who impressed me most at Nilokherri was an old man who came in to talk to us on the last day. He had not been specially invited, he had not asked to come, but he had been walking down along the Grand Trunk Road of India, with a staff in his hand, going from village to village, trying to get the larger landowners voluntarily to part with some of their land to the poorer people.

He was a famous man, in spite of the fact that he was too poor to use a bus; and when the management of the school heard that he was passing by, they seized the opportunity to ask him in to speak to us.

I wondered who the emaciated old man with a staff was who, on the last day of term, hobbled in wearing a *khadi* dhoti and wooden sandals. He was dressed in the manner that Gandhi used to adopt. One more old bore, I thought.

We had some particularly sententious speeches on that last day. And then the old man got up to speak.

He spoke English. Indeed, no other language would have been understood by all of us. He spoke well. Very softly, and yet you could hear every word he said, right at the back.

"You say you are going to do the work which it is right that every educated man should do," he said. "The only work that it is morally permissible for him to do. And that is to work to help the poor people. But if you really do this work, and not only *say* that you are going to do it, you had better know what it is like. I have spent my life working in the villages. I worked, as you know, for many years beside Gandhiji. I have worked for five years in a village to build something up. There has been a feud in the village. I have realized that, for the good of the villagers, I had better go. It is no use to stay and fight sometimes; when that happens you only cause more harm and unhappiness. You must go, and see five years' effort fall to ruin in a day.

"It is not the result of the work that is important, but the work, that you do it as a sacrifice. You must work because you know it is morally right that you should. Do not work because you hope to achieve something. Because you will not achieve anything. I have been bashing my head against that brick wall for forty years now. I am sixty, though I look eighty, and I shall go on bashing it just as hard until the day that I die. But if I do more than knock a bit of dust off the wall, I shall be surprised. . . ."

He spoke in such a quiet and gentle voice, with no ranting, and with such complete sincerity and such obvious knowledge of what he was talking about, that he held that unruly and extremely cynical audience for an hour. Even Madhusudan Singh had nothing to say.

He also quoted from the *Bhagavad Gita* to us.

In the *Mahabharata,* of which the *Gita* is part, it is related that Krishna, on the eve of the cosmic battle of Kurukshetra, gave Arjuna—the greatest of the heroes of the forces of Good—a choice. He said to Arjuna that he, Krishna, was willing to help him himself, or alternatively order his army to help him and himself stay out of the battle. Krishna, of course, was a god in the shape of a man, and he was at that time a powerful king with an army at his command. "But," said Krishna, after making this offer, "if I help you myself, then I must lend my army to the enemy, to help him. For that is fair. And I myself will not fight. I will drive your chariot, Arjuna, and help you with counsel. But I will not fight, and my army will fight against you!"

Arjuna unhesitatingly chose to have his friend Krishna help him, and Krishna's army went over to the other side. Owing to Krishna's inspiration, Arjuna won the battle.

"Now, see you don't make the mistake that Arjuna avoided!" said the old follower of Gandhi. "See you don't take the army, and leave Krishna!—take the material things and leave the Spirit!—go for the money and the machines and the material, but betray the spirit of Mother India!"

When we last saw him, he was hobbling off along the Grand Trunk Road again, with his staff, and with a few peasants who were going with him. Going to bash his head against that brick wall for a few more years I suppose.

Personally, I left Nilokherri with an Agricultural Extension officer, from Texas. We drove to Delhi in a large American car.

21

MY VILLAGE

I WOKE UP IN THE MORNING, after my first night in the village of Barwasni, to find three blanketed figures sitting in chairs in my room.

They were Chaudhri Mohan Dass, my host, Chaudhri Chhatter Singh, and Chaudhri Chander Bhan. (*Chaudhri* is the Punjabi Jat equivalent to our Mister.) They were waiting to take me for the early morning walk, which is customary in most parts of India, and also because they were consumed with curiosity to find out the strange habits of an Englishman.

I crawled out of bed, pulled on a pair of trousers and a shirt, flung a blanket around myself (for it was cold), and followed them out of my room, which was a sort of penthouse. Out we went—onto the flat mud roof of Mohan Dass's house, down a ladder into Mohan Dass's back yard, out of the gate, along the uneven and dusty roads of Barwasni village, into the dusty open country, along the bank of a large irrigation canal.

Then we dispersed and went our various ways for a few minutes.

My companions were most intrigued. Why did I not wash myself in the canal after our dispersion? "We wish that you should do as we do," said Chhatter Singh, who spoke some English. "We do not understand your customs!"

We strolled along farther, enjoying the coolness and freshness of the early morning. The sun was just coming above the flat horizon. Winter in the Punjab is delightful; it is the world's perfect climate. It was still cool, and we were glad of our blankets, but the sun promised warmth later. The Punjab is rich in birds, and we saw hundreds of them. Herons and cranes and other aquatic birds, ducks and teals on a small pond, weaver birds and parakeets and mynas and a score of kinds of birds I do not know. They were all tame; the people around there do not kill.

After perhaps a mile of strolling we turned back and re-entered the village.

"Now you will take your bath," said Chhatter Singh. It is taken for granted that at this moment of the day one takes one's bath.

Feeling perhaps that I should be shy to bathe in front of a mixed audience, Mohan Dass carried two buckets of well water up to my room. The floor of the room was of rammed earth and cow dung, as hard and as clean as cement, but in the corner was slab of real cement, because mud and cow dung will not stand up to water. On this cement slab I stood (my hosts delicately withdrew) and poured the water over myself and soaped myself and washed myself and dried myself.

This sounds spartan in such a cold climate, and indeed it was a little. But you can't let the old country down, can you?

Also, water drawn straight from a well is generally warmish. This certainly was.

Having taken my bath, I joined my friends on the roof outside, where chairs had been taken, and where the sun was beginning to warm things up. We sat in that pleasant early morning sun and talked for a while, and drank pint glasses of warm milk. Chhatter Singh and Chander Bhan both spoke some English. They were shy at first, but as time went on they improved. Chhatter Singh was secretary of several *panchayats,* or village councils, and had learned some English at school. Chander Bhan had not had much schooling but had been in the army, and had picked up some English there.

Other people came to see us; in fact, for the first few days in that village, there was a constant coming and going. I held a sort of perpetual court. People for miles around were anxious to view the strange exhibit, the Englishman who was living in a village. There was a lot of natural delicacy about this, though, and my hosts protected me from most of the visits. Only people they thought I should like to see did they allow to come.

At about ten o'clock the sun was getting too warm and we moved inside. And Chhatter Singh said, "Now we will bring your food."

I had stipulated that I should be given the same food as my hosts had themselves, and I was anxious to see what this was like. By that time in the morning, having had nothing but some milk and having been up since five, I was hungry.

A tinned-brass tray was brought, with a metal plate piled with about four *chapatis,* and four little brass dishes. One of the dishes contained curds, one lentils (cooked with chillies), one the boiled and spiced leaves of the oil-seed plant, which are eaten like spinach, and the last a mixture of some pulses and small beans. All hotly spiced. Oh, and there was a saucer full of slices of raw onion.

Chapatis are of many breeds. The simplest is made like this.

You take some whole-wheat meal, wet it, knead it into a dough, pat some of it out thin like a pancake, and plop it onto an iron plate which has been heating over the fire. After a very few moments you turn it over, then lift it from the iron plate, and throw it onto the fire itself, right onto the hot embers. This has a strange effect upon it. It blows up like a balloon. After a very few seconds you turn it around, leave it on the embers again for perhaps three seconds, then take it off. You have your *chapati*. The whole operation takes perhaps a minute and a half, but when you are cooking a number of them you do them in a kind of rhythmical series of operations: pat some dough out flat, take another off the hot plate, put the dough on, put the other on the embers, take a third off the embers, and so on; it goes to a rhythm.

Eaten hot and with the right curries, they are perfectly delicious. Whoever invented bread cooked with yeast was a fool.

But my *chapatis* had *ghee,* or clarified butter, on them.

I ate by pulling off a piece of *chapati* with my fingers, pinching up one or other of the contents of the little dishes and popping it into my mouth. About ten white-clad people sat on chairs or on the floor of my room as I did so, watching every mouthful. I sat on a chair and ate off a table.

As soon as the last *chapati* had followed the others, some more were brought. For they must be piping hot. I decided that this was the most delicious meal I had ever tasted. But then I was hungry, of course.

After this meal I tried to do some work. I asked my hosts and visitors to leave me (they had been warned by Madhusudan Singh, who had arranged this stay in the village, that they were not to worry me while I worked), and I sat down and started writing this book.

But I did not get very far. I was restless. I was nervous. I kept getting up and sitting down again. I paced the room. All the time I kept thinking of something. I was in the grip of a craving. And the craving was for tea!

I thought of tea I had taken in various parts of the world. The horrid little tea bags they hang in your glass on the Continent. The shallow china bowls with clear green tea in them, unsweetened, that you get in Burma. The times I had scooped a chipped enameled mugful of turgid brown liquid out of a four-gallon gas tin during the war. I just could not get my mind off tea.

In desperation I flung myself on the bed and went to sleep. And, as I live and breathe, I dreamed of tea!

Jumping up, I climbed down the ladder and shouted for Mohan Dass. He does not speak English, and there was no one there who did, but I indicated to him that I wanted to borrow his bicycle. I jumped on that machine and pedaled through the village, scattering the pigs and the small boys, out onto the open, onto the rough track that led to the near-by town of Sonepat.

I pedaled the five miles into Sonepat as if the devil were after me. On the outskirts of the little ancient town, so ancient that it stands a hundred feet up on a hill of its own making, a hill made of the crumbling ruins of the Sonepats of the past, I found a shack where they sold—tea! Glorious tea. I drank three glasses straight off. I sat down on a bench in the shade and felt my headache leaving me. My craving was assuaged.

Mounting Mohan Dass's bicycle again, I rode to where my friend Madhusudan Singh lives and has his office, and beheld that great bearded figure sitting in his office at work. "Hello, John!" he boomed. "Pleased to see you! Everything all right? Are they treating you all right? Come over to the house and we'll have some tea!"

I went to the house and drank three more cups, just to make sure.

When I went back to Barwasni, in Madhusudan's jeep, I clutched a two-pound packet. No more experiments of tea-lessness for me.

These Jat villagers just do not drink tea. They have never got around to it. Never having had it, they never miss it. Instead they drink some gallons of milk each day, warm milk in pint-sized metal glasses, sweetened with their own home-made sugar. They eat or drink virtually nothing that is not produced on their own land.

Madhusudan came up with me to my room, and there and then we gave Mohan Dass a lesson in the art of making tea. I had determined, at the start, to have exactly the same diet as the villagers had; but I had reckoned without the fact of my slavery to caffeine. Tea I could not do without.

While Madhusudan was still there, at about five in the afternoon, they brought me my second, and last, meal of the day. It was almost exactly like the first. Some of the little dishes, perhaps, contained different things. We often had potatoes, for example, which grow quite well in that part of the world.

For the month that I stayed in Barwasni I never had any other food than this. Two meals a day, and always the same thing. I never even began to get tired of it. In fact when I went into Delhi for a couple of days and visited a restaurant, I asked for exactly the same thing! I have never felt fitter, and I have never enjoyed food more.

We were strict vegetarians in Barwasni. All those Hindu

Jats are. They will not touch meat, or eggs, or fish, or fowl. They will not kill any living thing, and to them even an egg is living. Useless to try to explain to them, as Madhusudan did one day, that provided the cock was kept away from the hens the eggs were infertile.

I have seldom been more contented during my life than I was at Barwasni as a guest of the Jats. The fixed routine of living I found excellent discipline. Plenty of walking about the Punjab plain in the invigorating air kept me hungry and healthy. The friendliness, the warm, kindly, intense friendliness of everyone I met, was delightful.

The Punjab plain is as flat as a billiard table, and every yard of it, practically, is cultivated. If you climbed the tower of our temple in Barwasni you looked over an apparently limitless land. In that clear air the vision extended for a hundred miles perhaps, and the pattern was all the same: green fields of wheat in irregular rectangular strips and patches; tall, square, compact stands of sugar cane; patches of other crops; patches of fallow land; groves of fruit trees; occasional shade or timber trees, and villages.

The villages were far apart, on an average perhaps of six miles. They were all just like Barwasni, except that some were larger and others smaller.

Barwasni had perhaps a thousand inhabitants and a couple hundred houses.

The houses were all jammed together, most of them actually touching, sharing common walls in fact. Each house, of course, would front on a street, but possibly its back and both its sides would be touching other houses. This made the houses very dark inside, but it made for security. In that country there is a constant fear of armed robbery.

The houses were flat-roofed without exception, and all the same color—brown. The walls were built of big unburnt bricks plastered once a year with mud and cow dung. The roofs were made of hard dry earth, supported on closely laid lengths of rough timber, the earth first beaten down with wooden clubs and then well plastered with mud and cow dung. This roof is quite impervious to rain provided it is kept plastered and that there is sufficient run-off for the water.

But some of the newer houses were built of burnt brick, and their roofs were plastered with cement. These were called *pukha* houses.

Generally a house consisted of one very big room (the houses were by no means small), with its roof supported by ornamental brick "Moorish" arches, and three or four smaller rooms at the back and sides of it. The big room would be dimly lit from the door and windows in front (although the latter were generally kept boarded up), but the smaller rooms would often be pitch-dark; if you wanted to go into them you had to take a lamp.

Sometimes the cattle and water buffaloes were kept in the big central room, sometimes in one of the side rooms. The big room was the living room for the family. The baby's cradle was slung from the roof on two long chains; the cooking fires, of cow dung, were there, the cooking pots and water vessels, the farming implements, the milk churn, the hand mill for grinding the wheat. There would be some *charpoys* or wood-framed string cots, and maybe an old homemade chair or two.

One of the side rooms would just be a grain store; in it there would be a great pile of wheat, the staple food. Another would have in it a hard-mud rack containing perhaps a dozen or a score of great earthen pots, like Ali Baba's pots, containing what an English housewife would call her groceries. But these groceries were all—with the one exception of salt—grown by the householder himself.

Life at that time of the year, the winter, is not arduous in that district. The winter wheat was in and coming up nicely, just waiting for the spring sunshine to make it grow, and most of the other crops had long been harvested. There was, however, the sugar cane to cut.

All around our village were little sugar mills. The motive power of these was an ox, blindfolded, walking around in a circle, with a small boy walking behind it with a stick. The ox pulled around a pole, which turned a small cast-iron sugar-crusher. A man or boy squatted down beside the sugar-crusher (he had to squat low to allow the pole to pass over his head) and he fed the cane into it.

Not far away was a thatched lean-to; and in front of this four pans, two huge ones and two smaller, bubbled on a fire. The fire was built in a trench, and was fed with the crushed cane, from which the juice had been extracted.

By boiling the cane juice from the crusher, sugar was made. It was not in the form of white crystals, but was a brown, sticky, toffee-like substance, called *gur*. This *gur* is delicious. Once you get over the idea that sugar should be white and crystalline you find that there is no purpose for which re-fined sugar is as good as *gur*. The Jats, no doubt, will come to the stage when they will take their *gur* into town to sell to a sugar mill, and buy it back in the form of refined sugar; but eventually we will all reach the stage of civilization (if we are not stopped by an atom bomb) when we will return to using *gur* in preference to refined sugar. That will be a very high state of civilization indeed.

To leave or enter Barwasni you had to run the gauntlet of the sugar mills. The moment you were sighted from them, you would be hailed. There was no escape. If you pretended not to hear, a small boy would be dispatched to intercept you.

Over you had to go, and a place would be made for you on a string bed that always stood near the mill, and you would have to sit on it and drink a metal glass full of cane juice, and eat at least one large piece of *gur*. I will never forget the look of horror that came over the faces of the sugarmakers when an Englishman, who had come out from Delhi to visit me, offered to pay for this refreshment!

The string bed, by the way, plays an important part in the sugarmaking. For if a man tells you that it is his turn to go make sugar for the day, it really means that it is his turn to go sit on the string bed, taking his turn at a hubble-bubble, and occasionally getting up to go over and take a short spell at feeding the mill or boiling the juice.

The life of the villagers, I was told, was extremely hard at plowing and sowing times and at harvest. Then they all turned out—men, women, and children—and for weeks on end worked all day and half the night; sometimes all night.

But during the bulk of the year there is practically nothing to do. That is why they work so gently at the sugarmaking.

Gandhi realized this fact when he started his *khadi* cult. If the villagers, he believed, could be got to spin and weave and practice other handicrafts during their long slack seasons, there would be no need for them to buy anything at all from the town.

There the *ryots*, or farmers, sit; tough-looking men, roasted dark brown by the sun, mustached, most of them, with lean, aquiline features, turban-wearing, clad in voluminous white dhoties and homespun jackets, or with rough blankets wrapped around their shoulders. They talk, and as they talk, they smoke.

They smoke the hookah, or water pipe. The clay bowl of the pipe is charged with strong tobacco treated with molasses, and on top of the tobacco has been placed a large piece of smoldering cow dung. One man takes the mouthpiece, and, putting the long, curved tube up to his mouth, sucks at it through his hand. His lips do not touch the mouthpiece— he sucks the smoke through his clenched fist. There is a warm bubbling sound as he does so, and the smoke (in spite of the cow dung) has a scent of honey.

Two deliberate inhalations—no more, no less—and then, slowly and deliberately, he hands the mouthpiece to his neighbor.

The latter perhaps is talking. He takes the mouthpiece, continues talking for a while, pauses to take a long and deliberate puff, continues talking again (and no matter how impatient the man on his left is to get the pipe himself, he does not show it). The talker draws in his second puff and deliberately passes the pipe on. Like this it goes, slowly, urbanely, round and round, while the conversation pursues its even course.

You can only share a pipe with your caste brothers. Jats will smoke with Jats, but—strictly—with no one else. But several times towards the end of my stay I had the honor of being handed the mouthpiece to draw from.

The Jats are not only a Hindu caste of course, they are a race. They are descended from a wave of invaders that came from Central Asia perhaps a thousand years ago. Madhusudan's father (a Sikh Jat—that is, a Jat whose ancestors embraced the Sikh religion, but who remains a Jat) wrote a book proving that the Jutes, and other of the North European races, came from the same stock as the Jats. For all I know they did. I do know that the Jats I saw had faces very like brown versions of East Anglian farmers and farm workers I had known at home.

We had two temples in our village. Chander Bhan, the

ex-soldier, who incidentally kept the "co-op" store, went every evening to the orthodox temple, and one night I went with him.

This temple had been built by our village millionaire, a man who had made a fortune in Calcutta running a dairy. It was hideously ugly, and had cost somewhat more than five thousand dollars. I often heard people in the village say that the money could have been better spent.

It was a Siva temple, dedicated to Siva in his *linga,* or phallic, form. About a dozen men and boys were there when we got there and there was a small fire in a brazier. It was dark, and a cold wind was blowing.

We sat cross-legged on the ground, huddled in our blankets, on the platform outside the shrine, and they all sang except me. The song was lively in tempo, and went with colossal gusto. It was a delightful tune to listen to, and as they sang it they swayed backward and forward in time with the rhythm, and—it seemed to me—in tune with the wind. They seemed, in the dark there, to be swaying in the wind like ripe corn. An old man clacked cymbals together, to keep the time, and the small boys sang with fervor that showed in their faces.

The other temple was to Kabir Sahib.

My host, Mohan Dass, and a number of other people in our village, belonged to the Kabir sect. Kabir was a weaver who lived in the seventeenth century, and who turned poet and mystic and founded a new religion. This was an attempt at a synthesis between Hinduism and Islam, and the Moslems claim Kabir as a Moslem saint, but the Hindus claim him as a Hindu.

Our Kabir temple was a simple affair, just a large room with nothing in it except a bed, and on the bed was a large and ancient book wrapped in a blanket. The book contained the writings of Kabir Sahib.

On the night of every full moon the Kabir devotees would repair to this room, squat on the floor wrapped in their blankets, and take it in turns to chant the poetry of Kabir. One would chant, while another would pluck the time out on a one-stringed, one-noted instrument. The tune was pleasant, but monotonous; although from time to time there was a break in the rhythm, and sometimes even in the tempo. Every now and then there would be a murmur of approval from the congregation, and cries of *"Satsahib! Satsahib! Satsahib!"* (*Satsahib* was the greeting that we Satsahibists used to greet each other, instead of the usual Hindu *Namasté!*)

This chanting from the works of Kabir Sahib went on all night until the sun rose. I did not go on all night. I would creep inconspicuously off to bed after an hour or two. Of course, I couldn't understand a word of it.

My room became a sort of club. Madhusudan lent me a battery wireless set, and after my evening meal the room would fill up with people who had come to listen to the rural program from All-India Radio at Delhi. This was in the language of the district: the Rohtak dialect.

But they wouldn't listen to it for long if they didn't like it. If it was the singing of folk songs they would keep it on and listen to it with delight. If it was a couple of comic characters carrying on some cross-talk about farming, they would listen for a time perhaps. If it was a profane song, a song of love, they would immediately shout to have the radio turned off. Or if it was anything that they considered second-rate, they would not listen to it.

The folk songs of India are nearly all songs about God. For India is a God-ridden country. The songs they sing in the fields, the cheeky songs the women sing with laughter and side glances as they transplant the paddy, these songs are hymns. Every one in praise of Krishna, or Rama, or some other aspect of God. The names they give to their children are the names of God. The stories they tell at night are the stories of the Gods.

And my Jats were puritanical. They would not have naughty songs at any price. Chhatter Singh once told me that a nearby village had raised more than five thousand dollars by having a troupe of singing girls come and sing for a fortnight. The money was to be used to build a reading room. "But very bad thing," said Chhatter Singh. "In this village we will not do such thing."

"Does everybody oppose such songs?" I asked.

"Mostly the old people do," said Chhatter Singh. "The young people like such bad songs. And so do the women."

"But you are young?"

"But now I am bigger man in village. I am Secretary of *Panchayat*. I must not like such things."

"What is wrong with such singing, though?"

"Maybe some women listen, perhaps they are just before about to commit wrong with a man not their husband, they hear such songs, they then do wrong. We must not allow."

After the radio session, then we would talk.

Strangely, on some evenings I could join quite freely in the conversation. On other nights I was tired, and I could not; but when I could I did, and sometimes we would talk until very late—midnight even, which is late for people who get up at five.

There were perhaps half a dozen people in that village who spoke quite passable English, and they would translate for me. I picked up a little of the language, so that I knew which way the conversation was going all the time.

What lusty, zestful, vigorous fellows these Jat farmers are! My room sometimes would rock with our laughter as some fellow—often my host Mohan Dass, who was a great clown—

would play the fool to amuse us. At other times we would talk seriously. They were consumed with curiosity about England. I could never tell them enough about it. They all wanted to go there, and great plans were hatched of getting jobs on English farms. Mohan Dass was even going to buy an English farm, and an English wife into the bargain. Complicated arrangements were thought of so that Mohan Dass could spend half the year in England with his English wife, and the other half in India with his Indian wife, without letting either spouse know of the existence of the other!

But we would often talk on serious subjects. Politics, world affairs, the march of science, ethics, morals, comparative religion, and philosophy. They were interested, and often surprisingly well informed, about every subject under the sun. I sometimes used to remember during our conversations that these men were just small farmers and farm workers! Is there another country in the world where you could talk to such people about such subjects and have them understand and be interested in what you were talking about? They were mostly uneducated, although many of them had attended for three or four years at our village school and could read and write in Urdu or Hindi, but this real education had been in their close social life, their old culture, their verbal traditions, and their constant practice of the art of conversation. They have time to talk, these people, and to think. Ideas come easily to them.

They seemed pleased to have me there. One day they offered me thirty acres of land, canal-irrigated, and a house if I would come to Barwasni and settle. "Come and join us and become a Jat!" they said.

And they even said that they would throw in a wife!

22

MY UNCLE TOBY AND
CORPORAL TRIM

MY GOOD FRIEND Madhusudan Singh (we used to call him Sardarji; *Sardar* is the Sikh equivalent of Mister), my good friend Sardarji used to call for me sometimes in his jeep and take me off to various villages in which he was holding meetings. This was always interesting. We were welcomed with great enthusiasm, generally by the entire population headed by the barbers' band, and once we even had to walk down an aisle of small boys holding staves over our heads, like scoutmasters who had just got married. The meetings themselves never failed to be lively.

After we had consumed milk and candy, Sardarji would ask the people what they wanted done in the way of improvements to their village. Perhaps they would reply that they wanted a school. They already had a primary school, but they wanted a secondary one. Sardarji would say, "All right, you raise twenty thousand rupees, and the government will supply the rest and build another school." Then would come arguments of greater or less intensity.

The school will also take children from surrounding vil-

lages; why should not they also pay? A meeting is decided
on with the *panchayats* of the villages concerned. One man
gets up and demands a girls' school also. This arouses immediate opposition. What do they want to educate girls for?
Why put more ideas into their pretty little heads; haven't
they already got too many? Counter cries come from the pro-
gressives of the village. Sardarji gets up and makes a long and
eloquent speech in favor of a girls' school. Sardarji has tremendous force of personality. He dominates people. His tall-
ness, his large, brightly colored Sikh turban, his full, graying
beard, his deep and strong voice, his supreme self-confidence
and overbearing manner make him stand out as a natural
leader. But the Jat villagers are not to be led easily. If they
do not like an idea, they say so in no timid manner.

In every village we have a monkey argument. One man gets
up and says that he would like Sardarji to send his monkey-
killing gang to kill the monkeys. Sardarji has a gang of desperadoes, men who would murder their grandmothers for a
couple of chips, to ride around the countryside on bicycles to
shoot monkeys. The desperadoes are paid a rupee a head for
this service, and the villagers on whose land the monkeys
are killed have to foot the bill.

But the monkey killing is controversial. There is an uproar
at the suggestion. An old man rises to his feet and denounces
the killing of monkeys. The monkeys have as much right to
live as we have. Another man remarks that the old man is a
shopkeeper and has no land of his own; therefore he is indifferent to the monkeys. If he had land and was obliged to see a
quarter or more of the crop which he had grown in the sweat
of his brow being eaten by monkeys, he would pipe a different tune. Sardarji says that a Hindu will not kill anything
outright, but he will kill things slowly by letting them die of
starvation. Wasn't it true that that's what they did to their

bull buffalo calves? They only want cow buffaloes there, because they do not use buffaloes for draft purposes, and—somehow—the bull calves nearly all die mysteriously soon after
birth. They are not killed—no Hindu could kill anything
without danger to his soul—but they die. . . .

A roar of laughter greets Sardarji's remark, and people admit that it is true.

Sardarji then says that in parts of India there is famine.
Is it right that children should starve while monkeys flourish?
The majority shout no, but a minority of old men still stand
out: "The monkeys have as much right to live as we have!
It is not for men to say who is to live and who is to die. That
is for God to say. If He wants to remove the monkeys He will
do so. We must not interfere." This is, of course, the traditional Hindu argument. Gandhi himself would have argued
thus.

However, in these arguments one felt that the kill-the-
monkeys men would eventually have their way.

In one village there was a tremendous and, I thought,
rather moving, argument about cattle.

A huge herd of wild cattle, several hundred, were ravag-
ing the villagers' crops. They were cattle that had escaped
when the Moslems had left, or else unwanted beasts that people had turned loose in order to get rid of them without
committing the sin of killing them. The cattle were making
life almost impossible in the village. They were starving, desperate to get food, and, in spite of a ceaseless watch over the
crops, night and day, the villagers were losing most of what
they planted.

A man got up and asked Sardarji to remove the cattle.

"What do you want me to do with them?" asked Sardarji.

"Take them over the other side of the Jumna."

"There are farmers there," said Sardarji. "They also have too many cattle. They don't want yours!"

"Take them to the Himalayas," said another man.

"Everywhere where cattle can live in the mountains there are cattle," said Sardarji. "The mountains are terribly overstocked, worse than the plains."

There were several other suggestions, all equally fatuous, and then a man, a young one and a bold, said, "Kill them."

There was dead silence. No one wanted to oppose this idea, because they all dearly wished to get rid of the cattle, but no one wished to be associated with the heretical young man. Later, after the deed, they all knew that there would be a reaction. Perhaps a drought or some natural disaster would come to the village, and the blame would be put on to the impiety of killing the cattle, and the men who had spoken out for the cattle killing would be ostracized in the village. Sardarji had no compunctions about killing cattle. The Sikhs nowadays do not often eat beef, but this is because they have to live with the Hindus and do not wish to offend them. But there is nothing in their religion which specifically proscribes the killing of cattle. So, after a few moments of this shocked silence, he said, "I will lend you rifles and give you ammunition and you can kill them yourselves!"

There was an immediate uproar! Such a thing was unthinkable. No Hindu Jat could kill cattle. But why shouldn't the government kill the cattle? There were plenty of people who were debased enough to do the job for money. Christians, and Harijans, and the like. Even Moslems. Even, somebody was bold enough, to say, even Sikhs! Only Hindus cannot kill cattle.

But Sardarji said: "The government is your own government. You put it in. If the government kills cattle it is your own responsibility. Further, if the government ordered the killing of cattle, what do you think the opposition parties would say? What do you think would happen at the next election? The government would never dare to order the killing of cattle. If you want the cattle killed you must kill them yourselves!

A murmur went up at this. One old man said that the people would have to abandon the village and move elsewhere if the cattle were not removed. What would they do? The government were always exhorting the people to grow more food.

When we left the village the question still remained unanswered. Desperate though these people were, they would not agree to kill the cattle themselves at any price. Most of them would not have come out into the open in agreeing even that the government should kill them.

I asked Sardarji what he thought would be the eventual outcome of this cattle-killing problem and he said that he thought that in the end the Indians would come around to killing cattle. There can be no real improvement in the standard of life without it. It struck me as being noteworthy incidentally that at the school for project officers at Nilokherri there had not been one dissenting voice when a man had got up and said that India must start culling its scrub and surplus cattle.

This question of killing animals is a difficult one. I feel, when I kill an animal, that I am committing a murder, and doing something which I have no right to do. I have always felt this, although I have killed more animals perhaps than most people. The feeling of guilt grows as I get older.

And yet, when I reason it out, I *know* that Man, if he is to survive himself, must kill animals. If he does not kill he will be killed, or he will starve. We cannot have good stock unless we keep their numbers down to what our land will support

and also cull the bad ones out of our flocks and herds. This
is a thing that bears no argument; it is a matter of plain common sense. Yet, knowing all this, *still* I do not like the killing
of animals. But I know that the nonkiller of animals only
lives himself because there are other people who are willing
to kill animals.

In the end, I suppose, a lot of improvement will have resulted from Sardarji's work, from the Community Project
Scheme. Schools will have been built, village streets will have
been paved with brick, tube wells will have been sunk, agri-
culture will have been improved. But I have to admit that,
up to the time I left India, three months after the inception
of the scheme, little had been started.

This was certainly not Sardar Madhusudan Singh's fault.
If ever I saw a man work harder than he does, I do not remember it; nor did I ever see anyone better fitted for the
task he was doing. But he came up against bureaucracy on
the one hand and village apathy on the other.

The bureaucracy is apparently insurmountable. I went to
the head office of the Community Projects Scheme in the
secretariat in New Delhi once, and I found there an army of
desk sitters of such a size that if they had all been armed
with picks and shovels and sent out to do real work, they
would dig India out of her troubles within a year or two. But
sitting there, this clerical army just acts as a huge wet blanket,
a damper, a bar to any effort on the part of the men actually
out in the field. I knew a lot of Community Project officers,
and I do not believe that, up to the time I left India, a single
one of them had managed to get one single useful article or
piece of information from this vast machine.

The villagers are interested, but only passively. They are
waiting to see if the government is really going to do something for them, or whether the whole thing is just another

vote-catching scheme. I saw nothing of the intense enthusiasm that I had seen in Madras, in the Firka Development
areas, or in Ceylon. However, three months is not a very long
time.

One day I came back from a walk through our Barwasni
fields, to be greeted in the village by a short fat man wearing
a large sunhelmet.

He was very short, and very fat; his belly was a joy. As he
held out his hand to greet me he took off his solar-topi with
the other to reveal a shock of well-oiled iron-gray hair, every
individual hair of which stood straight up on end as though
they were all charged with electricity and were trying to get
away from each other, and from their parent scalp. He has a
dark, merry face and an enormous nose. The man indeed
appeared to be full of electricity himself. I never knew a man
with so much energy.

"Hello, sir, they have told me about you. Why did I not
have the pleasure of meeting your honor before? I have great
honor, sir, in introducing myself, if you don't mind. I am
Chaudhri Naidar Singh, sir, at your service, honored to meet
your good self!" As he said this he was pumping my hand up
and down and beaming at me. Without giving me time to
reply, he said, "It is all arranged, sir, I have arranged it all!
You are to take your evening meal with me, sir, in the school
where I am sleeping. I am A.D.I. Schools, sir, Assistant Deputy Inspector of Schools. I have held this post, sir, for thirty-
two years. After we have taken our food, we will witness the
boys of the school recite some verse and sing some songs, and
we will witness a short play I have myself made, sir, the purpose of which is to make the people give up their bad habits.
I am very much against bad habits, by which I mean smoking, particularly, and drinking and lie-telling and, above all,
abusing. And cheating and fornicating. I am against all these

things very much, you see, and I make such small plays which you will see, sir, and I have very much to tell you and you shall come on tour with me about the firka, and you shall see many things and I will show you all and you will see what respect the people give me, for I am thirty-two years in this same job in this same firka, not the one we are in, sir, but the next, and you will come with me and . . ."

During the week or so which I spent in this man's company he rarely stopped talking. He was tireless. He was insatiable.

Of course, I agreed to go on tour with him, and certainly never regretted it.

We rode on horses, the sort which you have to beat with a stick from the moment you get on them to keep them from lying down underneath you and falling asleep. Uncle Toby, as I very soon nicknamed my friend, for a reason which perhaps shall appear, was an indifferent horseman. I used to bait him by flogging my nag into a canter, whereupon his own would follow mine, and he, being unable to let go his grasp of the saddle in order to pull on the reins, would be put in great danger of falling off. He would shout to me to stop, in a most affecting manner, but I would pretend that I could not control my ardent steed. He never actually fell off; but he was a joy to watch hanging on, hopping from one side of the saddle to the other.

We made a week's triumphal tour of some scores of villages.

"I am a *desi*-man," said Uncle Toby (meaning he was country bred). "I am not a town man. I am simple, I come from this very Rohtak District, I am a Jat. My father was a farmer, I own land still, we Jats must own land, we will never sell our land for it is against our religion. We say that if you own land you own the sky above it which reaches right up to heaven. So if you own a piece of land you own a piece of heaven. But I am a *desi*-man, I am married in this firka. To-morrow we shall ride to my wife's village, you shall see. We are humble people, although you might not think so as I am having this government job. The same job for thirty-two years. And all the time I have been fighting against the bad habits. And against drinking buffalo milk. What is your own opinion about buffaloes' milk, sir, do you drink it in England?"

I told him that we did not drink it in England because we did not have any buffaloes. "I thought not!" he cried. "That I shall tell the people. In every village I come to I shall tell the people. You shall make speeches, sir, you make in English I shall translate! You will tell the people against buffaloes' milk!"

"But I like buffaloes' milk," I said.

"No, no, you say the English are not having. That is why. It is very bad, it makes people slow and stupid. That is why we Jats are slow and stupid, because the buffalo is a stupid animal."

So we continued on our tour of inspection, and our crusade against bad habits and buffaloes' milk.

I called him Uncle Toby because he had a Corporal Trim.

Every junior officer of the government in India has at least one peon. This man is supposed to act as a messenger for him, in government matters only, of course; and there are regulations to the effect that he should do no work of a non-business nature for his master at all.

But of course, in practice, the peon is a gentleman's gentle-man. He is more; he is a whole staff of servants in one. He is gardener, groom, chauffeur (if his master has a car), a baby sitter, butler, cook, everything you can think of.

Like the original Uncle Toby, my Uncle Toby had a hobbyhorse. Uncle Toby's hobbyhorse was God.

We went to bed as the guests of the leading citizen in the village we happened to be in when night fell, and before we went to sleep, at midnight, Uncle Toby said: "You will please, sir, do me a great honor! It will be a great honor, sir. My program is, in the morning I rise up at four. At four a.m. in the morning. I rise and repeat the name of God. If a man goes to sleep at ten or eleven thinking of God, and rises at four and washes his mouth and prays to God and repeats the name of God, he will be kept from bad thoughts, sir. He will be kept from all bad habits. He will be rendered pure, sir. Therefore, my peon and I, Kanwai my peon, this man's name is Kanwai, we will esteem it a great honor, sir, if you will join us in our humble prayers, if you will wake with us, sir, and repeat the name of God."

Anxious to get to sleep, I told him that I would repeat anything that would please him.

The next morning I heard a bustling, long before dawn. A sound of Corporal Trim getting up off the floor, and his master getting off his *charpoy,* and both rinsing their mouths with water and hawking and spitting, which is a thing all Hindus do immediately on rising, and wrapping their blankets about themselves, and preparing to repeat the name of God.

I pretended to be asleep.

Master and man were talking in their own language, but occasionally Uncle Toby would say something in English. As Trim knew very little of this language, Uncle Toby obviously did it for my benefit.

"Never mind," he would say. "He does not wish to join us. He is going on sleeping. Never mind, we will not mind. It does not matter. We will just continue quietly, as usual, with our program. We will continue with our program."

"*Om!*" intoned Uncle Toby.

"*Om!*" repeated Corporal Trim.

Om is the name used for God, meaning, "God is one." *Om* is the Essence. *Saying "Om" one calls forth; saying "Om" one recites; saying "Om" one sings aloud, to the honor of that syllable, "Om," with its greatness, with its essence.* Thus the Chandogya Upanishad.

Guiltily I sat up on my bed and wrapped my blanket over my ears. It was cold.

Uncle Toby sang aloud. As soon as he started a prayer or *mantram*, his peon would come into it and follow him. But it rapidly became obvious that the peon knew far more about it than his master. After about half an hour the master's stock of *mantrams* began to give out, and then Corporal Trim came into his own. *He* would begin a chant; Uncle Toby would have to crash in as soon as he could so that it would appear obvious that he himself knew the verse, but with patent annoyance that he should have been beaten to it by his peon.

And Trim was inexhaustible. He knew the lot. He must have known the Vedas, and the Upanishads, and the Epics, and Karma Sutra, and every other work all off by heart. In the end his master had to stop him. "We have prayed long enough," he said at last, in English. "Our hearts are pure. Now we will take our walk, and come back and have our bath, and then take our food."

When Uncle Toby reaches a village it is in a constant uproar until he leaves it. For no one can resist him. He makes speeches, has speeches made at him (only short ones, though), he goes here to see this, and there to see that, he inspects, he roars with laughter, and so do all about him. He eats and drinks and parleys with this one, and harangues that one, and intrigues with the other one, and whispers in this one's ear. He is tireless.

He knows everything about everybody. He seems to have relatives or in-laws in every village in the country. Before we rode into one village he gave me a two-rupee note and said, "You will meet my sister here. She is married in the village. You must give her this money. It is our custom here—we are very old-fashioned unenlightened people and have such customs." I did as I was told. His sister was a simple village woman. We sat in her house and drank some horrible tea (the more substantial villagers sometimes keep tea to serve to special guests, but they have no idea how to make it) and when we said good-by I gave her the two rupees, which she gracefully accepted.

But in the next village a man came and gave me *five* rupees! I asked Uncle Toby why, and he said, "It is our custom! You see, I am married not into this village, but my wife's brother is here. And because you are my guest, he must give you money. It is our custom." After this I insisted on producing the money myself, but was several rupees up on the business at the end of the journey.

As an interpreter, Uncle Toby was useless. Because he never translated a thing correctly. He simply listened to what the speaker said, then said what he *himself* wanted to say in the other language.

In every village I had to make a speech. Nothing would do but I must stand up (generally with a garland of flowers around my neck which always makes me feel an even bigger fool than usual) and make a speech either to the assembled schoolchildren or else the adults of the village.

As by this time we had probably had a very long speech from Uncle Toby, I would keep mine short. I would perhaps say, "I like this village very much. I like Rohtak District. I like India. I would like to live here."

"Now I will translate!" Uncle Toby would say.

And his translation would last an hour! Into it he would bring, for the tenth time perhaps, his dislike of bad habits, the pernicious effect of buffaloes' milk, the excellence of cows' milk, and all the rest of it. "The English sahib says they don't have buffalo milk in England," he would say, in his own language. "And he says they don't have it in America. Why? Because they are sensible. They are enlightened. We are not enlightened. We Jats drink buffaloes' milk and are stupid and dull. And have bad habits. And think bad thoughts instead of thinking only of God. All these bad things come from drinking buffaloes' milk. And from smoking. And from fornicating. And . . ." So he would go on.

Then would come the turn of the headman of the village to reply to my address. He would say, in Urdu, that he and his people were delighted that I should honor their village; they loved my country because the Jats and the British had always been friends.

The Jats were a martial race, and he himself, and many others in the village, had served under British officers in the army, and he hoped I would stay a few days, a month perhaps, or two, and return later perhaps, and a few more compliments of that nature.

But this would be turned, by our interpreter, into something quite different. "He says," Uncle Toby would say, "he says it is great honor that you come here. He says that all things are going to be done, in special honor of your visit. He says that all schemes that I, as A.D.I. Schools, have outlined to them will be done, immediately; they will start today, before we are gone, all only in honor of your visit. A new high school will be built, fifty thousand rupees will be raised for it, only in honor of your honor's visit! It was my suggestion. *There* will be the school," and with a wave of his hand he would outline a skyscraper against the sky. "And he says that so enraptured is he, so delighted, so extremely and highly honored, that tomorrow, today even, they will make pukha all the streets in the village," and with another wave of his hand he would lay a *lakh* of bricks, and so it would go on.

One evening we came, far from any village, to a great brick wall standing out in the flat fields. "We will go to the *guru-kul*," said Uncle Toby. "I am known there. Here we will sleep and spend the night."

A *gurukul* is the equivalent of a seminary. This one had been established by the Arya Samaj sect, and was to take boys from the age of about nine and make *brahmacharyas* of them. A *brahmacharya* is one who does not indulge in any sort of sexual activity. Hindu scripture lays it down that a boy should be a *brahmacharya* up to the age of twenty-five.

We rode through a high brick-vaulted gate, and our horses were taken by some little boys. We were greeted by the staff of the *gurukul*, half a dozen masters; none of them was the head, as they were all more or less of equal status. There were six hundred boys there, from the ages of nine to twenty-five, and they were all dressed in a simple uniform of shorts and a shirt.

They looked healthy enough, and some of them happy, and they were busy playing volleyball.

The masters were merry fellows, and we sat talking until after midnight. One of their number sat cross-legged and quoted the *Gita* to us for half an hour, and then we discussed what he had quoted.

While the recitation was on, incidentally, Uncle Toby suddenly said to Trim, "Kanwai, you're asleep! You're asleep!" Trim poked his head out of his blanket and indignantly denied it. "Yes, he was!" said Uncle Toby to me. "I heard him snore! He was snoring!"

We had an excellent conversation; the masters were lively-minded and intelligent. They were open-minded too, and were not annoyed when I criticized things I did not like about the *gurukul*.

"Do boys ever run away?" I asked.

"How can they?" said the master, who spoke the most English, happily. "They don't know where their homes are. They are taken away from home when they are nine and never go out of this *gurukul* until they are twenty-five. How can they run away? Their fathers may visit them twice a year, though."

"And their mothers?"

"No woman is allowed inside these walls. They never see their mothers."

I said what I thought.

I was told of the elaborate precautions taken to stop the boys from finding any sexual outlet, including having the masters sleeping down the middle of the two long dormitories. I had the delicacy not to ask a question that it occurred to me to ask when I heard this, but Uncle Toby had no scruples. "Who watches the masters?" he bellowed.

"We are all strict *brahmacharyas*," said our informant smilingly. "Even when we go home to our wives, once a year, we do not go for that purpose. We are completely celibate."

Whether they are or not, they are a very pleasant and amusing set of fellows, and the souls of hospitality. The little boys walk around in a line chanting until ten o'clock at night, sleep on hard plank beds, and go out for prayers at four-thirty in the morning. There was an English master there, newly appointed, and I believe he may have known fifty words of English.

Some of the more ordinary schools we inspected were good —and others less so. But they were all full of lively children, delighted at seeing strangers, bright-eyed and intelligent. And the masters and the children were as keen as they could be. Keen on the New India. Keen on finding out about the world.

Every village we visited vied with the others in showing us hospitality. We were given enormous meals, full of *ghee;* we were taken to the best houses, and given the best beds, and everything we might be thought to desire: everything in the *brahmacharya* way, at least. In one village we were set upon after we had gone to bed by *masseurs!* Large men came at us, and broke our necks to the left, and back again to the right, and pummeled and pounded and pinched us, and gouged our eyes, and half scalped us, and tweaked our ears, and wrenched our toes. I thought I would be left for dead, but Uncle Toby loved it, and grunted with pleasure, and belched and rumbled, and asked for more. A heavy-fleshed man.

I would have to write another book to describe all the adventures I had with Uncle Toby and Corporal Trim, and all the strange people I met, and the strange things I saw. But my lasting impression of the trip—and in fact of the Punjab generally—was one of bounding energy. Energy and endless zest for living. Coarse perhaps, lusty, earthy, but alive and intelligent and good-hearted, carrying generosity and hospitality to absurd lengths.

We ran into a village wedding. The young groom, a boy at college, had been forced into marrying by his relatives. Being educated, he had not wanted to get married until after his education was finished and then to choose his own bride, but it was not to be. He was most unhappy. He had to ride around the village on a horse, dressed up like a young prince,

with all the villagers in procession with him, the women behind clapping their hands and singing, and two men walking
beside his horse's head discharging shotguns. I must say, it
was a spectacle.

Some of his college friends were there, and we had a discussion about it. One of the other boys said, "They made me
marry too. My uncle was very ill, and they forced me to
marry by saying I must do it before he died."

"My grandfather is ill," said the reluctant groom. "That's
how they've got me to marry. Otherwise I should have refused."

Another boy said, "There's always *someone* who's about to
die—to make us marry!"

One of the college lecturers who was there to see his pupil
marry said, "But why do you do it? Why not refuse? Why
marry just because your father tells you? We must liberate
ourselves!"

This wedding, in a tiny village, cost nearly three thousand
dollars! The jewelry alone, which the groom's father was pre-
senting to the bride, was worth fifteen hundred. The family
was rich, of course.

All journeys have to end, and eventually I said good-by to
Uncle Toby and Corporal Trim, and rode back to my vil-
lage. And soon I had to say good-by to Barwasni too, and to
India.

I tried to persuade Mohan Dass to accept a small present
in return for keeping me for over a month, and he was deeply
offended. For a while I thought I had lost a friend.

Mohan Dass, Chhatter Singh, Chander Bhan, Sarup Singh
the goldsmith, and Kanwal Singh all came to see me off at
the airport. Before we arrived there, Mohan Dass took off his
turban and put it on my head. Among the Jats this is a
supreme token of friendship, and is only done between caste

brothers. Be that as it may, I felt a litle bizarre plodding about the airport, through all the customs and immigration formalities, with an enormous blue turban speckled with silver on my head, its tail hanging halfway down my back, and five stalwart men walking behind me, who obviously looked as though they had never been to an airport before, one of them wearing on his head a very peculiar trilby.

I kept the turban on, however, until I got into the Comet that was to take me back to England.

When I shook their hands and said good-by to them, standing there at Delhi airport with the other people who were sending their friends off, I felt that I was parting from some of the best friends I had ever made. I felt that instead of going home I was leaving it.

Perhaps I had arrived in India with a slight feeling of prejudice against it. Certain books may have been the cause of this. Western writers have been serving up such things as child marriage, monkey worship, untouchability, lack of sanitation, for over a century. But I believe that we have now heard enough about these matters. They are only a small fraction of the story of India, and a fraction which is rapidly diminishing.

But if I had arrived with prejudice, I left the country completely won over by the charm and kindliness of the people, by their depth of character, their sense of values, their culture, and their way of life.

India, one often hears, has many lessons to learn from the West.

It will be a good day when the West realizes that it has lessons of much greater importance to learn from India.